The Relevance of Philosophy to Life

THE
VANDERBILT LIBRARY
OF AMERICAN
PHILOSOPHY

The Vanderbilt Library of American Philosophy

The Vanderbilt Library of American Philosophy, under the general editorship of Herman J. Saatkamp, Jr., is a series devoted to past and current issues in American philosophy. The series offers interpretive perspectives focusing on both the historical roots of American philosophy and present innovative developments in American thought, including studies of values, naturalism, social philosophy, cultural criticism, and applied ethics.

Other titles in the series

RORTY AND PRAGMATISM:
The Philosopher Responds to His Critics
Edited by Herman J. Saatkamp, Jr.

THE PHILOSOPHY OF LOYALTY
Josiah Royce
Introduction by John J. McDermott

The
RELEVANCE
of PHILOSOPHY
TO LIFE

John Lachs

VANDERBILT UNIVERSITY PRESS

Nashville and London

First Edition 1995
95 96 97 98 99   5 4 3 2 1

This publication is made from recycled paper and meets the minimum requirements of American National Standard for Information Sciences—Permanence of Paper for Printed Library Materials. ⊖

Library of Congress Cataloging-in-Publication Data
Lachs, John.
    The Relevance of Philosophy to Life / John Lachs. -- 1st ed.
        p.   cm. -- (The Vanderbilt library of American philosophy)
    Includes index.
    ISBN 0-8265-1262-3 (alk. paper) :
    1. Philosophical anthropology. 2. Philosophy, American--20th century.
I. Title. II. Series.
BD450.L19 1995
128--dc20   94-44987
                                                                              CIP
                        Made in the United States of America

Vanderbilt University Press wishes to thank the following publishers
for permission to reprint several of the essays constituting this volume:

The Relevance of Philosophy to Life—from *Frontiers in American Philosophy*, edited by Robert W. Burch and Herman J. Saatkamp, Jr. (College Station: Texas A & M University Press, 1992) • Reflections on Current French Philosophy—from *Journal of Speculative Philosophy* 9 (1995) • Relativism and Its Benefits—from *Soundings: An Interdisciplinary Journal* 56 (1973): 312–22 • How Relative Are Values? or Are Nazis Irrational and Why the Answer Matters—from *Southern Journal of Philosophy* 28 (1990): 319–28 • A Community of Psyches: Santayana on Society—from *Rice University Quarterly* 66 (1980): 75–85 • Dogmatist in Disguise—from *Christian Century* 83 (1966): 1402–5 • Aristotle and Dewey on the Rat Race—from *Philosophy and the Reconstruction of Culture: Pragmatic Essays after Dewey*, edited by John J. Stuhr (Albany: State University of New York Press, 1993) • Violence as Response to Alienation—from *Alienation and Violence*, edited by S. Giora Shoham (Northwood, England: Science Reviews, 1988) • Persons and Technology—from *Personalist Forum* 1 (1986): 5–21 • Professional Advertising in an Ignorant World—from *Soundings: An Interdisciplinary Journal* 66 (1983): 439–500 • Education and the Power of the State: Reconceiving Some Problems and Their Solutions—from *Public Values, Private Schools*, edited by Neal E. Devins; the Stanford Series on Education and Public Policy (London, New York: The Falmer Press, 1989) • Law and the Importance of Feelings—from *Peirce and Law*, edited by Roberta Kevelson (New York: Peter Lang, 1991) • Questions of Life and Death—from *Wall Street Journal*, March 31, 1976 • Humane Treatment and the Treatment of Humans—*New England Journal of Medicine* 294 (April 8, 1976): 838–40 • Resuscitation—from *Frontiers in Medical Ethics: Applications in a Medical Setting*, edited by Virginia Abernathy (Cambridge: Ballinger, 1980) • Active Euthanasia—from *Frontiers in Medical Ethics: Applications in a Medical Setting* (Cambridge: Ballinger, 1980) • On Selling Organs—from *Forum on Medicine* 2 (1979): 746–47 • Personal Relations Between Physicians and Patients—from *Journal of the Indiana State Medical Association* 75 (1982): 310–13 • The Element of Choice in Criteria of Death—from *Death: Beyond Whole-Brain Criteria*, edited by Richard M. Zaner (Dordrecht, Boston: D. Reider Publishing Co.; distributed by Kluwer Academic Publishers, 1988) • Human Natures—from *Proceedings and Addresses of the American Philosophical Association* 63 (1990): 29–39 • The Philosophical Significance of Psychological Differences Among Humans—from *Southern Journal of Philosophy* 29 (1991): 329–39 • Persons and Different Kinds of Persons—from *Journal of Speculative Philosophy* 8 (1994): 155–63 • To Have and To Be—from *Personalist* 43 (1964): 5–14.

To three generations
of wonderful women
in my family

CONTENTS

CONTENTS

PART FIVE: HUMAN NATURES

SERIES EDITOR'S PREFACE

With John Lachs's *The Relevance of Philosophy to Life*, we inaugurate the Vanderbilt Library of American Philosophy, a new series of books devoted to past and current issues in American thought. Janus-like, the series will offer interpretive perspectives facing in two directions, leading both to the historical roots and to the present cutting edges of American philosophy. The primary goal of the series is to publish original works furthering scholarship in American philosophy. New editions of significant out-of-print books also will be included.

The Relevance of Philosophy to Life provides an appropriate starting point for the Vanderbilt Library of American Philosophy. The lineage of Lachs's philosophy itself is rooted in classical American thought, notably that of Santayana, James, Dewey, and Peirce. Yet this intellectual heritage is neither nationally parochial nor historically confined. Lachs traces the legacy of his work to major non-American philosophical achievements, including classical and current perspectives that provide insight to critical issues having no national borders. In the traditional thrust of American pragmatism, he assesses and draws conclusions concerning many barbed issues in contemporary life: dogmatism, the relativity of values, resuscitation, euthanasia, the right to die, violence, education, societal bureaucracies, and technological advancement. Lachs's overriding concerns are personal integrity and individual responsibility in a society where science, technology, and business dominate individual action and threaten to become predators of human choice and accountability.

These issues are not narrow ones generated by an isolated scholar. They are resident in the quotidian interests of alert and sensitive persons attempting to live meaningfully in the rapid stream of technological and societal expansions. Lachs's assessments inform the most sophisticated reader while making the issues, reasoning, and solutions accessible to the general public. Moral dilemmas require exacting analysis and personal resolve, and Lachs does not turn away from troublesome issues or unpopular views. Although some may sharply disagree with his conclusions, Lachs invites us all to join in the discussion and to do something more than simply talk.

The Relevance of Philosophy to Life ultimately highlights one of the principal reasons why many people become interested in philosophy in the first place: its applicability to the critical issues in life. Sadly, much of contemporary philosophy has lost this focus. Lachs's work is a clear remedy, replete with careful and articulate reasoning, good judgment, well-chosen examples, a sense of the practical, and a lucid explication of philosophical issues and their relevance to life. It is heartening that philosophical argument can be voiced in such a clear and jargon-free manner.

I invite your careful reading of this incisive book and of the forthcoming volumes in the Vanderbilt Library of American Philosophy.

HERMAN J. SAATKAMP, JR.

The Relevance of Philosophy to Life

INTRODUCTION

The professionalization of philosophy has distanced it from the concerns of daily life. Such separation offers benefits, providing thought with powerful tools and a wholesome reflective distance from the heat of action. It also exacts a toll, however, inviting attention to wander from what is ultimately important and to linger over abstract details of technique. Before long, philosophers forget what contribution they were to make to human life or else declare themselves unable to do anything concretely useful at all.

This self-created paralysis of the philosophical enterprise is particularly unfortunate at a time when rapid changes in the world make individual values unstable and social critique essential. We live in an age in which philosophy could and should make a difference: the proliferation of divergent commitments and lifestyles, our ever more problematic relation to the environment, the growing complexity and depersonalization of social life, and our expanding power to change human nature itself call for better understanding and thoughtful evaluation.

I argue that philosophers have not only an opportunity but also an obligation to address the problems of daily living. Moreover, they cannot pretend to be disinterested conduits for the truth or observers whose behavior may or must remain unaffected by their professional skills and knowledge. Thoughts and actions constitute a seamless whole. Kant might well have extended his metaphor of the relation between concepts and perceptions and said that thoughts without actions are empty and actions without thought blind. He could then have added that thoughts and actions out of measure with one another make for morally deformed and personally unsatisfying lives.

The essays in this book are united by the belief that philosophical reflection can yield results and by the desire to harness them to the service of improving life. For this reason and others, my work belongs squarely in the American idiom in philosophical discussion. This tradition has all the resources necessary for assessing how social changes we face relate to human flourishing. Astonishingly, however, it has fallen into neglect over the years; only in the last decade has it recaptured the attention of philosophers. In returning to it, my aim is neither to repeat what James, Dewey, and Santayana have said nor to provide a commentary on their thought. Instead, I utilize their terms and insights in an attempt to get clear about persistent problems of human happiness, social alienation, and medical ethics. I go beyond their work or differ with them whenever it seems desirable or necessary in order to understand our situation more fully.

The moral tone of these essays is one of tolerant concern. We are only beginning to learn the virtue of accepting the alien and of letting others lead their lives without interference or criticism. Loving someone whose values we cannot share, perhaps cannot even appreciate, is the experience that unlocks toleration. The epistemic foundation of such openness is doubt about one's ability to discern the good for everything that moves. Its ontological basis is the multiplicity of natures that surrounds us, every one of which demands its own proper fulfillment. A number of views called 'relativism' have been severely criticized in the history of thought, some quite correctly. But objections to a wholesome pluralism of perfections constitute only a philosophical rearguard action on behalf of intolerance. Both long-term social developments and the best thought point in the opposite direction.

Good sense also suggests that moral issues must always be considered in their broader, concrete social context. Attempts to gain clarity about pressing human problems on the basis of contentless formulas, abstract principles or some universal good are not likely to yield results. Facts and values are so inextricably connected that if we fail to locate our moral concerns in historically particular situations, we can contribute little beyond the affirmation of high-sounding platitudes or the repetition in fancy language of conventional thoughts. I do not deny, of course, that some values are more enduring or enjoy greater scope than others. But even this depends on the similarities among us and on the relative stability of who we are.

I strive to display the intricate and intimate relations between moral problems and social circumstance when I write about issues of medical ethics and the human costs of living in a world of giant institutions. My discussions of euthanasia display a twofold situatedness. In addition to trying to show why and in what contexts hastening death may become desirable, they themselves are set in the midst of particular controversies in a particular moral climate. In times when life is cheap, when death comes early and with ease, hastening it is not likely to occupy the moral imagination. But the question of when existence is no longer worth having arises inevitably once advances in public health and medical technology enable people to live longer than they want. Those who speak of the unconditional value of biological life affirm commitments proper under certain circumstances only. They overlook the way in which actual conditions affect the range and relevance of values; the young person's love of sex and achievement, for example, holds no power over the old.

My discussions of the costs of large-scale social life build on the theory of mediation and psychic distance I first presented in *Intermediate Man*. But they go significantly beyond the earlier work in clarifying my central ideas and in showing how much light they shed on a variety of concrete contemporary problems. They help us understand, for example, why individual powerlessness leads to social violence and how institutional structures designed to aid individual development soon come to obstruct it. The central fact is that we do not feel at home in giant institutions. To relieve our frustrations, we need to find ways to bring psychological and social reality into harmony; that is, we must help individuals with limited perspectives and resources to appropriate the vast, integrated social acts to which they contribute. We do this best by developing a sense of partnership in our actions and by making it possible for the lone individual to gain a hearing. The theory of mediation offers some useful suggestions for institutional and educational reforms to accomplish these.

We live in houses built by other hands. The careful reader will notice that Aristotle, Hegel, Mill, James, Peirce, and others have contributed rooms or hallways to my philosophical edifice. The dominant influences, however, are Santayana and Dewey. The best way to understand a significant portion of my work is, in fact, as an attempt to do justice to divergent, equally compelling, and not easily reconciled aspects of experience stressed by these two great philosophers.

Santayana and Dewey are at one in viewing humans as biological organisms in a natural environment. Both restrict knowledge of our nature to what can be learned of it by established methods of empirical inquiry. But Santayana thinks of human beings as individual animals fighting for food and air against hostile forces in an indifferent world. In a manner akin to existentialists, he sees the individual as insular, as the center and source of all action, as living its own life by its own values and dying, irredeemably, its own death. No one who attends to experience can deny the reality of this focused agency and of such private grief and joy.

Dewey, by contrast, operates with a social paradigm. His interest is focused on the complex social context, not the private individual. Persons and their environment are inseparable: we live in society and society, shaping us in its own image, lives in us. The continuities between humans and the fulfillments possible in social life call us to cooperative endeavor, and this mighty striving to make the world a better place draws our attention away from the quiet inner movements of the soul.

This ultimate difference of focus may explain why the two philosophers operate with such divergent ontological commitments. Dewey is so impressed by our social creativity that he sees everything we do, even our thinking, as constructive of new objects. He does not deny the independent existence of the elements out of which we make or reconstruct the world, but believes that our contact with them is mediated: each formed thing and thought bears the stamp of our activity and subserves our purposes.

Starting from the limited power of individuals, by contrast, Santayana views the world as a collection of ancient powers whose being and structure stand in no need of our creative endeavors. Though facts are contingent and beliefs uncertain, our knowledge attempts to capture local segments of this vast and fully formed cosmos. Truth stands as a permanent independent reality that limits what we can do and provides the standard by which our cognitive efforts are measured.

My theory of human natures rests on a foundation that incorporates both of these views. Good sense indicates that there are objective realities independent of us, powers that neither require nor permit reconstruction. Many facts, on the other hand, bear the mark of our purposes: how we organize, classify, structure, conceive, and value what we find in the world is at least to some extent a matter of choice.

Here too, however, animal needs intrude into the cognitive sphere to obscure the distinction. The desire for stability makes us into instinctive realists who suppose that socially passed on or newly invented classifications reveal the unchangeable order of things. We feel uncomfortable with change and find it especially disquieting to suppose that there are multiple ways of conceiving things, that our own may be no better than the alternatives and that we have the power to modify things simply by thinking about them in different terms. General recognition of the contingency of our modes of thought may be the next truly important evolutionary development of the human mind.

Manners of conception are, of course, organically connected with modes of action, so what we think and what we do always influence each another. The argument that being human is a choice-inclusive fact is, therefore, a step in the direction of securing a better fate for many individuals. Chances for humane treatment improve when we commit ourselves to viewing members of widely divergent races, cultures, religions, and political groups as human beings. But this inclusive notion of humanity needs to be counterbalanced by the idea that there are multiple human natures, many of which deserve to be allowed to flourish without interference. Rejecting a single ideal of proper human functioning enables us to appreciate the variety of perfections open to us. My argument for human natures is, therefore, an attempt to articulate the metaphysical and epistemic foundations of a tolerant, pluralistic society.

Through their daily practice, lawyers and physicians are exposed to the vast range of the actual: they see how what we think normal is crowded on all sides by cases of the odd, the peculiar, the uncommon, the irregular, and the bizarre. The experience of philosophers, by contrast, has been severely impoverished by their comfortable life in universities. Our focus on a small cross section of the usual has been a great obstacle in the way of understanding human life and appreciating the scope of experience.

One way to understand my work is as an attempt to direct attention away from words toward the world and there to provide a broader experiential basis for our theories. The idea of more evidence for more modest conclusions may not appeal to those who wish to stun everyone with accounts of the rational structure of reality or arguments for the unreality of time. But, along with scrupulous honesty in the form of not believing anything we cannot enact, it strikes me as the best hope for philosophy.

Part One

PREMISE

CHAPTER 1

The Relevance of
Philosophy to Life

When the time came for our children to receive their oral polio vaccine, we took them to their pediatrician. Surprisingly, the first question the doctor asked was whether the parents themselves had had their medicine-soaked sugar cubes. Noting the puzzlement in our eyes, he explained that he viewed his job not as the narrow one of taking care of a few children, but as a broader mandate to promote public health. He was convinced, he said, that the well-being of young people is inseparable from the quality of their environment and that it is difficult, therefore, if not impossible, to safeguard their health without taking an interest in their families and in prevailing social conditions.

Not all physicians share this attitude. But I cannot help thinking that those who do, take their responsibility more seriously than doctors satisfied to treat not the socially situated person but the disease. At any rate, I know that the more interested healer is the better one to have.

The contrast between a narrow and a broad conception of responsibility is not unique to medicine. In philosophy no less than in other professions, one may view oneself as a hired hand (or a hired mind?) paid to offer courses or to give lectures. But we may also think of our work as educating young people, as making available to them the skills necessary for a good life. The weight of tradition favors this latter view. The tenor of modern existence, on the other hand, encourages us to focus on professional standards and to be satisfied with a minimalist reading of our responsibilities.

In some fields, the distinction between these incompatible notions

of the scope of responsibility is of little significance. Even if pharma-
cists, nurserymen, and typing instructors fail to go beyond the skimp-
iest demands of their standards of competence, they will not do much
harm. To be sure, a broader sense of service could help them do more
good: the pharmacist might find a generic substitute for the prescription and save people money. But what is important in such fields is
adequately captured by basic competence; beyond that, not a great
deal is at stake. In medicine and philosophy, by contrast, the stakes
are too high for the meeting of minimal standards to be enough. By
not asking the additional question or not suggesting the innovative
treatment, physicians can endanger their patients' lives. By failing to
connect critical thought with the concerns of daily existence in the
minds of their students, philosophers contribute to the impoverishment of personal life and the persistence of social irrationality.

Philosophy is an ancient instrument whose use is all but forgotten.
It sits as mere decoration in the house of learning while the kitchen
and the garage hum with activity. We need to learn to play the instrument again, to remind ourselves of the power of its music. We must
go beyond scales and finger exercises until its melody becomes the
soul of the house. Our music is the outcome and completion of the
promising sounds of the kitchen, but also the tool that makes all that
busy activity meaningful and joyous.

Because so much is at stake in philosophy, we cannot rest satisfied
with a minimalist reading of our responsibilities. It is not enough to
teach philosophy as a set of facts about what people once thought or
as a set of verbal or conceptual skills. What Plato and Hegel believed
has direct relevance to our lives today. And as even Groucho Marx
knew, verbal skills can have important practical results. Our broader
concerns must, accordingly, focus on the application of philosophical
knowledge and skills to the pressing problems of personal and social
life.

Philosophers today consider themselves academics who offer pure
knowledge or, according to one view, none at all. The relevance or
human significance or concrete result of their work appears distant
from their minds. It is important, therefore, to inquire into the
grounds of our broader obligations. Of these I see at least five, each
powerful but none uncontroversial.

The purest source of obligation is fullness of soul. Such generosity
used to be called divine; according to one account, God's creation of
the world was itself the result of having wanted to share the goodness

of existence with as many beings as possible. Stoics who felt no need of worldly goods explained their motivation for teaching their discipline as gratitude for what philosophy has done for them. And even today, those whose lives have acquired added meaning as a result of philosophical reflection share the enriching aspects of their field with authority, enthusiasm, and success rarely seen in the classroom.

The problem here is that in a world that views teaching philosophy as a job, few attain fulfillment through its study. For many today, even the ministry is a calling only in name; in reality, it is something one does for a living. Philosophy has become a profession in just this sense, enabling those who have never profited from its enriching wisdom to profit by telling others about it. The obligation to share the benefits one has received from philosophy cannot amount to much if they come to no more than the pleasure of an occasional argument, steady employment, and modest status in the academic world.

The second source of responsibility is more compelling. Society supports the university as the last and best hope of preparing its young people for life. The aim is emphatically not only, and not even primarily, to equip them with skills necessary for narrow social roles. They are to be acquainted, instead, with the best that human beings have thought and done, with a view to their repeating or improving upon these achievements. There is a tacit contract between the university and its social sponsors for it to be something different from a technical institute and something more than a haven of abstract research. Through its faculty, it must, of course, pursue the truth relentlessly and convey it to its students. But it is expected to do more: to establish the search for what is true and what is decent as permanent dispositions of young people. Our children are to emerge, accordingly, not only skilled and well-informed, but also with secure habits and character-traits and values. They are to be ready not merely to think straight but to act right, and specifically to act on the basis of what they think and to think about what they do.

No doubt this is what parents who pay for the college education of their children want and need. And this is exactly what colleges and universities promise, if the mission statements in their catalogs are to be believed. What students actually get is another matter. When philosophers teach ideas without reference to their historical source, personal relevance and social consequences, they renege on their responsibility to help students take charge of their lives. When they teach philosophy as a collection of puzzles and mistakes, or as a string of deft verbal moves, they abandon their obligation to make intelligence an effective force in life. Because parents, having been educated by the likes of us, do not know any better, we can get away with this. But that is not something of which we should be proud.

The third source of our broader responsibilities is connected to this last. We are professors, teachers, educators. What we 'profess' and teach is not neutral material. We devote our lives to reading, thinking, and writing about it; we convey it to our students without embarrassment, perhaps even with pride. Our posture toward our subject matter is one of interest and devotion; we act as if philosophy mattered and especially as if it mattered to us.

But can it matter if we fail to act on it? Demands for action are by no means unusual in the professions or in specialized fields of knowledge. The French chef who does not eat his own cooking but goes, instead, to Burger King for dinner is rightly an object of suspicion. The cancer researcher who smokes, the biologist who defends evolution in print but confesses commitment to creation on Sundays, the theorist of democracy who never votes are not cases of charming inconsistency; they constitute failures to live up to the commitments tacit in their professional activities. In just this way, philosophers who fail to embody the principles of their field in their personal lives are suspect: their words ring hollow so long as they remain words only. Devotion to reason in discourse combined with refusal to honor reason by bringing our actions in line with what we say reveals a basic incoherence, a break in the unity and integrity of the person.

Should our students attend to what we say or to what we do? It is reasonable for us to demand of ministers that they not preach what they are unwilling to practice. It is no less sensible for us to require of philosophers who, after all, claim to apply reason to every sphere, that they employ it fully in leading their own lives. The objection that a society ought not to demand that its ministers or its philosophers be better than other people makes a valid point. But it is one that belongs to the realm of excusing conditions or to the movement of forgiveness rather than to the discussion of proper expectations. For the requirement of the unity of theory and practice in our lives is not inflicted on philosophers from the outside. It is the natural result of our self-confessed commitment to the rule of reason.

The fourth fountainhead of our special responsibilities is the very nature of our subject matter. Mathematicians may have little obligation to do anything of a practical nature about their reasonings or results. But nearly everything in philosophy repudiates the idea that thinking is a terminal fact. The mathematical properties of infinity neither suggest nor demand physical application. By contrast, when we reflect on right action, criteria of justified belief, human rights, duties to our parents, standards of inference, and the good society, every result cries out for embodiment in our lives. Philosophical reasoning points beyond itself and can gain fulfillment only when it acquires influence over our actions. Those who wish to liberate philosophy from the demand for practical results must restrict its subject matter to the narrowest spheres of logic.

If it is wrong for professors not to act on what they teach, it is absurd for philosophers to disregard the demands their work articulates. Much of philosophy revolves around criteria, standards of what to think, what to believe, what to do. Such standards lay normative claims on our behavior. The claims are of two sorts. The first tell us how properly to do something, if we should care to undertake it—how to reason, for example, if we wish to think. The second decree what it is appropriate or fitting to do, quite apart from whether we want to do it or not. The commands that injustice be resisted, freedom preserved, and innocent lives saved fall in this category. Our lives abound in occasions when such claims make action mandatory. When they occur, what philosophers do must be exemplary. Those who know or set the standards must be the first to meet them. People who know the rules of implication must excel at inference; the moral philosopher must lead the moral life.

The fifth and final reason to think that we have special responsibilities derives from a widely accepted analysis of belief. According to this view, whose first great advocate was Plato and which is a hallmark of the American philosophical tradition, to believe something is, among other things, to have a tendency to act on it. Belief and action are, in this way, organically connected, demonstrating the unity of our cognitive and conative parts. If philosophers believe anything they teach, therefore, they must be prepared to act on it when the occasion arises. Conversely, if they fail to have their principles shape their behavior, we must conclude that they do not believe a word of what they teach. There is something contrived about doubt that does not penetrate to the level of action and something deceitful about beliefs concerning matters of substance that issue only in words. The only alternative to embodying our commitments in our lives is that of pursuing our profession without commitments and beliefs—a momentous fraud.

What are the broader responsibilities of philosophers? As with physicians, a list of specifics is neither possible nor appropriate. The first requirement is the realization that there are times when we must act. This engenders an alertness to opportunities for putting our principles into action. What we must do clearly depends on circumstances and on what each of us believes. There is, in this way, no ideological demand that philosophers be liberals or conservatives, that they support a free-market economy or welfare-state redistribution, that they love utilitarianism or deontology. Anything intellectually defensible is worthy to guide action, even if others believe differently and I might join them someday. The commitment of physicians to radical mastectomy may change as evidence accumulates and the effects of the procedure are better understood. But that is no reason for failing to implement it so long as it is defensible as the treatment of choice. Seeing what happens when we act on a belief, even a philosophical belief, is one of the tests of its validity; it is, therefore, a fundamental misunderstanding to withhold this trial because the conviction may turn out to be false.

We have two general areas of responsibility. The first is to bring our lives in line with our beliefs. Philosophers have, on the whole, not excelled at this. We tend to be no better, and in our feelings and actions we are no more rational, than ordinary people. One might even argue, I blush to admit, that in these respects we are below average. In looking over the long list of professional philosophers, we find distressingly many cases of mindless ambition, pettiness, arrogance, insensitivity, and a devastating lack of common sense and good judgment. The absence of even minimal decency lays waste to many colleagues and makes the lives of their mates and children unbearable. Not many chasms are greater than that between the professed high values and the despicable practice of some philosophers. There is work to be done here by all of us, and by some a staggering amount.

Our personal lives are framed in the context of a community. The second major field of our obligations is, accordingly, the social and political world that surrounds us. The injustice and irrationality of people cannot remain a matter of indifference to us. The inhumanity of large institutions demands a response. The callousness of some who are in power must be exposed. All of these, of course, are my value judgments, and I must be prepared to act them out. Your thoughts may be different from mine, but your responsibility to give them flesh in action is the same. The fact that the social world is so much larger and more powerful than you or I is no excuse for inaction. One's obligation is not to succeed, only to try and to do one's very best. In this way, even if we fail to change the world, at least we point our own souls in the right direction and convert a social defeat into personal victory.

My argument so far has been a plea for what is usually called the unity of theory and practice. What this notion of the integration of human effort actually means, however, is not altogether clear. At least three different ideas are referred to by the same phrase, and they have not been adequately distinguished. The first is what I shall call the unity of theory and practice in theorizing. Perhaps the staunchest proponent of this view, surprisingly, is George Santayana. Dismayed by the discrepancy between what philosophers believe when they act as ordinary human beings and what they find themselves affirming as a result of arcane reasonings, Santayana issued a call for honesty in our intellectual endeavors. Speaking of himself, as he thought the philosopher must, but suggesting universal applicability, he declared, "I should be ashamed to countenance opinions which, when not arguing, I did not believe."*

Such honesty yields radical results. Santayana's intention was not to tie philosophical thought to the tangled prejudices of humankind. He believed, instead, that philosophy needs to be the critical explication of what we unconsciously assume in our active moments. There are certain beliefs we enact when we operate in the world, such as that time and space are real and that we are surrounded by mind-independent things that our agency can affect. Our job as thinkers is to discover these tenets of 'animal faith' or at least never to let our dialectic carry us to the point where we contradict them. In this way, our life activities determine or place limits on what we think, and as a result, our beliefs as active beings and our opinions as theorists always coincide.

This call for the unification of our theoretical and practical lives carries no prescription for broader action. It is explicitly restricted in application to how we ought to think. The second notion of the unity of theory and practice goes beyond it to disclose the full interconnectedness of action and thought. Many philosophers employ some such

* George Santayana, *Scepticism and Animal Faith* (New York: Dover, 1955), 305.

idea and give eloquent accounts of how our beliefs reflect what we do and our actions express, or ought to express, our thoughts. Sometimes the unity of the practical and the theoretical means simply the harmony of one's ethics and world view. In other thinkers, it refers to the identity of two forms of consciousness or the equivalence of two different sorts of action. The breakdown of the unity is supposed to cause ruinous inversions or alienation; its recapture promises fulfillment, or the final perfection of the human frame.

All of this talk of unity, however, is talk only. This is what I call the unity of theory and practice in theory, for very few philosophers who embrace it go beyond writing books. Yet there is something devastatingly hollow about the demonstration that thought without action is hollow, when we find the philosopher only thinking it. We can say all the right things and we can add that saying them is not enough—but none of this helps us escape the world of words. And words can never encompass the broader forms of action nor serve as substitutes for them. There can, therefore, be no true unity of theory and practice in theory, in our ideas, in our books. It can exist only through the unified twofold agency of living persons.

I speak of the unity of theory and practice in practice, where real actions follow real thoughts. Philosophy at its best irresistibly breaks the bounds of thought, seeps out of books to love, embrace and modify the world. Such unity cannot be found in the words of philosophers but only by comparing their books with what they do. Plato had it because he left for Syracuse and Mill attained it by running for Parliament. Marx achieved it when he agitated for revolution and Spinoza reached it by quietly converting his passive emotions into active joy. We can all come near it by acting on what we believe, by making our books the authors of our deeds.

The very fact that we are philosophers burdens us with special obligations. This should present no surprise: a high calling exacts a high price. This means that if we are to be true to our profession, we must be ready for extensive and perhaps even painful action. We must not only lecture our students but also present ourselves as living examples of what we teach. Those who are after virtue in their philosophical theories should capture some of it in their personal lives.

CHAPTER 2

Reflections on Current French Philosophy

What comes out of Paris today is a welcome change from what had for decades been oozing across the Atlantic from Oxford. We get a few new ideas, we are taught a fresh technical vocabulary, we learn to do the twists and tricks the novel approach makes possible. More important than anything stated or statable, our sensitivity to the contingent and the particular receives a boost. "Postmodern" thought helps our slow advance from a medieval to a properly modern view of the world.

In certain respects, of course, Paris is no different from Oxford. Both deconstruction and ordinary language philosophy are the invention of people who live in a world of words, people who are paid to talk and write and who find it congenial, therefore, to talk and write about how people talk and write. Both deconstruction and ordinary language philosophy, moreover, are fashions in the life of thought. Such academic styles come on shore with the tide; one needs to be an old-timer to know what happens to their practitioners when the wave recedes.

We need to welcome current French philosophy for at least one negative and a host of positive reasons. Whatever philosophy may be, it is not any one style or method or result. Acknowledgment of the legitimacy of multiple aims and starting points and procedures is always difficult to wrest from totalizing philosophers. Now that pluralism is at last accepted in our field, it would be unseemly not to make room for Derrida and Lyotard and those among our colleagues who are their American friends. We do not have to agree with them to live happily in the same departments and to wish them well.

What we broadly characterize as "deconstruction" offers significant benefits. First and foremost, it brings philosophy in closer contact, once again, with literature. This helps to counteract our three-hundred-year fixation on science by opening possibilities other than those that flow from the melancholy desire to recast philosophy in the image of physics or geometry or biology or logic or even history. Aristotle taught that we must allow the subject matter to dictate both method and expected results. Since each generation forgets this basic wisdom, we need all the reminders we can get.

Derrida and others have also taught us to read texts in greater depth and with more subtle discrimination than we have been able to before. Here the abhorrent example is analytic history of philosophy with its tendency to wrench great works out of social and historical context, to study them in poor English translations, and to bring them to the bar of judgment crippled in contemporary garb. By contrast, our deconstructionist friends read not only every line of the original text but even the spaces between them. As all interpretation, their efforts display an element of imaginative construction. But this fictive edifice is at least raised on a solid foundation, with due respect for the rich ambiguities of meaning.

We need to be reminded, moreover, that philosophers have nearly always looked for unities, for similarities, for the forms of things, for the universal, for what obliterates or overcomes differences. The healthy corrective of stressing the different, of calling attention to the irreducible and, in the end, perhaps unintelligible multiplicity of the world goes a long way toward curbing the pretensions of the history of our profession.

Such an exposure of the dark underbelly of everything we do and say has, of course, been attempted before. Its most sustained example, Hegel's dialectic of negativity, displays how need, particularity, immediacy, and the power of death provide the motive force of all life and development. Hegel's account, however, is in the service of the universal: immediacy finds its truth in structured thought, and negativity assumes its rightful place in the Notion. Everything can, in this way, be safely chewed over in philosophy and disgorged, as the bee spits out honey, in the translucent form of universal reason.

Différance, by contrast, is inassimilable to any universal concept; it cannot, therefore, be part of a philosophy. It comes closer to something we do philosophy *with*, something that helps us emphasize the particularity of the particular and display how the universal in every text undermines itself. Derrida thus represents the ultimate subversion of Hegel. In Hegel the particular liquidates itself to make room for the universal, while in Derrida the universal disintegrates into particularity.

At a time when totalizing social structures intrude ever deeper into every aspect of life, this ironic attention to the neglected, the omitted, and the ambiguous is altogether wholesome. We need to accustom ourselves to the fact that the distinction between the essential and the accidental is inessential, that everything in the world is contingent, that certainty is an elusive and misleading ideal, that power is a primary reality, and that the extent of human dissembling is matched only by our gullibility. These, too, are old insights, but the way Foucault and others deploy them has a freshness and charm we have not seen for years.

The ledger is strongly positive so far. Unfortunately, however, this is only part of the story. Speaking in general terms, which are the only terms possible and appropriate here, I find four objectionable features in much contemporary French philosophy.

(1) Its subject matter. Poetry is weakest when its only subject is poets writing poetry. Professions sometimes forget the useful tasks they have been developed to address: when they do, they get bogged down in a sequence of U-turns that makes their own art and their practitioners the focus of their interest. In this way, philosophers become fascinated with the work of other philosophers and spend their time analyzing the texts produced by their colleagues.

Did our predecessors, whose texts we study, write them about the texts *they* studied? The better among them were interested in casting light on the difficulties we face in daily life and on the great crises of the human spirit. Dewey used to say that we will accomplish little so long as we concentrate our efforts on the problems of philosophy rather than on the problems of human beings. What if we don't even get to philosophical problems, being too busy deconstructing philosophical texts? The world around us is in desperate need of what our thoughtful profession can offer. I lament each missed opportunity to make individual lives more meaningful or to contribute to the social good.

(2) Its reigning assumption. The idea that everything is a mode of consciousness migrated from Hegel across the Atlantic and established itself in one aspect of Peirce's philosophy as the view that everything is but an element in a semiotic stream. Seeing the world

as a sequence of signs is but a step away from seeing nothing but symbol systems and texts. Derrida and French philosophy are not alone in having taken this melancholy journey: Nelson Goodman also thinks we construct worlds by the manipulation of symbols.

Derrida and his followers waffle on this point: there is nothing beyond language, they seem to hold, though they speak also of reference and openness to the other. The reference itself, however, is subject to the conditions of *différance*, and *différance* is a structure or condition or constituent or feature or element of signification. But to speak of signification is to drag the nonlinguistic, screaming inarticulately, into the symbolic sphere.

The issue strikes me as ill conceived if we think of it in terms of reference. We do not need reference to conduct us to what is the other of language; we live in the midst of it. I, for one, find myself in constant physical or brute existential encounter with a world of unassimilated realities. What happens to meat at dinner is nonlinguistic to the core. Eating is, of course, overlaid with all manner of rituals and meanings, but it is absurd to suppose that the dead body of the animal we chew is but a symbol or a mode of consciousness or a tasty collection of universals. In spite of his bombast in calling even human beings signs, Peirce had a sound appreciation of such brute facts: he made room for them in his system as ineliminable seconds. These realities engulf us and set the parameters of human life, reducing language and every other symbol system to the shimmer on the surface of dark water. It would be sad for philosophers to imitate the small bugs that skate on the face of the uncharted deep.

(3) Its assessment of our prospects. On the whole, philosophers have been far too sanguine about the role reason can play in life. Recent French thought appears to want to counterbalance this by being far too pessimistic. The structures of rational inquiry now dominate much of our industrial and commercial life. The large-scale production of the necessities of life, the invention of lifesaving drugs, the development of rapid travel and of instant communication would have been impossible without the constructive application of human intelligence. Those writing against technology gladly embrace its benefits in the printing and distribution of their books and in jetting to their lecture engagements. Philosophers who admonish us to let being be do not mind interfering with the river to bring running water into their homes. It is not too farfetched to suppose that intelligence applied to personal and social life can yield at least modestly

satisfying results. All of us make choices nearly all the time; long and bitter experience has convinced me that with reflection I, for one, can make them better. This commits me neither to pristine reason nor to absolute good and evil, only to the task of slowly improving the future by learning from the failed experiments of the past. The collapse of the pretensions of Enlightenment reason is not the bankruptcy of intelligence. Yet French philosophy appears to act out the belief that if we cannot have it all, none of it is of any benefit. At the same time, the conduct of French philosophers is goal-directed and rational. Thought that overlooks its own behavior and fails to profit from what it clearly does leaves one of its main tasks unexplored.

(4) Its obscurity. Everyone can write murky and difficult prose. Deflecting the blame for this, however, requires special talent. I have long admired the ability of some philosophers to create an impression of profundity. This involves the poorly understood skill of making readers feel that the impenetrability of the text is due to their own denseness rather than to the abominable quality of the writing. My teacher, Wilfrid Sellars, displayed exceptional talent in this area: through twists of technical language and turns of idiosyncratic phrase, he managed to disguise his inability to write acceptable prose.

Much of French philosophy suffers from the same disease. Admittedly, clarity is a relative idea. But it is not so relative as to justify mistaking it for familiarity after the thirtieth reading. The claim that the subject is difficult may be true and yet serve as an excuse: better writers or writers who make a serious effort can render the same ideas much easier to grasp.

I suspect that in the case of many philosophers, opacity is a natural bent or a crafted strategy. It works well as a strategy because it makes us struggle; such investment of self creates allegiance. In doing so, it carves out a community, an intellectual elite satisfied in knowledge so arcane that no outsider can secure access to it. Obscurity becomes, in this way, a tool of professionalization and imprisons philosophy in the academic world.

The wholesome message of Paris is thus lost to the community at large. As philosophers, we are confirmed in our fantasy of being a privileged band rightly supported by the sweat of our neighbors because our shrouded knowledge is intrinsically valuable. Things need not go this way, and I hope they will not. But so long as philosophers talk about philosophical texts to other philosophers in a mysterious philosophical language, they cannot keep faith with their mission. Isolated and irrelevant, we will become the butt of jokes, and our departments will be marked, as they were in England, for eradication.

Part Two

VALUES
AND RELATIONS

CHAPTER 3

Relativism and
Its Benefits

Perhaps it is our animal urge for security that turns us into dogmatists in manners and morals. As dogmatists, we live in glorious and safe ignorance of alternatives; we find it not unlikely but actually inconceivable that a style of life and a form of behavior—perhaps even a mode of dress and a fashion of wearing hair—different from ours could have any legitimacy or value. Being essentially insecure, dogmatists pounce with fury upon each innocent change and contrary current: they sense danger, opposition, or conspiracy everywhere, and fight each deviation from their norms as if their lives depended on it. Steadfast dogmatists are, therefore, immune to external change. They may be destroyed, but they will not change their minds; they would sooner lose their lives than their illusions. In putting their lives on the line, they fancy themselves defenders of all that is good and wholesome; the collapse of their cause and their inability to impose their will on the rest of this restless world seem to them a tragic defeat of everything true and noble.

The dogmatist's faith in universal moral standards can survive every external test. Only the great internal crises of the human soul can shake the foundations of such deep and instinctive commitments. Sensitive dogmatists may someday find that judging by inflexible moral rules, they must condemn the person their heart adores. This conflict of abstract principle with love may bring the whole edifice of their verbal morals tumbling to the ground.

The disintegration begins when they first demand a justification for their moral stance. How could one justify condemning a friend or one's mother for lying? They could syllogize: all acts of lying are bad, and this surely was an act of lying; hence it was clearly bad.

Dogmatists could wipe their hands of the matter at this point and never give it another thought, were it not for nagging conscience. Why should we believe that lying is always bad? Lying is a form of deception, they might answer, and clearly all deception is bad. But this is no place to stop. That deception is bad itself stands in need of proof. How shall we demonstrate it?

Perhaps deception impedes the development of human faculties or interferes with their operation. And if they cannot stop here, dogmatists can perhaps maintain that such interference is bad because it causes pain or fails to create pleasure, or because it fails to maximize the social good, or perhaps even because God may not approve of it. But will the previous question not recur? What is wrong with not creating pleasure when we could or with letting the social good take care of itself? And why not try to enliven a dull eternity by refusing to obey God's will? Here we have come to ultimate values. There is no further principle to appeal to: reasoning ceases and the wheels of justification grind to a halt. Polite disagreement is abruptly left behind; ultimate commitments unfurled, we ride into combat for the true and good.

Faced with the need to show that their own ultimate values are universal and defensible, dogmatists can rely on two strategies. They may say that certain ultimate values stand in no need of being justified: they are self-evident and shine by their own light. Alternatively, they may admit that every moral judgment must be vindicated. Specific ones can be supported by showing their relation to more general principles we hold. General principles, in turn, are justified in terms of some being or attitude or nonmoral state of affairs.

Will these strategies work? Not much can be said for the first of them. It is reassuring to think that there are universal moral standards that can be known merely by reflection. If there were such principles, self-evident and knowable by mere intuition, moral disagreements could result only from haste in judgment or a clouding of the moral sense; nothing, surely, that sound education and a clear head could not cure.

Bishop Joseph Butler, the great eighteenth-century British moralist, wrote as if he believed this when he recommended that to be sure our judgments are right we reflect on them "in the cool of the afternoon." But is the matter quite so simple as that? We are all familiar with what it is like to be totally convinced of the legitimacy of a value or the universal applicability of a moral standard. Yet the very firmness of the conviction makes it suspect. Could it not be the expression or result of our gullibility? Does it really have the marks of objective truth?

What response can the defender of such ethical intuitions make to the person who is unable to see the self-evidence of some principle? What reply is possible to the philosopher who, after many earnest attempts, cannot see the universal truth of any moral judgment? What we want to say is that persons, actions, and consequences are good or bad as objectively as physical objects are red or green or blue. The colors are there for everyone to see. Similarly, the moral features of things are open to every sensitive person's scrutiny. Those who cannot recognize them are simply blind to the moral hues of life. The analogy of color vision is striking and inventive, but it does not work to the intuitionist's advantage. The color any given object appears to have is only partly the result of its objective properties. The light in which we bathe it and the nature and condition of the sensory mechanism involved are equally indispensable determining conditions. The color varies with changes in any one of these three factors, at least one of which is the psychological and physiological condition of the subject.

This is sometimes countered by the claim that although an object may appear to have a variety of colors, its real color is what an observer with normal sense organs operating under standard lighting conditions will perceive. The objection is, of course, worthless. The very fact that we have to stabilize the variables of lighting and sensory organs by calling them 'standard' and 'normal' constitutes an admission that all color determinations are relative to them. And what we shall call 'normal' is perfectly arbitrary. Standard lighting conditions are those that resemble sunshine in this epoch on earth. But what if our sun were a red star? Normal observers are those that can see a 'full' spectrum of colors, including red. But what if the bulk of the population were red-green color defective? We cannot talk of colors without tacit or explicit reference to the nature and condition of the perceiver. The shrill insistence of the majority cannot make the color they see the real color of the object. Though I may have to heed their view, it will always remain a fact that the object appears red to many but a rich brown to me.

The case of values is analogous. What appears good is only partly a result of the objective features of the action or event. The principles or categories in terms of which a given culture or subculture views an action are in some respects similar to the lighting conditions we may use on an object of perception. And the nature and condition of the sensory mechanism are paralleled by those of the mechanisms of desire and preference in the agent. Pleasure may appear good to some and evil to others. We cannot infer from this that one or the other side must be right though, as G. E. Moore generously conceded, it may be very difficult to establish which. If disagreement is genuine and ultimate, as in morals it often is, pleasure will seem as genuinely good for Aristippus as it is bad for Cotton Mather. The natural conclusion to draw is that 'good' and 'bad' are relational terms: as with colors, we cannot meaningfully speak of the value of persons, actions, and consequences without reference to the categories of a culture and the standards and commitments of the person who judges. The moral hue of the world of action will change with changes in our social milieu and in the organ of moral sight.

Clearly, then, there are no self-evident objective—that is, universally true—moral principles. But if absolute values are, after all, in need of justification, where shall we look for the principles that might support them? We may turn to four areas for the foundation of morals: (1) society with its rules and attitudes and institutions, (2) human nature with its structure and laws of operation, (3) nature and its purposive constitution, and (4) God as the infinite lawgiver of creation. Let me remark at once that if social rules and attitudes were to serve as the foundation upon which the structure of morality is erected, we could not legitimately say that values are absolute and unchanging. Persons, actions, and consequences would then be good as a result of their relation to socially established norms. Although every society would have some values, there is no reason to suppose that the values of any one would be identical with those of any other.

One might attempt to argue for the universality of at least such generic values as social cooperation and the survival of the members of the group. Yet this is a verbal gloss: it is a way of reading identity into diverse views and values by the expedient of calling them by the same name. 'Social cooperation' among primitive Eskimos involves different values and fundamentally diverse modes of behavior from what is required for it in a tour group from Hoboken or in the Pentagon. And even today 'survival of the members of the group' means radically different things in Washington and in Beijing. Generalities sometimes reach the stage of becoming vacuous or purely verbal: there is no better example of this than the claim that all societies share a single vision of the good. Values, if social in origin, vary with societies. If they do, the similarity of societies is the measure of the uniformity of the good.

A like observation should be made about the view that locates the source of values in human nature. If the view is true, values are uniform only to the extent that individual human natures coincide. It is clear, therefore, that absolute values could not be grounded this way without the ancillary tenet of a shared and unchanging human nature. Questions about our nature are notoriously difficult to handle. This is no place to handle them, even if I could. A few things, however, need to be said. They can be said briefly and with a reasonable degree of certainty. The question of what we shall be satisfied to call human nature is partly a definitional, and hence conventional, and partly an empirical matter. We always have the option of permitting our definitions to be guided by our preconceptions or our changing whims. We can go so far as to take the heroic course of disregarding most of the empirical evidence in our steadfast conviction that many of those who appear human do not properly deserve the compliment. If, however, we allow the suggestions of good sense to guide our concept formation, we shall find ourselves overwhelmingly committed to the view that human nature is no constant and that what we are dealing with is, at best, a wide spectrum of resembling individuals who do not share a single common essence. If human nature is to serve as the foundation of morals, the more reason we have to doubt the uniformity of that nature, the more we are entitled to deny the existence of universal values.

This leaves us with only two possible foundations for absolute morals. The first is the possibly infinite realm of facts we call Nature. Dogmatists might take a cosmic perspective and assert that the world is saturated with potentialities that demand actualization. It is a law of nature, we might think, that beings with specific potencies must strive to reach fruition: perfection consists in having what is latent discharged. Actualized being is both the aim and the result of potentiality; without it, everything would be frustrated and incomplete. Thus, value is or is grounded in the actuality that lures matter to create it.

The lawlike and natural connection between fact and fulfillment would amply suffice as the foundation of morals, were it not for the fact that it does not exist. The view that Nature is replete with potentialities aiming at self-realization and values that, although they do not yet exist, charm the world to make them actual is perhaps the most colorful of human fables. The natural world abounds with struggle and striving. But who would want to say that each of a plenitude of beings aims at achieving some minor element of the cosmic good? We can look at things this way, just as we can see shadows as giants and each frog as a metamorphosed minor royalty. In doing so, however, we commit a great blunder: we tacitly impute aim and consciousness to every natural impulse. The flux of nature has direction and frequently results in the production of some value. But to suppose that direction implies an aim, that motion requires an underlying love of the beautiful and the good to generate it, is to view simple physical fact as if it had an element of mind animating it at every turn.

If we examine the facts calmly and free of the persistent drive to find more rationality in the world than it displays, we are struck less by the remarkable adaptation of means to ends and the effort of every being at self-actualization than by the spectacle of the mindless indifference with which nature fulfills or frustrates its own potentials. There are millions of acorns for every oak tree: the phenomenon of discharged potency is the exception rather than the rule. Why should we disregard the wide compass of dysteleology and the plenitude of crushed potentials in nature? If we must see purposes in physical process, we might agree with the disenchanted Schopenhauers of the world that perpetual frustration of the will is the rule in nature and actualized good is for most a rare and furtive joy. In any case, to ground the concrete values of the moral life in some hypothetical cosmic principle that reads vestiges of mind into a mindless flux is as implausible as it is ill-advised.

Let me finally speak of God's decrees as a possible support for human values. In grounding the good in divine commands, we are presupposing the existence of a God who can make laws, proclaim rules of behavior, and create values at will. The existence of such a God seems highly dubious to me. I say this not as a person who believes in the existence of no deity at all or as one who refuses to accept the reality of a Christian God. My objection to the conception of God as an untrammeled creator of values and laws is precisely that it is not Christian enough, that it introduces the disturbing and religiously unacceptable element of arbitrary power into the concept of a being of pure love.

One could dwell on the grave philosophical difficulties of such a concept of God. But that is another story. For now it is enough to make two points. If God is the source of all values, in one important sense they are not objective or absolute. At a minimum, they are binding values only because God chooses them; only their relation to God makes them values at all. This should incline those who object to everything relational to mend their ways or at least to realize that they quarrel not with relativity but only with its terms. They think it all right for values to be relative to the whim of God, but not to the will of humans.

Second, what are the conditions requisite for making the commands of an Infinite Being relevant to our finite lives? No command, whatever its source, could be binding on a person who lacked the intelligence to grasp it or the capacity to act on it. One cannot command a stone, nor an Eskimo in Latin, no matter how elegant or fluent. Commands and values must suit the station and the circumstances, the nature and the capacities of the person who is to act on them or to adopt them. Hence even if all values have their source in God, their uniformity is not guaranteed. If human nature is varied, commands and values relevant to one person may be unsuited, perhaps even unintelligible, to others. The uniformity of God's effective commands thus becomes dependent on the uniformity of human nature.

Was Protagoras, then, right in the end and is nothing good but thinking makes it so? A few things are farther from the truth, but not many. We do not think or act as if mere thoughts and feelings could make much difference to what is good or bad. And if Protagoras were right, we could never be mistaken in our aims and values: whatever we desired at any time would then be good, at least for us. Yet what could be a more painful or pervasive fact of life than moral error in choosing our goals? Inadequate self-knowledge frequently makes us adopt ends that do not satisfy. Few humans, moreover, have not had the experience of choosing the lesser over the greater, the nearer over the remote, the apparent over the real good.

Such shortsighted and inhumane relativism could never account for the bitter complexity of moral experience. But there is a relativism that many candid and tolerant minds spontaneously believe. Human nature is various: this variety, due to biological, social, and psychological conditions, must be construed not as a threat or an evil, but as a God-given bounty of being. A variety of natures implies a variety of perfections. Only egotists, committed to seeing pale replicas of them-

selves everywhere in the world, would want to impose the same values and the same mode of behavior on every living soul. Sanity and
toleration demand that we allow each person to pursue his or her
own, possibly unique, form of fulfillment; if we had even a vestige of
Christian love, we would rejoice in seeing the growth of all human
beings toward their goal.

Values vary with the individual's nature. The good, therefore, is a
matter not of what we think or how we feel, but of who we are. A
person's nature, though not unchanging, is perfectly definite. This
makes progress in self-knowledge possible. It also renders the goals
that fulfill definable and our values precise. The good may differ in
part or whole from person to person, but one's own is always vital
and legitimate. Would moral or social anarchy not flow if we acted as
though this view were true? Not in the least. If the nature of individuals determines their values, similar natures yield similar commitments. The fact that human beings live in cooperative societies is the
best evidence that their natures are similar or at least compatible.
This resemblance is created, at least in part, by processes of socialization that are, on occasion, so successful that even people set free to do
precisely what they want continue to do their usual, useful tasks.
What little self-realization there may be that interferes with the fulfillment of others can be readily controlled by the threat or the application of force. In an orchestra, each instrument plays its own tune; is
this reason for saying that there is anarchy in the pit? The fact that
values are individual does not entail that people must fail to agree on
common goods and goals.

From the time that God or Adam called the first two philosophers
into existence, they and their descendants have argued about the ultimate source of values. Argument can go on too long. Today, the
interest of many philosophers in the sort of relativism I propose
would be to develop its technical details. This would enable them to
discuss it at length and to suggest minor changes in its formulation.
One feels intellectually clean after such an exercise: use of our train-
ing in drawing useless distinctions appears to justify it.

I earn my living by chopping my share of logic, so I cannot consistently denounce the procedure. And in reality it has an important
role to play: we must explore and appraise what precisely is worthy
of belief. I welcome that sort of hard-nosed inquiry into this view.
But another task is no less important. At some point, we must
announce results and go to the public to convince. The intellect's

obligation to pursue truth is no greater than the demand on the will to disclose it. Philosophy must have its own technology and results: if science yields refrigerators and the Salk vaccine, philosophy should give us the tools for wisdom and an improving public mind.

Consider the benefits that would accrue if we could make this relativism generally accepted. The view is a secular variant of the beautiful thought of many theologians that even the least of creatures has dignity and justification in the eyes of God. Sincerely believed, this thought could transform the soul. It would help allay our suspicion of all things alien. It could render us more modest and loving by showing the monstrous egotism displayed in judging another. As a result, we could develop a more tolerant and helpful attitude toward life styles and values different from those we like or admire; we could begin to appreciate moral variety and the bounty of fulfillment and perfection open to humans. The personalities shaped by such beliefs and attitudes would be attuned to the beauty and harmony of life. The vast energy we now consume in hate and in attempts to make others do our will could be harnessed to enhance our appreciation and joy. If such attitudes were dominant in it, human personality at large would for the first time resemble that of the great moral masters and cease to be offensive.

If private improvement would be extensive, public benefits would likely be immense. Children could be brought up with fewer useless precepts and damaging attitudes. Education, both of intellect and of character, could at last lose some of its rigidity. Human relations could be infused with elements of humane understanding, and cooperation might well take the place of blind antagonism. Condemnation of other persons and nations becomes difficult in proportion to our ability to see the legitimacy of differing ideals. Accordingly, justifications of hatred and war would be recognized as specious and dismissed by all who take the relativity of values seriously.

The greatest beneficiary of the universal acceptance of moral relationalism would, without doubt, be human liberty. There is a shrill, constrictive tone to many of our laws. They overrun fields where compulsory social prescriptions are inappropriate or unnecessary. If we were all relativists, most of the laws designed to enforce the uniformity of morals would be seen as unjustified. This would significantly increase the scope of choice and render now restricted human actions free.

Evidently, the firmest social and state controls are necessary to protect persons from the real harm others would do them. But due allowance must be made for the difficulty of generalizing about what is to count as harm. The experience that would be harmful to a child may well mean fulfillment to an adult homosexual. If we forbid that children be tempted into such actions, must we also forbid it to consenting adults? And what is the fancied public interest requiring that monogamy be the sole law of the land? Attention to differences in desires and temperaments would reveal such restrictions on human interaction as intolerant, if not insane.

Society would not collapse if we were to let a hundred flowers bloom. To be sure, it would be different in structure and operation from what it is today. It would be different and it would be better. But if believing and acting on moral relativism would bring about such a profound improvement in our lives, why have we not accepted it? Our beliefs and acts surely express our current, aggressive nature; what violates the integrity of our being or would tend to change it is difficult to embrace. Instinctive dogmatists, therefore, find it hard to see the merits of relativism on intellectual grounds alone.

Our best hope to escape egotism is by appealing to it. Our chance of making the world or even a small segment of it live by our values is negligible. With the increase in social regimentation and the growth of large impersonal institutions, we find, in fact, ever more trouble in making even our own conduct conform freely to our ideals. A cutback in scope promises increase in intensity: sound self-interest demands that each of us attend to his or her own life and leave the moral condition of others their sole business. The alternative is to lose control even of oneself, a frequent condition of ambitious egotists.

At stake is the eternal hope to tame human nature. Benevolence may be too high an ideal. Toleration of others would be enough or, as an absolute minimum, indifference to how they shape their fate. If we could only believe moral relativity, we would have the intellectual foundation of such indifference. Our nature could then be changed enough to merit being called truly human. We might even render our lives joyous and our survival assured. When shall we go to work?

CHAPTER 4

Values and Relations

With the exception of a few mad Platonists, philosophers have always believed that values are relational realities. As always, Plato himself avoided the excesses of his followers. He recognized that although goodness is a self-standing form, its embodiment in this twilight world involves the relation between the nature of a being and its activities. Nature, for Plato, is thus the foundation and measure of the goodness of any creature or its acts. A good dog and a good person are very different sorts of beings, and the actions we can demand from them vary accordingly. Plato goes so far as to suggest that perfection differs even within species: what is fitting for men and women ruled by appetite is ignoble for thinkers or warriors.

Such sensible stress on the role relations play in the generation and justification of values is ubiquitous in the history of thought. Even those who believe in absolute and timeless values gladly embrace relations. For some of them, the right and the good find their ground in a universal and changeless human nature. Only in relation to such a constitution, to its structure or to its demands, can anything, in their view, be considered valuable. Others lodge the foundation of the good in the nature or will of an eternal God. They believe that only in relation to His decrees can we praise or condemn any action, object, or individual.

For Aristotelians and for Thomists, no less than for Kantians and for the followers of Brunner, nothing is good simply in and by itself. For all of them, the value of anything is constituted or supported by a relation to something else. There is no disagreement among these widely different thinkers about the need for some relation. Conflict centers only on the being, event, or feeling to which the relation obtains and, derivatively, on the precise nature of the connection. Even the hedonistically inclined utilitarian agrees with this line of thought, believing that the value of actions is a function of their relation to pleasure. And let me emphasize that the relations of which I speak need not be, and in fact for most thinkers are not, the relatings accomplished in judgments. On the contrary, they are fully objective, real connections that obtain independent of the work of mind.

These remarks are particularly suitable to introduce a demonstration of the metaphysical underpinnings of morality. And that topic would have attracted me ten or twenty years ago when metaphysics was still in ill repute. But times have changed and, for now at least, it is not necessary to work that ground again. I want to address, instead, a surprising conjunction of views. Most of the philosophers who readily acknowledge the central role of relations in the analysis of values steadfastly deny something they call 'relativism.' This is all the more baffling because in a perfectly obvious sense, all of these thinkers are relativists. They believe that everything good is of value only in relation, or relative, to such things as the decrees of God or the demands of human nature. Why, then, does it appear attractive to them to escape the relativist label?

The answer is not that these philosophers want to strike a blow on behalf of absolute, in the sense of intrinsic, self-standing, or nonrelational, values. They want, instead, to fixate the good and to give it universal scope. By connecting value with an eternal God or with timeless and unitary human nature, they hope to bestow on it the dignity of what never changes and applies everywhere. Viewed from a practical perspective, and ethics is nothing if not practical, this is no mean feat. It assures us that the values now commanding our thoughtful allegiance need never be revised and that they are authoritative for human beings of either sex and every race and all sorts whenever and wherever they happen to live.

Relating values to an eternal deity would unquestionably establish their changeless universality. But the difficulties of interpreting the assertions and ascertaining the intentions of God are notorious. The stability and uniformity of the good can acquire no greater certainty in this way than the assurance with which we can say that there is a God, that His commands are just these and no other, and that these orders have a self-evident and invariant meaning through all of history.

There is a more direct and more promising way to secure unity and scope for values. If we suppose that they acquire their authority because they express the demands of a shared nature, we can conclude that they apply to all humans everywhere. Our goods can then be seen as identical because all of us are human beings with similar needs seeking the same fulfillment. Values relative to a single, unchanging human nature hold absolutely for all who partake of that essence.

The assumption of such a unitary, shared human nature haunts the entire history of Western thought. Normally, it takes the form of the insistence that we are all ruled by reason, but it also shows itself in the, typically unsupported, supposition that we all have the same faculties. Our emotional makeup is thought to be closely similar, and even our lamentable animality is assumed to be of a single, tiresomely predictable sort. With respect to their fundamental constitution, human beings are considered to be devastating bores: it is as true of them as it is, according to a previous president, of redwood trees that once you have seen one, you have seen them all.

We must not underrate the attractiveness of such a view. It establishes the foundation of a universal human community and through that the possibility of intercultural understanding and of communication across the ages. It can serve as the normative basis of worldwide political action and as the foundation of a universal religion. Of course, it can also ground intolerance and is open to disastrous abuse. It can be employed to sanction the repression of minorities and the extirpation of deviants. And it is easy for those in power to invoke it when they attempt to force everyone into a single mold, coercing uniformity in institutions, beliefs, behavior, even in taste.

Utility apart, however, do we have reason to believe that something in the world answers to the idea of a single, universal human nature? Let me begin to frame an answer to this question by distinguishing two ways in which the human essence can be supposed to inhere in us. According to the traditional view, which goes back to Plato and Aristotle, however much social interaction it takes to accomplish this, each individual manifests more or less fully the entirety of the human form. The alternative conception, which became popular in German idealism, takes the human essence to be communal and not individual. When, for example, Marx says that man is a species-being, he has in mind that no single person and no group of persons smaller than the entire human race can ever embody our nature. Our form, therefore, is not like that of number, which 1 and 2 and 75 each manifests individually and quite well. It is, rather, like the form circle, whose embodiment requires a very large number of points, all suitably arranged, none of which displays circularity alone or in smaller groups.

It is attractive to think that the human essence is historically evolving. And in an expansive mood it may not sound completely absurd to assert that we are everything we shall become. But neither of these ideas requires us to believe that only the organic state or the human race as a whole manifests our essence. In thinking that they do, such philosophers as Marx and Hegel simply fail to distinguish forms from the conditions of their embodiment. We are social creatures and this means, among other things, that no one can become a full-fledged human being without the help of others. Nurture and the transmission of culture are necessary for children to attain fully developed humanity. Once they have done so, however, each manifests individually the characteristic traits of our species. Even if some of these human features or skills require a social context to be displayed (language and love normally involve others), they are not socially possessed. The situations that permit us to actualize our nature are not parts of it.

If the human form is individual, do we have reason to suppose that it is the same form in every individual? Many philosophers think we do, but I believe they are mistaken. The notion of a single, uniform human nature has been kept alive by two of the less admirable characteristics of philosophers: empirical inattention and the penchant for high-level generalization. It does not take an intimate knowledge of anthropology to become familiar with the variety of beings we call human; a few thoughtful trips to the penitentiary, the emergency room, and the mental hospital, even to the grocery store and the local bar, suffice. Academic institutions and middle-class suburbs are safe havens not well situated to expose us to diversity. Yet the broad spectrum of our abilities and activities, affections and afflictions, faculties, needs, and destinies is undeniable.

Even the suspicion of such diversity mobilizes philosophers to search for a shared essence. Unity and simplicity are attractive features of thought and we may expect, on occasion, to attain them. But what constitutes a hope for some tends, for philosophers, to be a demand, perhaps even a demand of reason itself. Accordingly, they not only seek unity but take steps to achieve it, even at the cost of a generality or indefiniteness that renders the result vacuous. And it is, of course, always possible to reduce the obvious multiplicity of human natures to a single essence, if we are prepared to move to a high enough level of abstraction.

That a human being is a rational animal, for example, has long been recognized as the affirmation of hope rather than an assertion of fact. How can we make it true or at least not blatantly false about all human beings? We can move from actual reflection or rational behavior to the possibility of it and boldly announce that we have the *power* to think, even if we choose not to use it. But then we are confronted with people unable to reflect beyond the level available to lions and baboons, with congenital idiots, hydranencephalics, and catatonic schizophrenics. Such devastating counterexamples, however, do not for long stop the searchers after essence: they invent the idea that all of us have the *power to develop the power* to reason, even if obstacles prevent the least actualization of this initial potentiality.

Such forced constructions are of little value. We can, of course, assert many general truths about people, such as that they all need food to live and that they display selectivity in their behavior. But these statements call attention to traits we share with creatures of other species and, therefore, fail to identify a form all and only human beings embody. It is reasonable to conclude that, though human beings have much in common, they lack a single, universally shared essence.

In anchoring our good in who we are, therefore, we are inevitably carried to the acknowledgment of multiple goods and a diversity of natures. According to this view, all value has a foundation in fact, and only its special relation to some nature confers worth on any action. But someone may object that this permits an event to be both good and bad. So it does, though without contradiction. Since good and bad are relational properties, they can characterize the same object in its different connections. We do not hesitate to speak of a fortune as both great and small, depending on the sum of money to which it is compared, and of a person as both short and tall, depending on who happens to stand nearby. Should we then fear trouble when we discuss right and wrong?

I am afraid we should, for at least two reasons. The first is an experience of loss, the second a concern based on misunderstanding. If we take the view that values are grounded in individual nature, the reassuring simplicity of the moral world disappears. We can no longer rest content with determining the moral properties of actions once and for all. These features, along with all the other characteristics of things, are subject to change. Moreover, because any object can display a number of such apparently contradictory relational properties, the simplicities of conventional belief are inadequate to capture them. This spells the end of the mean pleasure that condemnation from a distance affords. It is also the end of laziness in moral matters, of feeling justified in not thinking about the value of things because others have.

The loss, as you can see, is palpable, though not one over which we need to grieve. The concern is of greater philosophical weight. In viewing values as relational properties and in rejecting a uniform human nature, we appear to be relativizing the good to the point where it loses its normative force. Value becomes, in this way, a function of our current condition, possibly even of our opinions or feelings. If anything anyone at any time considers good is truly so, moral improvement is unnecessary and the enhancement of moral knowledge is impossible. Improvement, on the one hand, is unnecessary because everything is already as good as we think it. And, in any case, should we wish to have things better, all we need to do is to form a higher opinion of them. On the other hand, our knowledge of values cannot be enhanced because each moral assessment or feeling is an independent fact and none represents an advance over any other. In this view, evaluation *constitutes* the value of the object. For this reason, it can never be incorrect, nor can it ever be corrected or improved.

These are legitimate concerns, and philosophers have been right in attacking such extreme relativisms from Plato's day on. But it is clearly a misunderstanding to suppose that a position even vaguely resembling this follows from what I have said. Life has too much pain and disappointment for us to be able sensibly to deny the reality of error about values. The good has, and must in our accounts be shown to have, a normative force: when we disregard it, misrecognize it, or fail to achieve it, we suffer the consequences. It has, moreover, far greater stability than the tie to fickle opinion can provide. My view, accordingly, maintains that the generation and justification of values occur in relation to the nature of individuals, not to their passing emotions or thoughts. This nature sets a standard, which is no less compelling for being individual, and confers rewards for meeting it. Values enjoy, in this way, an objective, real foundation in their relationship to the needs, activities, and other facts constitutive of persons.

What might such a theory of individual relationalism look like? It must begin with the acknowledgment that values are grounded in the fact that we are needy, less-than-perfect beings. Food is good only for creatures with alimentary tracts that they must fill at regular intervals or else face pain and death. Clean air is of value only to a being whose existence depends on the work of lungs. Beings without need, perfect beings, may be able to understand that some value food and air, but they would find no intrigue in them. To dispassionate reason, to pure understanding nothing is preferable to anything else: even valid reasoning and truth derive their value from the need and the drive of hard-pressed organisms to sort out the world.

Our needs give rise to active tendencies to meet them. I am not satisfied that there is a single word in the English language that accurately captures the nature of these tendencies. 'Interest' is bland and fails to suggest activity; 'impulse' remedies this, but at the cost of focusing on sudden, uncontrolled actions of short duration. 'Habit' rightly stresses the sustained nature of these tendencies, but carries connotations of mindless passivity. 'Drive' restores the activity, but suggests lack of intention and autonomous control. 'Desire' conveys a connection with action and is commendably neutral on its scope and complexity. But it has misleading mentalistic overtones and too close a tie to articulate consciousness. Let me, therefore, adopt the phrase 'active tendencies' to refer to the activities, budding and actual, of people in response to their needs. Active tendencies are frequently purposive and sometimes conscious. They can be of short duration or established as permanent dispositions of the organism. Some of them are relatively focused, while others are diffused; many are guided by intelligence, though more than a few suffer from being impulsive and blind.

Active tendencies are always selective: they fasten on certain objects and events in preference to everything else. It is easiest to see this on the biological level. Hunger is focused on objects that can be used as food and on such events as chewing and swallowing. But the same selectivity prevails in more subtle psychological, cultural, and even spiritual matters. When we wish to pray, for example, we prefer speaking to swatting flies and scratching, we think it better to say quiet, respectful words than to tell fish stories or to cuss, and we choose a certain form of words, such as the Lord's Prayer, over those prescribed by an ayatollah or over Buddhist chants.

By a chemistry I cannot explain, the objects and events on which our active tendencies fasten frequently appear not only chosen but also good. I am confident that seeing them as good is not the result of judgment capturing their intrinsic features. We simply find that, quite without thought, spontaneously and sometimes inexplicably, we experience certain objects *sub specie boni*. Later, of course, the mystery is dispelled as we learn of the involvement of our active parts with the objects or events we deemed good. It is no wonder I think of how good a steak would be if I missed both breakfast and lunch. This does not mean that goodness is identical with the interest my active tendencies take in what they seek. The tendencies are best described in organic terms, and goodness, as it is experienced, cannot readily find a place among biological categories. It would be better to suppose that our experience of goodness qualifying an object is one way—a characteristic, important, and irreducible way—in which the work of our active tendencies rises to consciousness.

When needs engender activities and those, in turn, achieve their objectives, the organism flourishes. This prosperity, relative and temporary for the most part, rises to consciousness in the form of satisfaction. 'Satisfaction' denotes something broader than 'pleasure,' which is burdened, in any case, with sensory and animalistic overtones. I mean by 'satisfaction' agreeable consciousness of any kind, whatever its source or duration. Every active tendency that rises to consciousness endows its object with value, and every objective achieved yields a consummation. This difference between the good in prospect and the good enjoyed establishes the first possibility of moral error. The distance between expectation and reality measures not only our mistakes but also the opportunity to eliminate them in the future. Almost the entirety of the project of moral education, which is a central part of family and community existence, is deployed around this process of learning from our errors in the art of life. Those who take the view that morality is discontinuous with the ordinary valuing activities of people are unable to understand and account for the immense civilizing influence of this education. My view, by contrast, sees moral error and moral improvement as organically connected. We learn to pursue our true good the way we learn to fish: by experience that is sometimes sad, we must identify the right places to look, the right species to hook, and the right technique to capture what we want.

The second opportunity for moral error arises from the periodic discrepancy between short-term and long-term goods. Some of our active tendencies are directly or closely connected with the deep, established interests of the person. Others, though strong for a time, are peripheral or at odds with what the individual needs to flourish over extended stretches of its life. The impulsive force of narrow tendencies focused on immediate satisfaction sometimes overpowers the drives that aim at more inclusive goods. It is not that violent impulses fail to generate value. They are fully justified from their own perspective, so in acting them out, we prefer value to value. But the good we choose is impoverished by comparison with what we forgo: our momentary gain comes at the expense of the comprehensive, life-enhancing interests of the organism.

To be sure, some people opt systematically for the powerful, immediate drives. If the organism brings its interests fully in line with the object of these active tendencies, we have no basis for condemning what it does. But if it wants to live long and well, going with impulse is a moral error. Can Odysseus censure Achilles' choice? Not from the standpoint of the young man who cast his lot with passion. But in his own case, impulse and final good are not identical. He can, therefore, see the mistake of living at white heat and choose a different course for his own life.

The view I have sketched can be summarized by saying that value consists of two three-term relations. The first identifies the generative conditions of the good and involves a connection between the active tendencies of a person, the value-experience in the form of which these rise to consciousness, and some object or event that is deemed worthy of pursuit. The active tendencies begotten of our needy nature hold the causal key in the generation of value. But without the form of the good, which we all know from direct experience, there would be no value, only striving in the dark. The thermostat whose active tendency attempts to keep the temperature at seventy degrees does not see the equilibrium as good. That is why such stable comfort is of value only to us and not to the mechanism that assures it. The object or event, finally, that we see as good may be anything actual or possible. The momentous scope of the things we can embrace is perhaps the most instructive part of anthropology. If you decide to explore the matter, do not neglect textbooks of abnormal psychology.

The second three-term relation captures the epistemic conditions of value. Here desired objects and events serve as signs of active tendencies. When we find some object bathed in the light of the good, we can reasonably infer that there is something in our nature that seeks it and whose needs it might well satisfy. The meaning of this sign-significate relation is interpreted by later experience. The satisfactions that follow upon attainment of the object sought confirm the successful embodiment of the value relation. Alternatively, if capture of the desired good fails to yield satisfaction, we have evidence that object and need do not match, that the sign relation is wanting in this case.

I want to stress that this account of the generation and the recognition of value is neutral with respect to how widely human natures differ. Even if all of us share a single essence, my relational view of how the good, satisfaction, and our active parts connect is left untouched. The important idea remaining is that the good finds its source and consummation in individuals; whether these persons are similar or not, we can lay aside as an ancillary question. In fact, we find people significantly different with respect to at least some of their needs and a good many of their active tendencies. This suggests that they value a wide variety of things, and the diversity of their satisfactions confirms the hypothesis that their divergent values reveal divergent natures.

I think, however, that leaving the issue of the diversity of human natures as a purely factual one is a mistake. We note our differences, but we also make decisions about the differences that will exist in the next generation. The question, therefore, is not only how dissimilar human beings are, but also how dissimilar we ought to be. This is the point where the metaphysical foundation of ethics naturally flows into the philosophy of education. It is reasonable to suppose that a certain amount of diversity is desirable; human beings are not machine parts that must be uniform and interchangeable. But differences should exist within limits: the natures we create should be such as have a high likelihood of being satisfied and whose satisfaction does not endanger others and the life of the community.

Our power to engineer our similarities and differences is, naturally, far from absolute. There will always be some whose divergence, due to genetic or environmental factors, exceeds the accepted limits. How shall we treat these brothers and these sisters devoted to the pursuit of alien goods? With the greatest toleration the safety of the community and our own pursuit of nonmilitant values will allow. My view of the generation and justification of multiple goods is meant to provide the conceptual groundwork of such toleration.

CHAPTER 5

How Relative Are Values?
or Are Nazis Irrational and
Why the Answer Matters

I embark here on a dangerous course. I intend to argue that Hilary Putnam's claim* that Nazis are irrational is mistaken. I shall try to show that Putnam's notion of human nature is too narrow, that at least some of his premises are untenable and that, in any case, belief in the supremacy of the cognitive, which he adopts without support, is precisely what any serious Nazi must reject. On one level, therefore, Putnam does not even manage to engage the Nazi. Where an engagement occurs, the implausibility of Putnam's assumptions renders his view unworthy of belief.

My course is dangerous because, in criticizing Putnam's attack on Karl the Nazi, I may come to be seen as Karl's advocate. My objections to Putnam might then appear as a defense of wicked people and an inhumane system. If this view of my efforts is permitted to take hold, the more persuasive I am intellectually, the more monstrous I will seem from a moral point of view.

To forestall any possible misunderstanding, therefore, let me declare at once that my aim is not to justify Nazi ways. Putnam is right that given the shared, or at least the official, commitments of the liberal West, the values Karl's life displays are unacceptable. But this point is irrelevant. Both Putnam and I are after bigger, and less malodorous, fish. The case of the Nazi is used merely to highlight the issue of our proper relation to deviant minorities and to measure the range of our toleration. On this last point, I must note with regret

* *Reason, Truth, and History* (London and New York: Cambridge University Press, 1981). *Reason* hereafter.

that, Putnam's recently expanded philosophical reading notwith-standing, his sympathies have not been much enlarged. Although he pays lip service to the legitimacy of individual differences, his idea of human perfection is restrictive and monochrome.

Here is one way we might think of our relationship to people unlike us, Nazis included. We might reflect on their beliefs and val-ues to see if they have anything to teach us. If we decide that they do not, we forget about them. If we find it difficult or unpleasant to get along with them, we leave them alone. If they do not leave us alone, attacking the values we treasure and interfering with our attempt to lead the life we choose, we indicate our displeasure and take steps to dissuade them. If they do not cease their aggressive activity, we fight them. When our values are safe and our security is reestablished, we once again leave them alone.

This appears to be a perfectly sensible way of dealing with people who are in important ways different from us. Yet many human beings find it wanting: they are not satisfied unless they can pass judgment on the actions and the character of their fellows. Nor do they think it adequate simply to fight for their values; they desire an elaborate cosmic justification of what they are inclined to do. The best among these, of course, is that our enemies are wicked, caring neither for God nor for the good. This places us on the side of the angels, and we can fancy that we are in the enviable position of fighting not for our chosen way or grubby selves but for what is truly good and right and natural.

Instinctively self-certain people need no such justification: to them, fighting for what they believe feels natural and cosmically right. But ours is a reflective and discursive culture and many of those in the business of handing it on feel that actions we cannot verbally defend are somehow illegitimate. Accordingly, they have made innumerable attempts to formulate rules to justify what we do and principles to justify these moralizing justifications. The critical venom of these stu-dents of moral language and moral thought is directed at each other. They are prepared to question every account of universal or objective moral claims, but not why we should ever want to make such claims at all.

Hilary Putnam goes a step beyond the usual moral smear cam-paign against our enemies. He argues not only that Karl the Nazi is wicked but also that he, and other people whose values differ signifi-cantly from ours, is irrational. In addition to not acting right, such

individuals cannot think straight, for if they could, they would understand the folly of their ways. If they were rational, they would ask
the relevant questions and they would give cognitively acceptable
answers;* in this way, they would quickly become convinced that our
values alone are objective and defensible.

The disarming naiveté of this view is only thinly guised by the
sophisticated arguments that support it. In fact, Putnam displays the
not uncommon inverse relation between technical brilliance and
sound judgment. The clarity and neatness of abstract arguments can
mislead logicians into supposing that the world, and disagreements
in the world, share these properties. Putnam extols the virtues of the
imagination but fails to avail himself of them when it comes to dealing with the messy but very real self-justification of alien forms of life.

What makes Karl irrational? In the prevailing view of rationality,
the role of reason is restricted to the specification of means: ends are
chosen and embraced, intelligence serves merely as the tool to get us
what we desire. We can be wrong, therefore, only concerning the tendency of what we do to bring about what we want; there is no sensible way to criticize the value choices any of us makes.

Putnam is right in attacking this view of rationality. Means and
ends are not rigidly and externally related to one another but compose, instead, a single, unbroken chain. Many things we desire as
ends surprise us by turning into means (to further ends) once they are
attained. And habitual means can easily become ends desirable on
their own account. The claim that only means are open to rational
examination becomes vacuous the moment we realize that everything
we treasure as an end is also, in another of its functions, an instrument to further satisfactions.

This intimate connection of means and ends leaps out at us upon
the least attention to human activity. Of all the elaborate and deli-
ciously complex actions that constitute making love, which are the
means and which the end? The act as a whole is not a single goal;
many of its constituents make sense only because of where they lead.
Yet the orgasm is surely not the single enjoyable end to which the
entire process, like a burdensome instrument, points. The plain fact is
that each portion of the act is enjoyable for its own sake, and yet
serves, leads to, elicits the next. Each is both means and end, sought
for its own sake and for the sake of its causal properties.

* *Reason*, 202.

The universal coexistence of means and ends undercuts both the fact-value distinction and the instrumental theory of rationality. It makes it possible for us to apply intelligence across the full spectrum of human activities and enjoyments: we can assess the cost and value of any means or end by giving due consideration to its conditions and consequences. John Dewey has explored these issues in detail; ignorance of the advances he achieved is a devastating failure in nearly all contemporary moral thought.

Without showing much sympathy with his work, Putnam mentions Dewey and quickly dismisses him.* There is too much relativism in Dewey, Putnam avers, for him to be able to denounce the Nazi as irrational. The truth of this claim is by no means obvious, and Putnam does not stay to debate it. But the comment calls to our attention that even in Dewey's view, there are some ultimate, largely uncriticizable facts involved in valuation. What we enjoy or find satisfying serves as the foundation in terms of which costs and benefits are defined, and the taste for such enjoyments may well be a primitive, hard, and final reality about our constitution. We can criticize it only in terms of other basic satisfactions it makes too costly or impossible.

This is the root of ethics in our nature, and Putnam himself acknowledges its legitimacy. What seems to bother him is that Dewey remains respectful of the facts and allows for the possibility of divergent human natures. Putnam, by contrast, is committed to a single, uniform constitution for us all and to a correspondingly narrow conception of human flourishing. Our deeper differences call, in Dewey's opinion, for education; for Putnam, they demand condemnation. He is pleased to reject alternative ideals of human perfection "as wrong, as infantile, as sick, as one-sided."†

Given a certain nature, intelligence may be able to devise a way to fulfill it. Those who settle for less than it is possible for them to achieve and enjoy can, presumably, be criticized for making a mistake. If people born with "normal human potential," for example, settle for lives fit only for pigs, we can convict them, Putnam argues, of a "cognitive shortfall."‡ They are irrational because they never made vivid to themselves certain goals and activities that, if they only knew of them, they would "doubtless prefer." If, therefore, the fans of Motley Crüe could just imagine the pleasures of Mozart, they

---

* *Reason*, 167–68.   † *Reason*, 148.   ‡ *Reason*, 172.

would become permanently attached to chamber music. Those who like to drink beer, chew tobacco, and spend their Saturday nights watching monster trucks compete in pulling large logs out of mud cannot even be said to have chosen these activities because they did not give adequate consideration to Carnegie Hall or Shakespeare in the park.

Astoundingly, Putnam is satisfied with this justification of high culture. The central fact, for him, is that such "pig-men" have the same potential as philosophy professors, and thus we have something in them, some latent goals, to which we can appeal. Since intelligent people generally agree that a cultivated life is better than swinishness, all we have to do to make good ole boys see the light is to render them intelligent.

I find it hard to see how the weakness of this argument could have escaped as fine a logician as Putnam. The priests of high culture are a self-selected lot: they choose Mozart and tuxedos and then they praise the choice. But would everyone who gave adequate attention to Wagner's *Götterdämmerung* and an evening of football in the bar head directly for the opera? Of course not. And it is simply false that those who opt for beer did not really envisage the alternative; it is precisely the thought of having to listen to all those sounds that filled their minds with dread. If there is a failure of imagination, it cuts both ways: pig-men know little about opera and professors fail to understand the redeeming power of mindless fun. But actually, I think both sides are perfectly clear on the alternatives; what they cannot imagine is not how the others live but themselves liking it. And this comes near to an ultimate disagreement on values that cannot be settled by enhanced knowledge or by reasoning.

The argument does not fare any better if we make it turn on the foolishness of leaving some of our faculties undeveloped. In the name of what standard can we say that pig-men are worse off than if they led "more truly human lives"?* To be sure, as Putnam points out, they would be ashamed of their past if they ever turned highbrow. But then professors would violently regret their lost years if they ever caught on to pleasure. Although it is a favorite maxim of competitive society that we should never settle for less than we can get, I find it hard to see that as the heart of rationality. Religious communities have long believed that focus on a special few of our talents

* *Reason,* 172.

is the way to salvation. Although the resultant lives may seem stark and impoverished from the outside, they appear poignant and rich to those who lead them.

The pig-men (and, for the sake of these fellows, I hope pig-women) presumably have something in common with us, some latent goods or elements of their nature to which we can appeal. The case of the Nazi is more difficult because there is nothing in him that we can address. He is simply different from us: he lives and acts and dies by alien values. He is not as different, of course, as Putnam's hypothetical beings from Alpha Centauri;* he feels pain and he can understand passion and death, even though his values make him attach a different meaning from ours to these phenomena. Can we call such a person, devoted to spontaneous destruction, not only wicked but also irrational?

Putnam's overwhelming desire is to call such people sick. Like his super-Benthamite pleasure seekers, they suffer from a sick system of values, a sick conception of human flourishing, and possibly even sick standards of rationality.† Factually, the word 'sick' means that these human beings are different from us; normatively, it suggests that they ought not to be that way. The real wallop comes from the emotive side, for it is clear that Putnam's aim is not diagnosis but blame. Nazis, super-Benthamites, and their kin are not sick in the sense in which we get sick with the flu, but in the sense in which kids say to each other, "You're sick." They are monsters and perverts and pigs.

Venting these emotions gives relief. But Putnam knows that calling people names is not an argument, and he does not want to settle for the incommensurability of divergent values. Accordingly, he produces a bit of reasoning designed to show that it is legitimate for us to interpret other cultures in our terms and to judge them by our lights. This argument, designated 'transcendental' by Putnam, is the centerpiece of his discussion of morality and the foundation of his claim that Nazis are irrational.

To understand the beliefs others hold and the values by which they act, we must state them in our own terms. This is possible only on condition that we equate their concepts with ours. For we could never grasp the propositions another affirms unless we had a clear fix on their constituent terms; any difference in beliefs presupposes the

---

* *Reason*, 168.   † *Reason*, 140–41.

similarity of the ideas used to frame them. Putnam puts this neatly as the contrast between concept and conception.* Sharing concepts, he says, is a necessary condition of disagreement about our conceptions or views of the course of nature and of the condition of human beings. This implies that no matter how far our opinions may diverge, our basic ideas always remain identical: all human cultures we can understand share, for example, our notions of the reasonable and the natural.† And as if this were not enough, the principle of interpretative charity requires that we construe not only the ideas but even the beliefs of members of other communities as closely similar to ours. They must be seen as "believers of truths and lovers of the good," so long, of course, as truth and the good are conceived in accordance with our ideas.

It should be obvious at once that the concept/conception contrast will not stand scrutiny. It is simply false that two cultures can be said to have the same concepts if they have systematically, and perhaps radically, different conceptions. That opinions are constituted by relating concepts to one another is only one side of the story; the other side is that how we relate the concepts changes them. If one set of predicates is thought applicable to a subject-concept in one age but a different set at a later time, it is reasonable to suppose that the concept changes as a direct result of our changed opinions.

When we advance, for example, from thinking that machines are clocklike contrivances to the belief that they are computerlike, we alter the concept of machine. Concepts and conceptions are organically connected; we cannot change one without changing the other. If the beliefs of two cultures differ, so do the ideas that constitute the beliefs. If, on the other hand, their notions are shared, as Putnam supposes, their views and values must also be closely similar.

This last point constitutes an absurd result. We cannot seriously entertain the idea that all communities and all ages have used the same conceptual framework and believed the same things. Philosophers have been given enough grief concerning their idea of a perennial philosophy; imagine if we added to this the notions of unchanging science, universal morality, and immutable commonsense! Putnam's argument requires the immunity of concepts from differences of belief, but such isolation of the building blocks of thought from their context is impossible. Without this independence

* *Reason*, 116–17.   † *Reason*, 119.

of concepts, the argument collapses.

Putnam's position has some additional peculiarities. Experienced translators know that concept matching, even in related languages, is a difficult, risky, and inexact affair. There is little need for interpretative charity in such matters; the identification of foreign concepts with our own is the unavoidable essence of translation. Our duty, accordingly, is the exact opposite of what Putnam prescribes. We need not strive to make others sound like us; we must, instead, do all we can to help them retain their voice. We can do this only by constant reminders of the inadequacy of translation and of the differences between the ideas we are rendering and our own. The violence of wrenching concepts out of their living context to equate them with something alien inevitably distorts them. We must compensate for this disfigurement by stressing how the thoughts and feelings of others differ from our own.

Concepts live in a language, and language structures and expresses the life of a community. Understanding the conceptual framework of another society or of other people is, therefore, far from a purely linguistic enterprise. It involves interpretation of the actions, tendencies, and traditions of others, of their values and of their cast of mind. Just as the translator of a poem must know the language of the original along with his own, the interpreter of a culture must have firsthand acquaintance with the alien form of life no less than with his own. This immediacy with others enables us to recognize differences beyond what their language and conceptual apparatus might reveal.

Putnam is correct that our aim must be to render such foreign worlds intelligible to us. But he also makes the unfounded claim that the behavior of people in these communities must be shown to be "reasonable by our lights."* What strange people do in odd places on the globe tends to be anything but reasonable given our values and history. The war-loving antics of headhunters and cannibals may be perfectly understandable if we consider their background and circumstances. But they are certainly not reasonable in the sense of constituting behavior we can judge sensible, acceptable, or sound. When we call on people to be reasonable, moreover, we ask them to be moderate and to listen to argument. Many cultures, and many individuals in our own, find reasonableness in this sense unthinkable; they consider moderation a sign of weakness and conversation about matters

* *Reason*, 119.

of substance absurd.

Even if not all actions and values and forms of life are reasonable in our eyes, it may still be possible to render them intelligible. But here 'intelligible' means no more than that we can imagine how people living under certain circumstances and by certain commitments might well do what they do. That these actions form some sort of imaginable whole does not imply that they are rational in any discursive sense. Nor does it mean that we can appropriately apply a standard of cognitive acceptability to them.

This goes to the heart of Putnam's misunderstanding of Karl. In a possibly unconscious and certainly unexamined fashion, Putnam embraces the dogma of the primacy of knowledge. To want to judge forms of life for their rationality is to demand that they report for cognitive sanction. The test of rationality, in this view at least, is always discursive: it is the relevance of questions, the acceptability of belief statements, the justifiability of action proposals. The supremacy of the epistemic leads, therefore, directly to the kingdom of words, where discussion precedes and must in retrospect sanctify every action.

Karl rejects this entire world of principles and talk, of calculation and justification. He repudiates it, of course, not in a self-referentially disastrous way by saying so and then arguing for his view. Instead, he gives moral knowledge and rational vindication exactly what they deserve in his universe: no heed. He acts on impulse or instinct, perhaps destructively but always full of life. There is not likely to be much consistency in what he does, although he tends to favor violent, explosive and emotional displays. Like a warrior, he lives at white heat, yet shows no interest in maximizing any value. He may learn from the past, though not consciously, and modify his behavior, but not through deliberation. He seeks no understanding and no justice. Movement and fantasy absorb him: he acts, he laughs and he sleeps.

Karl is obviously not the petty functionary who made the Third Reich move. He is an innocent and dangerous soul, almost an animal. From our perspective, of course, he is a soulless monster, yet he cannot be the source of the systematic horror bureaucrats visited on the world in his name. Karl is no organizer; he is closer to a spontaneous Nietzschean man. That connection reveals him as Western rational man's deepest alter ego. Nazism is a garbled ideology foisted on him. He puts up with it because it permits his playlike and violent sides to show. But he has no native system of beliefs. Words and ideas lack cognitive content for him; they are triggers to action.

We meet this dark person again and again in Western literature. But we also see him in the local pub, in the marketplace and at the grocery store. All of us include an element of him and many comprise not much else. Can we maintain that this amoral person, this proto-Nazi, this ideal other of the cognitively controlled Enlightenment self, is irrational?

The answer must be no, unless we frankly admit that the judgment is external. Karl rejects the terms and conditions of any such assessment, just as we repudiate the structure of his life. There is no basis to convict him, because we lack commitments in common. It would be absurd to charge him with a cognitive shortfall, if knowledge has no function in his life. Should we blame the oyster for not singing or the canary for failing to grow pearls? Karl rejects the supremacy of the cognitive; by calling him irrational, we do no more than groundlessly affirm it.

Karl's challenge to the order of our lives is not easily dismissed. Those who hope for a fully rational world must reckon with the subterranean forces of unreason. And those who take satisfaction in condemning alien goods must remember that, potentially at least, the deviant minority is each of us.

CHAPTER 6

A Community of Psyches:
Santayana on Society

Readers of Santayana know frustration and delight. To the literate among us, little gives greater joy than to be borne by a rich current of words to insights that burst on us like the morning light. Yet much in Santayana's fabric of thought dissatisfies. Some think him too poetic, others too deeply devoted to reason and to science. Positivists find him too metaphysical, metaphysicians too positivistic. Stern moralists condemn him for having embraced an aesthetic or spiritual life; religious people bemoan that he is not spiritual enough.

Perhaps one could explain these frustrations as due mainly to our natural hope to find in others what we think is right. But there are two areas of Santayana's thought where his readers' pain is too universal to explain away. One is in literary criticism, the other in his social and political views. How can Santayana both condemn Emerson and praise him? How can he celebrate Shakespeare and also consider him a barbarian? And what does he really think about democracy? Which is the best form of government and the best community? How should the individual relate to the laws and the state and the international order that may come someday?

I will not discuss literary criticism here, although I think that what I will say about the source of our anger with Santayana over his political theories can also be applied in that area. I will develop Santayana's view of the relation of the individual to the community and do so in detail for two important reasons. The first is that there has been very little serious consideration of this part of his philosophy. More significant, there is no problem more timely, more pressing, or more difficult than the precise nature and proper form of this relationship. Confusion about it has become a hallmark of American society even while other nations assume thoughtlessly that they have the right idea. I do not wish to flatter thought by saying that if only we had the intellectual answer, it would gain acceptance before long. But it is no joyous task to go stumbling without sight. It may be profitable to see more clearly about matters of such moment.

Why does Santayana seem indecisive about the good society? How can he describe widely divergent social arrangements with equal sympathy, seeing the point of each and refusing to condemn? He has been severely and perhaps unjustly criticized for his ready acceptance of fascist Italy. Yet he deplored his sister's love of fascist Spain, launched a searing attack on imperial Germany, freely publicized his admiration of Britain, and on occasion confessed a quiet love even for the imperfect democracy of the United States. I know no other thinker who could write equally eloquent defenses of a secular, cosmopolitan world order and of a society of fanatical monks.

Are such broad sympathies due to a lack of principle? To the contrary. They are the deliberate and adequate expression of Santayana's most deeply and sincerely held beliefs. For Santayana is a relativist concerning values, and this naturally makes him a relativist about social arrangements.

We should not be distressed at hearing the word 'relativist.' Many of those who believe that values are absolute and unchanging do so because they think of them as relative to or dependent on the will of God. Relativism has received a bad name because Protagoras and selected undergraduates maintain that good and evil are created by what they or anyone thinks. This sort of relativism exalts the power of thought less than it insults the significance of evil and leads to a number of silly consequences. It is not the sort of relativism Santayana has in mind. He thinks values are relative to the established nature of individuals.

If we now ask, "Why individuals?" we suddenly find ourselves at the level of Santayana's deepest metaphysical commitments. He is convinced that value links up with desire, living tendency, and action, and he sees the individual as the only center and source of agency. Of course, the individual is not, for Santayana, some disembodied soul or amphibious person. All motion is in the end physical, and the meanings that convert motion into action are themselves the products of consciousness, which is physically based. The individual, then, is primarily a biological organism, an animal fighting for life and love in a violent world.

Attentive reading of Santayana reveals that the generative image in his mind is that of the single animal attempting by cunning and force to thrive or at least to survive. The world of space and time is a field of action, and substance, he says, is universal food. The best evidence for the unity and continuity of nature is the symmetry of action: all agencies are capable of affecting one another, of aiding or impeding each other's activity. The final reality, then, is to eat or to be eaten, to prevail or to be annulled.

This ultimate rule of existence is converted into value with the emergence of special, self-maintaining vortices in the flux. These organisms, each a controlled and complex set of habits, have the capability of sustaining and restoring their activity. They are enduring, definite beings for whose perpetuation not all contingencies are equally welcome. The definite constitution, the established potentialities, the living momentum of these organisms ground value; all creatures seek and avoid, embrace or abhor on the basis of who they are and in what they are engaged.

Humans are no different from other organisms in this respect. Their habits may cover a broader range; they may be more adaptive or more unstable. But in the last analysis, each individual human being is just such a center of selectivity and agency. This swirling center of activity is what Santayana calls the 'psyche'; it is the individual as a totality of dynamic tendencies. The unity of the psyche is, Santayana readily admits, mythological: it exists only for the observer who wishes to think of immensely complex affairs without having to focus on each complexity. In reality, the psyche is a moving spatiotemporal region that displays a staggering variety of loosely coordinated activities. I see a confirmation of this every time my toenail grows while I think of God.

In this conception of the soul or psyche, as in many other of his philosophical ideas, Santayana draws heavily on Aristotle. The insistence on activity, the language of potentiality (even of first and second act!), the ultimate unity of source of the vegetative, conative, and cognitive functions all remind us of Aristotle. There is one important difference. Aristotle thinks that the individual is a substance that engages in activities. Santayana, by contrast, maintains that the psyche is simply the sum total of its activities. If we insist on using the language of substance, and Santayana is by no means reluctant to do so, only the entirety of the field of action, the sum total of the physical world, is a substance. The psyche is a mode of matter.

This last claim, however, while true, is seriously misleading. Although the psyche is a mode of the physical world, in another and very important respect it is a substance. Thoughts and values are modifications of this mode; in relation to them, the psyche functions as source and substratum. This means that the individual is a moral substance; it is the ultimate and only creator of the goodness of whatever is good and of the evil of what it abhors.

That there is no significant argumentation in Santayana's works in support of this position is perhaps not altogether surprising. For activity, desire, and consciousness are primary conditions of value creation. What beings other than individuals can display these properties? Surely not atoms or molecules. The only other candidate is some larger unity, such as the state. Hegelians have made much of this, but throughout the long years of Santayana's productive life, Hegel was thoroughly discredited. Santayana did not think it necessary to argue for a position that seemed to him as obvious as the moral ultimacy of the individual.

It is not difficult, however, to reconstruct the sorts of considerations that would have seemed persuasive to Santayana, had he bothered to array them and to develop them in detail. First of all, nothing in the state or society could be read as a valid analogue of desire or consciousness. Collections of individuals simply lack the unity and the biological sensitivity necessary for awareness. Unless one defines consciousness in some excessively abstract metaphysical way—such as multiplicity-in-unity, in which case every modulated belch would have its attendant cognition—society lacks the organ of awareness, and we lack all reasonable evidence for supposing that there is anything beyond the perceptions and thoughts of individuals. As to desire, all we can detect in communities is the contagion of seeking and of wants. There is no indication of an added immediacy, of an experience of communal desire in some social mind.

Second, we note that each 'action' of every community is, in fact, an action performed by individuals on its behalf. To say that on December 7, 1941, Japan attacked the United States is shorthand for what a number of sailors and pilots did at Pearl Harbor in the name of the emperor. To be sure, there are many things individuals would not do if they were not in the company of others, or if they did not think that what they propose is sanctioned or required by the rules that unite them. But this constitutes no evidence of agencies more cosmic than ordinary mortals. Whatever is done must be performed by men and women singly or in groups. It is just that one among the factors determining their will may be their perception of what the state or their community demands.

Let me say at once that this analysis appears to be correct. To maintain that Japan attacked the United States by means of its sailors and airmen, just as I scratch my nose with my fingers and thumb, is to lose sight of a critical condition of agency. Players in the field must be able to be found. There is no problem in locating me or my fingers. It is not unreasonable, therefore, to say that my fingers were not the ultimate source of agency when they wandered to relieve an itch. But in spite of the fervent testimony of sociologists that institutions are real, who has ever encountered a state? Is there more to General Motors than the patterned activities and possible activities of a large number of people? To explain the supposed efficacy of states, we need have reference to nothing beyond what physical individuals do in the physical world and what meanings they perceive or what rules they find compelling.

I am not, of course, denying that institutions are in some sense real. But the task of the philosopher does not end—in fact, it only begins—with this acknowledgment. For reality comes in many forms, and it is a disastrous error to identify all of them with power. Mathematical relations are real, yet it would be silly to think that they bend the mind to compel recognition. Physical laws are real, but the law of gravity would never keep me tethered on the ground. The joy of sun that lingers into evening is real and beautiful and rare. But it is the rich expression of a healthy life, not the force that makes us carry on. The philosophical task is not to distinguish appearance from reality or truth from illusion. To do justice to the complexity of the world, we must sort out and learn to appreciate the different kinds of reality that surround us. Santayana undertakes this mission in a clearheaded and resolute way that could serve as a model for all of us. He sees the claim and place of every sort of being; concerning reality, he is the greatest pluralist.

Our culture, interested in power without responsibility, is insensibly turning Hegelian. We see power everywhere and want to exercise our own namelessly, as though it were a part of the nature of things and hence could never be called to account. People now widely subscribe to the fiction that true agency, and therefore responsibility, resides in institutions or 'the system.' As a result, we readily blame government, big business, or the oil companies, while we insist that in our role as employees of these institutions we must not be blamed. If ever there was an inverted moral order, we live it: we say the fictive system does it all, while the agents hide behind their roles or seek innocence through committees and the collective act. Santayana saw the early stages of this trend and recognized it as a sad inversion. It is time for us to unmask it and to take corrective steps. The trouble with our society is not that we are excessively individualistic, but that we are not individualistic enough. For the individual as single agent carries knowledge of his or her acts or at least responsibility for their consequences. Only such persons can constitute a community, a human world that is not a mere social machine.

Santayana's view that values are relative to psyches and his conviction that individuals are ontologically ultimate in the social world should give us at least the beginnings of an understanding of why he appears to be elusive about the good society. For, to him, no society is good simply because of its structures or processes. Such formal features promote the possibility of certain perfections, but all perfections presuppose underlying natural organisms. The value of a community, therefore, is largely a function of the nature of its constituent psyches. Since human nature is neither stable nor uniform, psyches can differ widely, though not indefinitely, within changing parameters. As a result, a society that permits ideal self-expression to one sort of psyche may be the paradigm of evil to another type. There is no one good or best society because there are many good ones, each best for a certain type of soul.

Let me now develop Santayana's criteria for the goodness of communities in somewhat greater detail and more systematically than he did. His central and most general idea here, once again, has Aristotelian overtones. Psyches have definite potentialities. By and large, these potentialities determine what the psyche desires and what in fact would satisfy it. The notion of the good life is thus the notion of discharging what is latent in us. The good society, in turn, enables or allows all or a very large number of its members to lead the good life. Given the essential interdependence of human beings, the community functions as a condition of individual self-fulfillment.

The matter is, of course, not quite so simple as this would suggest. For there are significant problems in determining the individual's good and there are nagging difficulties in the treatment of minority psyches. The individual soul is not, for the most part, a rationally or even neatly structured unity. Long-term constitutive interests vie for dominance with stray impulses directed upon momentary but very real goods. None but the most impoverished psyche may hope for fulfillment by the satisfaction of all its desires; for those of us in whom life runs hot and thick, internal strife is a daily spectacle. Hence we must distinguish the 'real' from the 'apparent' good of every creature, and for someone with Santayana's sensitivity for the reality even of the apparent, this can be done only in terms of the contrast between narrow short-range and richer long-range goods. The good life for an individual, then, is one in which he or she is able to satisfy the richest set of most intense desires or attain the largest number of fervently sought compossible goods.

The interest in this harmonious maximization is what Santayana calls 'reason.' To be sure, there is nothing compulsory about reason or uniform about its products. Those in whom the impulse for harmony is weak may live and die, as did Aristippus, in a golden haze. We can say of them perhaps that they had a good time, but not that it amounted to a satisfying life. There is no legitimate moral criticism of those who opt against reason, so long as we are not asked to bear the cost of their choice. Fortunately, we would not have to criticize for long in any case: those who steadfastly reject maximization have no reason to embrace the life-enhancing and soon expire of a passing passion.

That reason is uniformly the impulse for harmony may mislead us into supposing that it yields uniform results. But maximization is a formal principle. It orders our desires without determining what they shall be and without creating new ones that, in some abstract way, it might be better to fulfill or to possess. Reason, like married love, works with what there is. It was reason that shaped the life of Casanova no less than it rules the latest pope. Achilles and Saint Francis abide by it to varying degrees; in each, it is the gardener that trims natural growths. The good life, governed by reason, is not restricted, therefore, to one or a few ways of valuing and behaving. It requires a measure of unity in the soul and the opportunity to express our nature, no matter what flowers our native soil may grow.

This discussion of reason and the good life gives us the clue to a fuller development of Santayana's view of social authority and the proper treatment of divergent psyches. Ideally, the good society facilitates the fulfillment of all its constituent psyches. Such social harmony has been a human ideal since Plato's time or before. But once again, being rigid about the specific features of such a society would be a mistake. It may operate by inflexible rules and demand unconditional self-sacrifice, if such a life fulfills its citizens. It may, on the other hand, be an association of anarchic sybarites, each psyche a lovely note but the whole composing only a loose, uncertain melody. Santayana has no quarrel with the varieties of life so long as they are authentic and satisfying to the people who lead them.

But such universal fulfillment is an ideal not only in the sense that it would be good to have. It is also beyond the pale of reality. Under the best of circumstances, some souls are still left out; even in the bravest new world, deviants and malcontents abound. What will a good society do about them? First of all, it will try to keep their number as low as possible. And second, it will leave them as much room to fulfill themselves in their own way as it can without abandoning its grounding principles. Toleration, the maximal bending of rules consistent with the genius of a community, then, is a necessary feature of any good society. Let me stress at once that no precise or determinate amount of toleration is necessary. Different social organizations can and should permit differing magnitudes of dissent and deviance. Santayana's point is not that toleration should be infinite, but that intolerance should not be unchecked and gratuitous. His condemnation of militancy is founded precisely on this point. For a militant society is less concerned with assuring the fulfillment of its faithful than with frustrating the will of everyone else. Militancy always involves the effort to impose an alien will. Pursued on a small scale, it is lamentable; when it becomes a way of social life, it often yields disaster.

But why is a society of total toleration not better than all others? Because the very notion of such a community is a meaningless abstraction. Human nature is so varied that the desires and operations of the people in a community are never completely compatible. Conflicts naturally arise; wills cross in the process of seeking private goods. Those who think that without social rules we would grow like flowers never had a garden to observe. Without rules, toleration would be restricted to the strong or crafty; everyone else would soon be oppressed or dead. Toleration must, therefore, always remain a limited and relative matter, for from the standpoint of the leaders of a society, there is no difference between tolerating intolerance and perpetrating it.

Must we then suppose that militancy is unconditionally bad? If that were true, it would at once destroy Santayana's moral relativism. And, I must admit, the deep respect I feel for individual autonomy inclines me to think—better, to feel—that imposing an alien will by force is always evil. But the moment we reflect on the great militant spirits of history and view their actions from their own perspective, the pervasiveness of evil disappears. Attila and the Grand Inquisitor, Stalin and Savonarola all had a perfectly good time attacking or persecuting. But do not let me hang the matter on how they felt. Only an external unsympathetic view can overlook the inner cogency and justification of the life of militants. We may call their reasons rationalizations, but from their own point of view they are valid and compelling. For true enthusiasts, militancy is not a pose but the only form in which their nature can gain expression. To condemn them, we must compare their views with ours and find them wanting. Or we must be able to show that their nature is depraved or worse than ours. Such comparisons are not impossible. But they take place in the private imagination, an organ notoriously bathed in prejudice. They all presuppose standards and perspectives far from neutral, so that their results become predictable.

Militancy is, indeed, bad from the standpoint of the person overwhelmed. But it is the only form of life worth the effort for some vigorous wills. This is as far as argument can go; the rest is left to physical encounter. For moral and political arguments soon come to an end, and we face one another with guns or at the ballot box. But preferably at the ballot box? Clearly for you and me, today. But with guns if circumstances change—if not to impose our will on others, then at least to prevent them from forcing theirs on us.

The outbound militancy of a state is aggression; directed inward, militancy becomes oppression. There are good societies, Santayana thinks, that are natively aggressive. They offer their citizens not balanced lives but glorious demise. But no good society is oppressive to any significant extent. There is a subtle but important difference between not allowing people to do what they want and forcing them to do what we desire. The former is best done by such rules as the criminal law, the latter by force or ruthless terror. A good society, then, will try to make room for deviant psyches. If it comes to the point where deviants must be controlled, it will proscribe rather than prescribe, stop harmful behavior instead of twisting natures.

The kinship of their natures or their souls renders groups of people true communities. This does not mean that communities are accidents of nature. On the contrary, the native bent of every society carries it to communion. We all tend to create replicas of ourselves in our children. The process of socialization reinforces our similarities. The power of a society in defining wants and channeling efforts, in creating desires and providing for their satisfaction, is unparalleled. The result is a staggering, though largely unnoticed, uniformity among the psyches that constitute a nation. In spite of individual differences, our habits and values are confined within modest parameters: the Reverend Jones of Jonestown fame resembles a self-effacing American hermit more than he resembles a mad ayatollah.

The similarity of psyches, once it is sensed, establishes the foundation of legitimate authority in the state. Those who speak for alien goods receive no hearing in the soul. Authority has a vital basis: only when the voice of our own values calls are we impelled to action or sacrifice. Yet even this voice, spoken through the laws or government, is inadequate to integrate us into a community so long as we think we can do it all alone. Santayana is less eloquent on this point than many of the great proponents of human unity. But he sees it clearly enough: to make a community, we must view one another as necessary friends. Each must regard the others as having legitimate claims to fulfillment, and his or her own welfare as being organically tied to theirs. We must see the free self-expression of all, to rewrite Marx, as a condition of the free self-expression of each.

Political philosophies may fail in many ways. They have the usual difficulties attendant on description, generalization, and the avoidance of contradiction in complexity. But, in addition, they also face special problems associated with the fact that they have normative elements and stand, as does any theory about society, a good chance of being self-falsifying. In writing of values, Santayana is a devoted follower of Spinoza: he attempts to give a calm, descriptive account of human valuation instead of telling us how everything should be. Yet we find that with the growth of the organic state, Santayana's claims about the primacy of the individual recede from the descriptive to the normative level. It is as if we found human history bent on convincing us that Hegel was right, after all, that ultimate agency resides in units much larger than the single person. Individual agency is now ever more difficult to trace and personal responsibility is deflected or cast aside; what used to be obvious fact must now be disentangled by analysis. In such a world, Santayana's claim that the community is built of single units, that its legitimacy derives from you and me, is more of a call to action than a true account. I agree with the call, but it is important to see how easily even descriptive naturalists can find themselves in the pulpit preaching of threatened values to a yawning world.

Political thought may be self-falsifying, as well. Overstating the social impact of Santayana's thought would be easy; I certainly do not wish to do so. Yet it has made some small contribution to public knowledge of the cost of relativistic individualism. And this cost is high. A serious commitment to the primacy of the individual puts choice and accountability on our reluctant shoulders. And if we believe in the relativity of values, we rob ourselves of the joy of condemnation. Responsibility without solace is what we face if Santayana and his soul mates are correct. Is it surprising, then, that we do what we can to render their thoughts false?

Yet these are not the ultimate problems with Santayana's view. One issue that grows out of the essence of his project presents a nagging, gaping failure. Santayana's attempt is to understand all without passing judgment. This cognitive ideal has been deeply embedded in philosophy. It was profoundly attractive to Santayana, who was by nature reflective, a spectator. But understanding is not the only function of thought; we cannot leave the physical world to brute, untutored action. Santayana's own master, the great Peripatetic, taught that in addition to the pure joys of intellectual life, there is also moral virtue guided by reason through sound habits and the practical syllogism. Here Santayana has little to offer. There is understanding but no guidance for life. If anything, we understand so much that we know not where to turn. The legitimacy of all styles calls our own in doubt.

Let me be clear about what I have in mind. Schopenhauer thought that all life was equally legitimate. He inevitably concluded that we must never impede the will of any other creature and hence should choose a course of resignation and saintly death. Santayana refuses to draw even this conclusion. For the psyche, he thinks, is primed to live and act; even after, as philosophers, we achieve understanding, it is best to leave it to do its thing. But this presupposes that the potentiality of the psyche is fully formed and unchangeable. And it commits us to the view that thought either makes no difference or can create no improvement.

I think these assumptions are false. There is no better way to demonstrate the problem than by focusing on children. Every community's future is locked up in its children, and each wants to control it through education. To parents, raising children is a world-creative act. Obviously, we cannot make our children into anything we want. But there are options; there are futures to consider, choices to make. In doing so we seek, perhaps more than we ever sought for ourselves, what is rational and good and satisfying. What shall we make of our children? On what principle shall we choose the psyches with which we endow them for life? It is inadequate to say that we must do what our psyches now demand. For in such soul-making we transcend our ken, and, as the future opens, our own values lose sacred primacy.

I know that soon enough we learn how we shall have raised our children. But that is not to know how we should do or should have done it. In raising children, the values that structure our own psyches and our community need to be questioned first of all. How shall we ground our judgment? Moral and political philosophy must have an answer. Santayana's, unfortunately, does not.

CHAPTER 7

Dogmatist in Disguise

No one who has spent ten minutes reflecting on moral decisions will deny that in making them we pay attention to the nature of the predicament that demands them. A grasp of the concrete features of the situation is indispensable for decision. Otherwise we may not know that a decision is called for, certainly not what principle to apply.

These statements are prompted by Joseph Fletcher's celebrated *Situation Ethics.** The 'new morality' Fletcher presents is, in fact, as old as the hills and as tangled as the underbrush on them. That decision is context-bound has been well known at least since Aristotle and his theory of the practical syllogism. Hence the novelty or importance of Fletcher's view does not lie in its demand for giving the concrete situation its due in our decisions. It is more nearly correct and perhaps more enlightening to say that the core of the new morality is simply the call for decision. Rigid codes, the 'new moralists' tell us, are no longer enough to handle the complex moral issues of our age; rather, they exalt flexibility, intelligence, and undogmatic love as characteristics of the proper Christian response to the problems a moral agent encounters.

It is by an understandable egotism that we speak of our own age as the one in which codes can 'no longer' meet the demands of morality. The facts are, however, that codes have never sufficed to solve a single moral dilemma, and that unthinking adherence to them has never guaranteed the worth of any agent. Decisions have always been

* *Situation Ethics* (Louisville: Westminster Press, 1966).

essential to the moral life. But all along most people, indeed most Christians, have refrained from decision making largely because this necessitates thought. Thus, a telling objection to Fletcher's view is that it is altogether impractical. The majority of people are neither willing nor able to deliberate and decide with the care and rational foresight demanded by genuine morality.

The ideal of the unthinking advocate of law-morality is that of a computer divinely programmed with the list—no doubt infinite—of all the individual right actions that may be performed. If we had such a list, our moral problems would certainly be solved. In any problematic situation, we would check the alternative courses of action that appeared on the list and hope that in each case the machine would approve at least and at most one such alternative. Fundamentalists have on occasion attempted to use the Bible as such a computer, but the list of right actions derivable from it by even the most careful study is too incomplete and too schematic to give more than general guidance.

What renders laws useful and even indispensable for the person who finds thinking difficult is the unavailability of specific commandments to cover every conceivable situation. Following a code—the Ten Commandments, for instance—does not guarantee that the right thing will be done in every case. But it does ensure that people who unflinchingly act by the code will do the right thing much more often than if they acted out of instinct or private 'inspiration.' If Aristotle was correct in declaring that in any situation there are many ways of doing what is wrong but only one way of doing what is right, the chance that people will hit on the right action by following a hunch is not very good. Choice has many advantages over simple adherence to law. It is by no means clear, however, that choice yields actions with a higher probability of being right than does code-governed behavior. In his legitimate attempt to expose the inadequacies of codes, Fletcher seems to forget their genuine and useful function in guiding the conduct of the many. Decision ethics cannot become universal so long as human nature remains what it now is.

In ethics as in everyday life, we speak sometimes of moral actions and sometimes of moral persons. The word 'moral' has different senses in these different contexts. To say that people are moral might mean that they are likely to do or to intend doing the right thing. To say that actions are moral, on the other hand, might mean that they are likely to produce good consequences. Further, a person thought moral is considered worthy of being rewarded, while an action thought moral is considered worthy of being performed. There is general agreement that people's moral worth should be determined on the basis of their intentions, their dispositions, and their character traits. But there is great disagreement as to what makes an action right. Some hold that certain actions or certain types of action are right in and of themselves, and that any adult with a developed moral sensibility can tell whether an action is intrinsically right or not; and that is the end of the matter. Others maintain that the rightness of an action is conferred on it by the intention of the person performing it. Yet others—perhaps the majority of moralists—declare that an action must be judged right on the basis of the good consequences it produces.

These are simple but central distinctions in ethics. Yet Fletcher seems to lump them all together. On the issue of what makes actions right, he appears to hold every possible position. He gets off to a good start by denying that an action can ever be right in and of itself (pp. 59-60). But soon we find him retracting this view in favor of one maintaining that actions are right "when or while or as long as" they are loving, simply because they are loving (p. 141). Since "loving" is something we do (p. 61), we could simply say, then, that actions are right in and of themselves if they are 'loving.'

This last might be a defensible position. Fletcher, however, is apparently not satisfied with it. He goes on to explain that the morality of an act is really a function of our purpose in performing it. If our purpose is loving, the action is right; if the good intention is missing, even conformity to the moral law will not make the action right (p. 65). This too might be a defensible position if it were held consistently and alone. But it flatly contradicts Fletcher's previous view (that loving actions are intrinsically right), as well as the next view he adopts.

This third and final theory maintains that an action is right if it creates a greater amount of value than any alternative action could create. Actions, we are told, are justified by their "agapeic expedience" (p. 125). This means that they are right when their consequences are good or when they help create the greatest possible amount of love in the world (p. 156). Fletcher is quick to discern the close similarity of this view to utilitarianism, and with the qualification that the ultimate value is love not pleasure, he hastens to ally himself with Bentham (p. 95). Thus, by a few bold contradictions, he succeeds in combining in the same book Bishop Joseph Butler's view of intrinsically right actions, Immanuel Kant's insistence on the central importance of intentions, and John Stuart Mill's plea for the primacy of consequences

If I had no theory about the cause and cure of such miscellaneous contradictions, it would be pointless or unkind of me to dwell on them. Let me say, then, that the reason Fletcher is unclear about the morality of actions is that he is confused in his concept of love. Love is central in his 'new morality.' The presence of love, he says, is pivotal in the moral life, and in ethical theory everything hinges on it. Yet nowhere are we told in detail what love is. Instead, we are given an astounding series of half-developed and contradictory indications. Love is first said to be something we do: it is thus (1) an action or a way of behaving (p. 61). This definition is quickly revised: love becomes (2) a characteristic of certain human actions and relationships (p. 63). Again, it is (3) the purpose behind the action (p. 61). Toward the end of the book, it becomes (4) the motive behind the decision to act (p. 155). Elsewhere, love is (5) an attitude of persons, (6) a disposition to act in certain ways, (7) a preference for certain values, and (8) goodwill or a conative predisposition to take certain attitudes (pp. 79, 61, 104, 105). And it is also said to be (9) a relation, (10) a formal principle, and (11) a regulative principle (pp. 105, 60, 61).

Surely, love cannot be all these things. If love is (1), it cannot also be (2), since actions cannot be the characteristics of actions. If love is (9), it cannot also be (4), (5), and (6), since relations are not motives, attitudes, or dispositions. If love is (3), it cannot also be (10) and (11), since no conceptual dexterity can identify purposes with principles. This central confusion about love explains why Fletcher is confused about the morality of actions. For if he holds that love, which he considers the only ultimate value, is (1) a kind of action, he is naturally led to the position that right actions are right intrinsically; that is, simply by virtue of their being loving regardless of their antecedents and consequences. If he maintains that love is (3) a purpose, (4) a motive, or (5) and (8) a conative attitude, he must obviously embrace the view that the value of an action derives from the intentions or personal traits of the agent who performs it. And if he avers that love is (9) a relation between persons, he will inevitably adopt the opinion that the morality of an action must be judged by its tendency to bring about such ultimately valuable relations.

Although he presents no clear ideal of its nature, Fletcher is admirably single-minded in maintaining that love alone is unconditionally good. In consequence, it is difficult to take seriously his assertion that situation ethics is a method only (p. 34). In fact, situation ethics is both more and less than a method. On the one hand, to designate something as the summum bonum is to do far more than merely to provide a method of making moral decisions. If love is the only thing good as an end, we know not only *how* to make choices; we also know *what* to choose. On the other hand, to bid us make decisions is to fall vastly short of providing a method for decision making. The injunction "Take the circumstances into full account" does not amount to a description of a procedure that would reduce decision making to an ordered sequence of steps. Nor is it helpful to introduce the hedonistic calculus. That approach never brought much order or mechanical regularity to moral deliberations. Rechristening it "agapeic calculus" merely compounds its own problems with the difficulties of specifying the nature of love and measuring its extent and intensity.

By an exercise of Christian benevolence, one might attribute all these weaknesses to the difficulties inherent in working out a revolutionary new Christian ethics. The reason Fletcher's view appears revolutionary is obvious: he claims to be a relativist. No one loses sleep over relativity in physics; yet the bare mention of relativity in the realm of values evokes an outcry that brands the moralist as a radical. Nevertheless, most of the great systems of Christian ethics have been relativistic. In theological ethics, the good has traditionally been conceived as relative to God's will or God's intellect or to the total configuration of God's nature. In natural law ethics, excellence is conceived as relative to and determined by the essence of existing types of being. Such traditional relativisms upset no one. After all, it would be an exaggeration to call Augustine and Aquinas radicals today. Relativisms that establish fixed and universal values appear to be generally welcome. What motivates the rejection of other sorts is the fear that they might make values varied, changeable, and individual. Most Christians are instinctive dogmatists, firmly convinced that unanimity in belief and uniformity in behavior are indispensable conditions of the moral life.

Fletcher announces his bold break with the dogmatists and promptly rushes headlong into the most unstable and absurd relativism. He quotes Cicero's remark that only a madman would hold the difference between virtue and vice to be a matter of opinion (p.

77), and then he cheerfully introduces himself as such a man. In short, his position seems to be Protagorean: anything is good and any action is right for the individual so long as he or she honestly thinks so. This is a view magnificent in its simplicity. Fletcher gives a fair sample of its wisdom when he says that "if people do not believe it is wrong to have sex relations outside marriage, it isn't" (p. 140).

But surely, this is not Fletcher's basic view. He is quite explicit in maintaining that love is good intrinsically, that it is supremely valuable whether anyone thinks so or not. A person who says that love is not good or that it is good only because he thinks so is simply wrong. And here for a moment Fletcher displays his colors. Love, it turns out, is good not only independently of opinion; it is "always good and right . . . regardless of the context" (p. 60). As the end of all ends, love is an absolute and unchanging value; its goodness is neither relative nor contingent (p. 129).

Here Fletcher's vaunted relativism and contextualism vanish. The nature of agents and the context in which they operate, says Fletcher, have no influence on *what* is valuable; they govern only *how* something of value may be best achieved. Thus their relevance is restricted to moral means. In other words, the good is fixed and unalterable, and in any moral situation firm, discoverable causal laws make possible the production of a definite amount of good; the moral agent's obligation is simply to discern the good and to discover the means by which it may be realized. Since the nature of the good, the quantity of good realizable in a given situation and the means to such maximal achievement are all fixed and determinate, virtually no room is left for choice, decision and the varieties of individual conscience. In this way it becomes easy to separate the sheep from the goats. Those who are intelligent enough to recognize the good and industrious enough in their pursuit of it are morally justified; the others must be condemned for a failure of intellect or will. Residual credit may be given those who earnestly try, without success, to make the right decisions; but the fact remains that their decisions are wrong, their choices mistaken, and their values confused.

It should be clear by now that what lurks behind the new morality is the old dogmatism. To render the old moral dogmas acceptable, Fletcher dresses them in today's garb. There is much talk of relativism, and on some individual moral issues, concessions are made. Free love, abortion, and euthanasia appear to be condoned. At first the reader thinks that a genuinely Protestant view of morals, insisting on the primacy of individual conscience, is about to emerge. But in the end Fletcher seems to believe that the values *he* favors are objective and universal, and that no one else's values have any legitimacy. This urge to disclose the universal good and this ambition to prescribe values for everything that lives and moves are prime characteristics of dogmatists, who in their vast immodesty presume that they may speak for others in matters of moral commitment and values. It is no surprise, then, to find Fletcher delivering imperial judgments on sundry moral problems. He seems to take it for granted that every reflective person will agree with him, or will at least demand general agreement. From his point of view, every moral problem has its solution; and when the solution is not provided—as in the case of the four problems with which he leaves us at the end of his book—we shall find it ourselves if we have been attentive students of the new morality. Thus making moral decisions is, like elementary mathematics, a search for right answers. The skilled moralist always gets the right answer. But woe befalls the person who, in this game for the highest stakes, has not learned the rules and so makes a mistake.

Nowhere is Fletcher's promise of a genuinely Protestant, individualistic ethics fulfilled. A fruitful Christian relativism is indeed possible. Not, of course, the Protagorean relativism that Fletcher flirts with; for if values were relative to opinion, our lives would fall into a disconnected series of momentary commitments. No value could be consistently judged lesser or greater, and belief would float erratically about, unattached to any firm basis in compelling fact. Still, opinions about the good must touch the world of facts somewhere, and the contact can occur only in living, judging persons. If we were omniscient, we would share God's knowledge of whatever universal norms the unchangeable divine nature might dictate. As it is, we must be content with the modest conviction that values vary with the nature of finite individuals.

Such might be the complexion of a warm, generous, Christian relativism. The theory that values are relative to a universal human nature does violence to the facts of our plasticity and straitjackets the rich variety of our perfectibilities. The theory that the good is individual, however, sounds alien harmonies. Christian humility debars us from judging the lives or ways of others; Christian love demands that we accept their different goods as equal in legitimacy with our own, and that we permit, even help, them seek their own perfection. The theoretical basis of such loving toleration is that natures differ, that one's values are a function of one's nature, and that a unanimity greater than constitutional likeness allows is useless in morals and unnecessary for harmonious social existence.

For human beings caught in this valley of doubt, there can be no higher morality than to live by the most inclusive values their nature dictates. The test of their achievement—and its reward—is the satisfaction without which life has no meaning and in whose presence one can feel no lack. Fletcher hints at this view when he says that all ethics is happiness ethics and that everything turns on what makes the individual person happy (p. 96). If we add to this the criterion (also briefly mentioned by Fletcher, on p. 140) that self-realization should not be allowed to proceed at the expense of hurting others, we have the rudiments of a sane value-relativism that may revolutionize Christian ethics. Minor concessions on issues of sex or business practice cannot save the old dogmatism, nor can they do justice to the radical love message of Christianity. The 'new morality' will have to be a relativistic ethics of total toleration. And there will be little that is new even in that, for it is simply the all-forgiving love-ethics of Christ.

CHAPTER 8

Grand History and Ordinary Life

O nce every thousand years, near the end of the millennium, es-
chatological fever spreads like an epidemic among intellectu-
als. Everything is declared to be at an end: we are told that
God is dead and hence religion is finished, that the modern world
killed art, and that philosophy killed itself. A few years ago, before
the disappearance of the Soviet Union, the entire world faced nuclear
annihilation. Now we learn that even if the world may survive, its
history is surely at an end. That, at least, is the message of Francis
Fukuyama, the newest voice in this tradition of thinkers who read the
portents of doom and salvation. In a celebrated article in 1989 and in
his subsequent book entitled *The End of History and the Last Man*,
Fukuyama declares not only that history is a thing of the past (with
which we might agree), but also that it is over once and for all.

To say that history has ended sounds surprising. Does it mean that
the next presidential election is too late: whoever wins will not be
recorded in the books and taught as part of what happened in this
country? Does it imply that nothing anyone does from here on will
have significance for the future of the human race? Obviously, such
claims would be absurd, so the end of history cannot mean the cessation of important national and international events.

History, for Fukuyama and others who speak of it as over, is a specific developmental pattern that played itself out between the earliest
manifestations of human conflict and approximately 1990. It is a history on the grand scale. Its players, as Hegel pointed out, are states
and its movement constitutes the drama of the development and the
fulfillment of human nature. The moving force behind this inspiring

story is the human spirit itself with its needs and talents and devotions. This powerful and pure spirit, manifesting itself through generations of grubby individuals, is both author and actor of the play that is history and achieves rest only when it has worked out all of its internal contradictions and met all of its own demands.

Departing from Hegel, Fukuyama suggests that these demands include rationality, freedom, and happiness. Of the three, freedom is the most central. Reason achieves self-actualization in the way modern natural science organizes our relation to nature. The application of intelligence, in turn, makes it possible for us to satisfy our desires and thereby to achieve happiness. The central element in attaining freedom is the search for recognition in the eyes of our fellows. Initially, we attempt to gain such standing through war. But this liberates only (or not even) the winner, and the human spirit demands freedom and mutual respect for all. The development and the recent ultimate and peaceful victory of liberal democracy assure civil, religious, and political rights to everyone* and thereby fulfill this central requirement of human nature.

Fukuyama thinks that the collapse of fascism and communism amounts to the final and ultimately worldwide victory of liberal democracy. In his initial article, he viewed this victory as the end of historical development and forecast nothing but boredom for the future.† In his book, he is a little more ambivalent about what lies in store for us: he at least leaves open the possibility that competitiveness and ambition may in the long run subvert the stability of the social and political structures that guarantee human dignity. But until that comes about (if it ever will), he thinks we will remain, like Nietzsche's last man, devoted to petty pursuits and to the satisfaction of our individual material needs. The idealisms that led to wars, the readiness to risk everything, even to die, for an idea will have died with the end of history. Paradoxically, when universal respect for human dignity enables us at last to actualize our nature, we sink back to the level of contented, mindless animals. We come to conceive of happiness as pleasure, and thus we choose, in Aristotle's words, "a life suitable only to cattle."‡ The last man, according to Nietzsche and Fukuyama,

---

* Francis Fukuyama, *The End of History and the Last Man* (New York: Free Press, 1992), 42. *Last Man* hereafter.

† Francis Fukuyama, "The End of History," *The National Interest* (Summer 1989), 18.

‡ *Nicomachean Ethics* 1095b20.

is one who thinks that love, creation, and longing involve too much exertion. Such humans have their "little pleasure for the day" and their "little pleasure for the night,"* but their activities are never strenuous. Their tired enjoyments make everything safe, everything agreeable, everything ultimately small.

The message about the end of history, therefore, is bittersweet. On the one hand, we are told that we will be safe, we will have our desires satisfied, and we will be happy. On the other hand, we hear with distress that everything spiritual, human, and truly interesting is about to disappear. Is life worth living if we can be no better than animals? Should we even consider continued existence if we have neither the opportunity nor the desire to sacrifice it for some higher cause?

Lest we despair and decide that life without a chance to die for our favorite ideology is below us, we should examine the plausibility of Fukuyama's central claims. It would be easy to show where he misunderstands Hegel and Nietzsche, and how his attempt to combine Plato's view of a tripartite human nature with Hegel's account of the development of consciousness yields an unstable, self-liquidating mix. Such niceties are the stuff of scholarship, but they miss everything about what is of human and of immediate interest in Fukuyama's ideas.

Instead, we should begin by acknowledging that he addresses something of great contemporary significance. The sudden and surprising collapse of communism has, we all suspect, some profound and now poorly understood bearing on what will come our way. It is something momentous that can be easily seen as the permanent victory of democracy over its rivals. The closer we find ourselves to such astounding events, the more obvious and inescapable appears their meaning. "How could it be otherwise?" we ask and feel satisfied that we see the pattern. Universal commerce has at last replaced war. Dictatorships are falling everywhere. Recessions are overcome and opportunities for endless trade will create wealth for all. It is difficult not to think that we live in historic times, and it takes but a small step from there to suppose that after these days nothing will ever be the same, that we see the end of everything we have known.

But now consider an alternative story. Instead of identifying the

---

* Friedrich Nietzsche, *Thus Spoke Zarathustra*, in *The Portable Nietzsche*, trans. Walter Kaufmann, (New York: Viking, 1954), 130.

aim of history as the realization of freedom and dignity, let us say that it is the total degradation of the individual. This happens through the invasion of privacy made possible by such high technology tools as video cameras, hidden listening devices, interactive television sets, and computers. The constant surveillance, the momentous stores of information about each of us in computer banks, the easy traceability of everything we do destroy the spontaneity of our actions. Instead of exercising our freedom by doing what we want, we learn to do only what looks good or at least acceptable to the faceless observers behind the machines. The community derives its power over us from its ability to know what we desire and what we do. This knowledge, when its extent dawns on us, turns into control. Reluctantly, though without overt coercion, we surrender our self-determination and fall into the ranks of the indistinguishable masses.

History, according to this reading, is the story of the control and eventual elimination of the *individual*. This history is by no means over, but it has taken an ominous turn with the development of the computer. In earlier ages, government incompetence left room for individual freedom. The computer eliminates the ignorance at the base of this incompetence and makes total control for the first time possible. Is the story about the ultimate victory of liberal democracy any better than this story about the victory of the computer? No. Does one of them capture what is *really* going on more accurately than the other? Of course not. If what one describes is really occurring, can the other line of development not be taking place as well? Of course it can.

This is so because what happens in the world is thick or indefinitely rich, as is our imagination in seeing patterns in it. The patterns are thin nets we throw in the roiling stream. They bring up some fish and a few crustaceans, but not *all* the fish and not the rocks and not the water that runs continuously through the webbing. We might be tempted to say that what we have caught is the mother of all fish, but the fingerlings next year give that boast the lie.

History thus is a collection of all manner of stories, of which some are more pleasing to some people and others to others. None is *the* story, though any number might show fine plot development and a satisfying moral. New stories begin when old ones end, but history, as the thick strand of all the stories, ends only with the human race. Remarkably, whether a story about the past is really good, whether it captures something of broad and continuing significance, can be determined only in the future. The truth of what we say about past developments is borne out, if at all, by what is yet to come. This suggests that the course of events is continuous and that even the idea that history has ended implies more history as needed to confirm it. The continuity and the richness of history make our grand theories about its meaning selective of the facts and forever unfinished and incomplete.

What can we say, then, of Fukuyama's claims about the end of history? They make an interesting story, though not one likely to be true. It certainly does not capture *all* the developments of which the life of humankind consists. The processes he weaves into a story are selected on a basis both unacknowledged and undefended. The immediate use of the story is that it calls our attention to some trends, such as growing ideological exhaustion, that we face today. Its ultimate value depends on how sustained those trends prove to be. In all, therefore, we are justified in saying, "Very interesting. Now let us wait and see."

Since history is the field of surprises, I would gladly let Fukuyama bear the risk of his hypothesis and leave the matter at that with a smile, were it not for three pernicious errors that his enterprise embodies. He thinks, mistakenly, that history has a grand internal logic and is driven by a single, intelligible dialectic. He displays, lamentably, a profound disdain for individuals and their values. He supposes, intolerantly, that there is but one human nature, that he knows what it is, and that any view acknowledging a multiplicity of perfections must be false.

Although Fukuyama says that the future belongs to liberal democracy, his own theory of history, glorifying struggle and the value of ideological commitment, is not one usually associated with it. The thought that everything of significance is accomplished or governed by a hidden force is a convenient excuse for remaining in power on the part of those claiming privileged insight into its workings. It was no accident that Hitler believed the power of history lay in the mysterious hands of race and nation; he claimed to be their spokesman. Lenin and Stalin also believed that events revealed a single dialectic, the nature of which they felt in a unique position to interpret. Such claims of occult rationality are the residue, or as Hegel said the truth, of the time-honored idea that God guides history. But those committed to democracy have always thought that such guidance comes through inspiring the will of individuals, not through large-scale infusions of divine power into the marauding actions of some class or race or state.

Theories of unimodal causation and views that postulate a cunning rational force behind history have for long and for good reasons been discredited. Such approaches to understanding human life selectively disregard evidence, reinterpret the obvious meaning of facts, overemphasize the significance of limited perspectives, and underrate the role of contingency. Nothing is simpler than to look back on a few large facts and to detect a pattern. That is what Hegel invites the philosopher to do: the job of this devotee of reason is to make sense of the welter of absurdity and confusion that constitutes life. There is nothing wrong with such aspirations so long as we remain, as Hegel did not, modest and self-critical in acting on them. Modesty requires that we claim only that ours is a likely story told for whatever light it sheds and held subject to whatever confirmation it may receive. Self-critical reflection demands that we recall how many past stories sound silly now and how many others evoke but a knowing smile. Only if we view our efforts in that context can we avoid the puffery that has made the modern world think of philosophers as buffoons.

What, in the end, is history? Is it the movement of impersonal forces, the struggle of nations, the contest of disembodied ideas? If one conceives it this way, the individual dwindles to insignificance, and a time filled with the happiness of people becomes, as Hegel said, a blank page in the history of the world. Fukuyama looks ahead, sees only the satisfaction of private persons, and sadly concludes that history must be over.

This strikes me as a colossal inversion of values. The theme of the insignificance of the individual is powerfully sounded by Hegel, who said that "the individual must . . . forget himself; less must be demanded of him, just as he in turn can expect less of himself, and may demand less for himself."* The world-historical destiny of the human race appears to be undercut or abandoned, Fukuyama thinks, when all our efforts result in no more than universal happiness. "No more than universal happiness"! Indeed. If war, starvation, premature death, senseless conflict, disease, frustration, insecurity, lifelong suffering, poverty, injustice, discrimination, hatred, stunted development, and debilitating handicaps were, against all odds, eliminated, we should have to mourn because that would leave no history. The

---

* *Phenomenology of Spirit* (Oxford: Clarendon Press, 1977), 45.

history whose passing we would mourn is the endless procession of morally corrupt leaders, of megalomaniacal warriors, of expansionist states and murderous factions. Let us all be distressed because without Genghis Khans and Napoleons, without Hitlers and Stalins, without history, all we will have to do is get on with our boring lives. If this be history, it cannot end too soon; it should have ended long ago. It will be missed only by those who would be great dictators themselves and the enthusiasts who like to trace the course of military campaigns in the library.

Fukuyama has evidently read too much Hegel and Kojève and too little of the great American poet Walt Whitman. With Whitman, I celebrate the ordinary person and everyday life. He says,

> Grown, half-grown and babe, of this country and every country,
>   in-doors and out-doors, one just as much as the other, I see,
> And all else behind or through them.

> The wife, and she is not one jot less than the husband,
> The daughter, and she is just as good as the son,
> The mother, and she is every bit as much as the father.

> Offspring of ignorant and poor, boys apprenticed to trades,
> Young fellows working on farms and old fellows working on
>   farms,
> Sailor-men, merchant-men, coasters, immigrants,
> All these I see.*

These are the people the great theoreticians must see also; they constitute the human race. Of the great ideas that supposedly govern history, none is greater than the thought that efforts at improvement must focus on the lives of these little people, that is, of people like you and me. We have heard enough about saints and heroes and all the high moments of human history. The hagiographers fill our ears with stories about the fine and the few. But were the high really so fine? At what cost to the daily lives of countless others did they perform their mighty exploits? There is no better gauge of the worth of an age or a nation than what ordinary people wake up to in the morning and what their days amount to by the afternoon. Life is a collection of ordinary days and humankind a collection of ordinary people; only

---

* Walt Whitman, "A Song for Occupations," in *The Complete Writings of Walt Whitman* (New York: G. P. Putnam's, 1902), 1:259.

the features of the ordinary can measure the quality of life and the level of the development of the human race.

The grand ideologies, the gory and glorious conflicts of world-views have not helped us ordinary people very much. Our lives have improved slowly over the ages in spite rather than because of what the ideologists have tried to foist on us. The great enthusiasms of the human race—the mad wars of religion, class, race, and national pride—are like fevers from which it is best to recover without a memory of their hallucinations, recalling only how horrible they were. None of this means that ordinary people might not want to act on high ideals or to reach for the finest experiences possible for them. But such ideals tend to be concrete, focusing on the future of family and kin rather than on the stereotypical great deeds of crushing wicked foes and sacrificial deaths.

History is constituted by the ordinary lives of ordinary people. These lives, full and rich at their best and sometimes monumental in courage and perseverance, form the stream of human events in which the nets of our theory are cast. The fish we land obscures the significance of the water that raised it. So Fukuyama finds grand struggles interesting, but the lives of all the extraordinary everyday people involved in them boring or at least lacking in grace. In terms of his own image of the wagon trains heading west,* only the journey through the badlands, suffering Indian attacks attracts him. He seems to bemoan the fact that such fine journeys lead to nothing but new settlements, stable communities in which people can get on with their lives. Yet is there another reason to undertake them? For once we colonize the land, we can plant groves of orange trees and pistachio nuts for us and for our children to enjoy. The majority of the colonists came to this country not out of missionary zeal but in search of a better life. The genius of America is that it allows the individual to flourish, that it does not permit ideological repression of middle-class life.

Fukuyama's third fundamental error consists in his adoption of the now widespread gratuitous attack on pluralistic democracy. The assault is disguised as a high-minded rejection of relativism, but it comes in reality to a declaration of war on any social order that allows a variety of values to flourish. Without some absolute good, the argument declares, without some value that holds universally, even the

---

* Fukuyama, *Last Man*, 338–39.

fundamental principle of human equality must fall. Such principles cannot be supported by the contingent and divergent allegiances of people pursuing their own interests; if each value is as good as the next, equality cannot be better than inequality, and we have no basis for choosing tolerance over intolerance.*

This line of argument is familiar from the work of Allan Bloom, Fukuyama's teacher, and the wicked relativism it supposedly exposes is normally associated with Nietzsche. As an argument, this set of ideas is totally without merit. Those who wish to refute such a 'relativism' tend to present the most misleading and the least defensible versions of it. What they need to deal with is not the equivocations of ancient sophists, but a serious and thoughtful account of how individuals may hold different values and yet cooperate, and therefore of how societies may be both tolerant and stable.

Democratic pluralism may be easily and fruitfully conceived on an Aristotelian model. We may think of values as grounded in and expressing our nature: who we are determines what we choose and what ultimately satisfies us. The instability of the good is, in this way, eliminated—the truly valuable is a function not of what we think or how we feel, but of the permanent dispositions that constitute our being. We have, of course, little reason to suppose that our natures are identical. The Greek ideas that all humans share a single essence and that the human race is an unchanging, uniform, and sharply circumscribed species can sustain neither philosophical nor anthropological scrutiny. So just as the objective reality of nature establishes the stability of the good, individual variations in nature define the diversity of goods.

The multiplicity of values presents no special problem so long as acting on the basis of one does not require the frustration of others. Achievement of one good may incidentally be incompatible with achievement of another; you and I cannot marry the same person or hold the same job. But that leads only to healthy competition. The structuring values we cannot permit are those whose aim is the frustration of human beings and whose satisfaction is, therefore, possible only by defeating others. These are the values, as Schopenhauer put it, of wickedness and cruelty for which "the suffering of another is no longer the means for attaining the ends of its own will, but an end in

* Fukuyama, *Last Man*, 332.

itself."* Systems of formal and informal education, which are the social tools we use for creating natures, must therefore leave room for all manner of individuals, though not for ones who seek happiness by dominating or destroying others.

If values are divergent and all are equally legitimate, how can members of a pluralist democracy share them, and what will justify their allegiance to them? The answer is simple: we share values to the extent our natures resemble one another. Such resemblances exist due to biological factors and socializing activities: almost all of us seek life, for example, and the satisfaction of our needs in the midst of our fellows. Commitment to our good does not require that we think it absolute or universally justified. It is enough if I realize that my good is absolute and all-encompassing for me, just as yours is for you. The recognition Fukuyama thinks we all seek is acknowledgment that our values are legitimate, that our special perfection—though perhaps neither sought nor shared by others—is nonetheless acceptable in their sight.

Such diversity of perfections, tolerated and celebrated, is the very essence of pluralist, liberal democracy. If grand, ideological history is over, good riddance, I say. Its demise will permit us perhaps to begin with good conscience the pursuit of our private good in a caring, tolerant community. Undisturbed by the fanaticism that uses force and war to remake the world in its own image, we can create history in its true, rich, human sense.

---

* Arthur Schopenhauer, *The World as Will and Representation* (New York: Dover, 1969), 1:363.

Part Three

𝓇

PROBLEMS OF
SOCIAL LIFE

CHAPTER 9

Aristotle and Dewey
on the Rat Race

Aristotle put his stamp on the history of Western thought by inventing the concepts of activity and process. That is not the
only way in which he exercised a formative influence over
much subsequent philosophy nor are these the only novel concepts
that flowed from his fertile mind. But these ideas became corner-
stones of a distinguished series of metaphysical systems. They also
came to articulate a vision of the good life or the life proper for humans.

The observation underlying the distinction between activity and
process is that some actions appear to be complete while others seem
to point beyond themselves for their completion. In digging and
pouring foundations, for example, we find that the acts make sense
only by reference to further things to be accomplished in the process
of building. Foundation work is, in this way, intrinsically incomplete:
it requires a significant sequence of additional performances to render
it meaningful or whole. A moment or two of pleasure, by contrast,
demands nothing further: it is experienced as complete and satisfying simply by itself. Extension of the feeling is, of course, welcome
but it is not necessary to render the initial pleasure a complete and
self-contained moment of joy.

On careful inspection, this incompleteness is revealed as not a ran-
dom or accidental feature of some acts. Complex physical performances, in particular, appear to be rent by a sort of fragmentation that
renders them imperfect and unsatisfactory. The reason is their integrated complexity itself. Within such processes, each part is tied to
the rest, and none makes sense alone. Pouring the foundation is

incomplete without building the basement, nothing can be a basement without a first floor, and before the structure can become a house, we must build each of its parts in its proper place and in the right sequence. This seems neither surprising nor altogether bad, and we may well decide that such processes achieve completeness only when finished: they are whole in the totality or whole of their existence, but always fragmented in the parts. This whole, however, never actually exists because the parts that constitute it are successive. Past and future infect the entire process: all the parts necessary to make it whole never coexist, and paradoxically, at the moment when it reaches completion with its last constituent act, all of it has sadly ceased to be.

Sequential actualization is, in this way, essentially imperfect since it is structured by time: it must always rely on the dead or the yet-to-be for its completion, which means that it can never be complete. Its fate, both as human action and as metaphysical event, is expectation and grief. It is a yearning after what is to come and the sadness over what is irretrievably gone. Aristotle and others have, therefore, concluded that it can serve neither as a foundation for our understanding of what *is* nor as a design for how to lead a satisfactory life.

In sharp contrast with this, activities are complete at each moment of their occurrence. Their simplicity assures that they can be actualized at once. In this way, they liberate themselves from the tyranny of time; even when they exist for a while, as when happiness endures for a precious hour, they are complete and self-contained at each portion of that stretch, gladly accepting continuance, but losing nothing if it fails to be granted. Activities constitute, therefore, human acts that are gems: they are meaningful, self-contained achievements free of the corrosive influence of time, of all expectation and sadness. They are eternal not in the sense of lasting forever, but in that they transcend or defang the temporal to reach perfection in a moment.

This notion of timeless actuality became the foundation of our understanding of the divine. Aristotle himself thought of his odd god as consisting of just such an eternal act in which the timeless timelessly contemplated itself. Thinking of God as being constituted of activity assures divine completeness and perfection. One of the ideas of substance—that of an existent in need of nothing beyond itself in order to be or to be complete—captures this notion of a being shielded from time, growth, decay, need, desire, and imperfection. This manner of conceiving the ideal being permeated not only theology: it became the grounding notion of many of the great metaphysical systems. It has a remarkable history through the Middle Ages and was memorably introduced to the modern world in Spinoza's *Ethics*. It haunted German metaphysics after Kant, as a long series of system builders struggled to work through their love-dread relation to Spinoza. In one form and context or another, it has survived to ground much of the metaphysics of the twentieth century.

Despite this distinguished past, the idea of activity would not command the interest it does if its use had been purely theoretical. Conceptions of God, however, typically also articulate ideals for human life. Activity was viewed precisely in this light from the first. Aristotle thought of it not only as a way of understanding God, but also as an ideal to which we needed to aspire in order to actualize the best in us. He knew that, as temporally embodied, we could never escape the world of labored processes. But contemplation of the changeless beckoned to him as at least a momentary completion of imperfect lives and, therefore, as a manner in which we could be godlike. The same ideal, in typically exaggerated form, was present in Spinoza, who saw absorption into eternal, pure act as the only life worth living.

A fundamental disagreement separates Aristotle and Spinoza. The resolutely sensible Greek could think of no way of breaking down the distinction between process and activity and of thereby escaping temporality and death. As natural creatures with minds, we always remain both temporally fragmented and, potentially at least, eternally complete. The Stoics showed Spinoza a way to avoid this undesirable ambiguity in human life. Their belief in the power of the mind convinced them that the distinction between process and activity was not absolute: by taking the correct attitude to what we do, they maintained, we can convert any process into an activity. If what renders an action a fragmented process is that it is performed to obtain an ulterior end, all we have to do to change it into an activity is to do it, and each part of it, as an end in itself. This breaks the process into a sequence of activities, each of which is meaningful and complete without reference to anything beyond. The Stoic insight suggested to Spinoza that a life in the eternal was really possible. His account of how passive emotions can be converted into active ones was his version of the transmutation of process into activity and his explanation of how, though finite, we can completely fade, or rather brighten, into the eternal.

The ideal of self-contained activity, of life in the eternal, has remained powerful to this day. Some people advocate attitudinal adjustments to unpleasant tasks; others continue to draw a sharp line between the realm of means and those things that are of intrinsic value. Many condemn commercial and industrial life because of its endless cycle of fragmented acts and trivial demands. All of these critics tacitly assume the process/activity distinction and embrace pure act in some form as our only hope of satisfaction.

A fine, though perhaps surprising, twentieth-century philosophical articulation of the same ideas can be found in the work of George Santayana. Although he studied with William James and found himself in sympathy with some of the central ideas of pragmatism, when it came to thinking through the nature of the good life, Santayana reverted to Aristotle's time-honored distinction. He viewed the physical world as an endless sequence of events and animal life within it as a cycle of needs and fleeting satisfactions. Nothing caught in this web of the tenuous, not even the temporarily successful life of reason, could escape the ultimate inadequacy of all processes.

Santayana was more explicit than Aristotle in identifying process with the material world and activity with a phase of consciousness or mind. Accordingly, he maintained that nothing is of ultimate value except conscious feeling. But even the realm of mind is permeated by the anxiety and incompleteness characteristic of temporal process: since, referring to what is beyond, neither belief nor emotion shows itself satisfied with the immediately present content of consciousness, they cannot constitute self-complete moments of activity. We reach fulfillment only in the spiritual phase of awareness, which is free of all restless striving and of all reference to the absent or the beyond. Santayana deliberately identified this 'spiritual life' with activity in Aristotle's sense.* It consists of a string of pure intuitions (contemplative acts of consciousness), each complete in itself and presenting some form for cognitive grasp or direct enjoyment. Placid aesthetic immediacy is thus the only thing perfect in the world, the only act whose performance does not in the end dissatisfy.

The broader context of Santayana's theory of the spiritual life was naturalistic. He thought that absorption in the given constituted a perfection open to certain animals, and that it required the continued support of a living body. Nevertheless, the view amounted to a reaf-

---

* George Santayana, *Scepticism and Animal Faith* (New York: Dover, 1955), 217.

firmation of the supremacy of mind and, in the form of aesthetic immediacy, of a sort of cognition. It also identified time and its attendant imperfections as the enemy. We could not hope to defeat this antagonist but, by momentary escape, we could cheat it of victory.

This depiction of Santayana's view of the perfection open to us reveals its remarkable similarity to Schopenhauer's theory of art. Schopenhauer thought of the aesthetic intuition of universals as one of only two ways of escaping the ravages of an ever-hungry and never satisfied will. The ultimate form of escape was denial of the will-to-live; if resolutely executed, this terminated life. Contemplation of the beautiful offered a less radical, and therefore less permanent, solution to the problem of endless frustrated striving. It enabled one to eliminate desire for a moment by providing absorption in a pure, uselessly beautiful object.

The resemblance is important to note because it shows the close connection between application of the process/activity distinction to the question of how to live well and the deepest, most devastating pessimism. So long as we think that time is the enemy and set ourselves an ideal of godlike, eternal act, we cannot avoid seeing much of life as worthless, if not positively evil. In such a sea of imperfection, with nothing but momentary glimpses of beauty to redeem us, we can readily decide that life is without hope and significance.

If we think of divine perfection in terms of activity, we can hope to achieve a state similar to God's blessedness by engaging in activity ourselves. Our inevitable failure to sustain such pure actuality need, then, not plunge us into ultimate despair; with God, we can have the promise of another life in which eternal activity will go on unabated. The pessimism of Schopenhauer and Santayana becomes unavoidable if we retain the process/activity framework but eliminate the theocentric metaphysics that has been its historical partner. Contrary to what some philosophers think, Schopenhauer and Santayana were not pessimists simply because they failed to believe in the existence of God. Their hopelessness was due to rejecting God's existence and the promise of a future state while, for purposes of elucidating the ideal human life, they retained the very concepts that, employed in metaphysics, lead at once to God. The lesson may well be that we end up paying a high price if we refuse to employ a set of concepts in one area while we retain their related use in another.

The process/activity distinction rests on the claim that there is an essential incompatibility between ends-in-themselves and means, between ultimate value and utility. Philosophers since Aristotle have, accordingly, maintained that whatever aims at some goal beyond itself cannot also carry intrinsic worth. Astoundingly, no one challenged this idea until the twentieth century. Much in Hegel hinted at its wrongheadedness. But Dewey was the first to bring it into question and to develop an alternative conception.

In *Experience and Nature*, Dewey acknowledges that much of what we do "in home, factory, laboratory and study"[*] is devoid of intrinsic value. The ends we prize, by contrast, are "spasms of excited escape from the thraldom of enforced work."[†] Labor is merely useful while enjoyment is good in and of itself. Its value resides in our being satisfied with it independently of where it may lead or precisely because it leads nowhere beyond itself. It appears, therefore, that work is intrinsically incomplete process, enjoyment luminous and perfect activity.

Dewey, however, is quick to dispel this appearance. In reality, work can be seen as useful only if "we arbitrarily cut short our consideration of consequences"[‡] by focusing on the commodities it produces to the neglect of its cost in the quality of human life. Enjoyments, in turn, approximate ultimate ends only if we detach them from the full context of their conditions and consequences and thereby convert them into passivities devoid of meaning. The process/activity distinction applies, therefore, only to life fragmented by improper institutional arrangements and to events we abstract from their place in experience. The extent to which it applies is a measure of how far "experience fails to be art."[§]

To speak of experience as art is to say that in it means and end, the useful and the valuable all fully coincide. This sounds at first as a restatement of the idea of activity: since such divine acts are performed for their own sake, they display no distinction between means and end. The reason, however, why we can see no such distinction is that activities contain no means at all. Means are realities not in themselves desirable that tend to bring about what we seek. We turn to them for their causal features or for their mediating role in leading us where we want to be. There is no such mediation in activity; we perform what is wanted directly, for its own sake. In activity, we tran-

---

[*] *Experience and Nature* (New York: Dover, 1958), 362.
[†] Dewey, 360–61.
[‡] Dewey, 362.
[§] Dewey, 61.

scend time and achieve perfection by refusing all contact with the merely useful.

Dewey speaks of the genuine unity of means and end, not of the absence of means. This demands rethinking the traditional notion of means, which is the "coerced antecedent of the occurrence of another thing which is wanted."[*] Such causal conditions, serving as external necessities, appear to have nothing in common with the ends they help bring about. Dewey rejects this as the only, or the proper, idea of means and introduces in its place a notion according to which the means is an intrinsic element of the end. In addition to being a causal condition of the end to which it leads, a means must meet two criteria: (1) to be freely chosen and used to bring about a consequence, and (2) to be an integrated portion of that consequence.[†]

It is generally agreed that if they are not chosen and used, causal antecedents result in effects without being means to them. Dewey goes a step beyond this and notes that, under normal circumstances, the love for the end extends to whatever helps us attain it. Achieving results by control over the generative conditions of things and events is a characteristically human endeavor. Such deliberately and intelligently caused consequences are, in Dewey's language, 'meanings.' The need for meanings runs deep in our lives; their attainment constitutes art.[‡] The first criterion connects means, therefore, with the prized and enjoyed ability of humans to take control of their lives, or at least of important portions of them.

The second criterion amounts to a rejection of the separateness of causes and effects. Affecting the tone of an exasperated instructor, G. E. Moore thought he wreaked havoc with Mill's wayward attempt to show that music, virtue, and money could have both instrumental and final value.[§] Dewey picks up Mill's mantle and maintains that nothing can be a means *unless* it is both useful and a part of the desired end. He presents telling examples of means that are, at once, elements of the whole to whose creation they contribute. Flour and yeast, he argues, are both means to bread and ingredients of it. And a "good political constitution, honest police system and competent judiciary, are means to the prosperous life of the community because they

---

[*] Dewey, 366.   [†] Dewey, 366–67.   [‡] Dewey, 370.
[§] G. E. Moore, *Principia Ethica* (Cambridge: Cambridge University Press, 1951), chap. 3.

are integrated portions of that life."*

Dewey's attention to the notion of activity, of what can be done as an end directly, is the idea of action that is both means and end. Events in experience present this double face: they play a role in the sequential (causal) order and also display qualities we can immediately enjoy. Dewey does not think that these divergent features of actions are matters of perspective. Everything actually has both relational and intrinsic, both instrumental and consummatory, properties. We need neither adjustment of attitude nor act of will to gain access to them; a growth in sensitivity is enough. Such growth, if Dewey is right, enables us to realize that instrumental and final values are not incompatible. Accordingly, intelligent human beings will seek satisfaction by participating fully in both the labor and the delights of life.

This notion of means-end integrated actions is a far more worldly ideal than Aristotle's. It abolishes the supremacy of the cognitive and the contemplative, and opens the entire range of human activities to the legitimate search for satisfaction. It eliminates the prerogatives of the eternal and turns attention away from the age-old fixation on transcending time to the use of the time available. It restores the dignity of everyday activities and establishes them as proper elements in meaningful human lives. It refuses to view the totality of our condition as flawed (along the lines of the idea, for example, that we are rational beings tied to absurd bodies in an irrational world) and looks, instead, for concrete ways to enhance enjoyment in the present and to increase it in the future.

Dewey's claim that we can perform actions both for their own sake and for the sake of what they bring is heartening. If true, it would make life richer and satisfaction in it easier to attain. By redirecting our efforts in accordance with it, we could engage in actions that are both fulfilling and useful; we would not have to sacrifice pleasure to service. But is Dewey's claim true and his ideal workable?

Utopian thinkers have an easy way of sidestepping these questions. Dewey himself readily admits that many of our current practices fall short of being both means and ends; they include "much of our labors in home, factory, laboratory and study."† A single easy step from here could take him to the declaration that means-end integrated actions constitute an ideal in the sense of what defines how things would be if humans were rational, the world sufficiently pli-

---

* Dewey, *Experience*, 367.   † Dewey, 362.

able, and social arrangements optimal. Such standards beckon from afar: nothing need live up to them now or at any time until the millennium or some astounding change in human nature. This insulates the ideal from criticism as impractical; its function, it might be urged, is precisely to articulate a standard that is difficult, if not impossible, to meet.

Such an approach has satisfied framers of abstract ideals throughout the history of thought. To his great credit, Dewey sees no appeal in it. His denotative method requires him to anchor all his views, including his ideas of the good, in actual experience. We must, therefore, be able to find cases of action that are valuable both as means and as end, and that we undertake to do in order to secure both sorts of good. Such actions, Dewey asserts, must be both instrumental and consummatory simultaneously "rather than in alternation and displacement."* Moreover, much of the rest of what we do should be reorientable so that it approximates this ideal of the coincidence of utility and intrinsic value.

At least two sorts of ordinary practice qualify by Dewey's criteria: love and play. Kissing, done in the right context, clearly displays both instrumental and final values. Unquestionably, it is pleasant and tends to lead to additional fine activities. As enjoyed for its intrinsic qualities, it is an end; as freely chosen to bring about a larger, more orgiastic, consequence of which it is an integrated portion, it is a means. Persons engaged in it may, moreover, be reasonably viewed as initiating and continuing it for the double reason of how nice it is and what exciting things grow from it. It is, therefore, both instrument and consummation, as is every other element of the act of love.

The same holds for games and for play. Dribbling the ball downcourt is not a coerced antecedent of going for the layup. It is an activity enjoyable for its own sake, but also for the sake of the basket that may come from it. As freely chosen instrument of scoring and as an integrated element of the larger scoring drive, it is a means; as fun experience and display of ball handling skill, it is an end. People who like playing the game, moreover, dribble for both reasons: they enjoy fast movement with control of the ball, and they look forward to the opportunities for scoring it creates.

Unfortunately, not many other examples of human conduct appear to qualify as optimal by Dewey's high ideal. Some ends we seek,

---

* Dewey, 361.

such as entertainment and beer-soaked highs, lack useful outcomes. The majority of actions we perform as means can be enjoyed only by idiots or by those sufficiently unconscious not to note or object to repetition. Means and ends are, in this way, fragmented and sequential, and we pay a high price for fleeting satisfaction. At first sight, therefore, Aristotle's view of the human lot as pervaded by incomplete and ultimately unsatisfying processes appears more accurate about the bulk of life than Dewey's more optimistic assessment.

Two well-known psychological phenomena operate to reduce the onerousness of means. The pleasure of attaining the objective tends to spread to the instruments that helped us in the quest. Shaving, an otherwise unpleasant or indifferent act, can in this way become suffused with excitement if it is a condition of morning love. Brokers on the floor of the stock exchange report that long train rides to work cease to be objectionable when their trading goes well. Such anticipatory pleasures do much to make life bearable, even if the delight they offer is bittersweet or ambiguous.

The second psychological mechanism of relief is the remarkable human capacity for acceptance. Unavoidable, debilitating routines can become bearable with the years. Their assurance and predictability offer comfort, and the force of habit makes them expected, even essential, parts of life. Boring and menial work may seem a depressing way to earn one's living. But vacations reveal how much even such miserable routines can come to function as important elements of at least acceptable days. Given a choice, perhaps only a few would opt for such lives, but swallowed up in them we do all we can to make the pain subside.

Although these mechanisms render existence centered on unpleasant instrumentalities a little better, they fail to achieve satisfaction beyond the compensatory. They fall far short of endowing instruments with intrinsic value or of making dehumanizing tasks a pleasure to perform. So long as there are disagreeable but necessary actions, they are, therefore, inadequate to attain Dewey's ideal of means that are at once consummations.

Must we, however, always face disagreeable necessities? We face them now and, if they are to disappear, it will be either because we refuse to view them as unpleasant or because they will no longer be needed. The former leads us back to the attitudinal adjustments of the Stoic and is unlikely to gain Dewey's support. The latter points to increased control over the conditions of our existence and thus to applied intelligence and technology.

We find that many onerous tasks have been eliminated in the last few hundred years. We no longer have to gather wood for heat, haul our own water, or take an oxcart when we visit friends. In many respects, we live in what James called a "wishing-cap world," in which:

> We want water and we turn a faucet. We want a kodak-picture and we press a button. We want information and we telephone. We want to travel and we buy a ticket. In these and similar cases, we hardly need to do more than the wishing—the world is rationally organized to do the rest.*

In such a world, we have to do much less, or at least much less that is objectionable, to attain our ends. One part of the reason is that we have reduced the amount of human labor necessary to meet our desires; the introduction of machines, for example, makes our efforts more efficient. Another is that much necessary work has been shifted to others who, since they are specialized and have access to the right equipment, can do it more easily or better. Very few people raise their own food, for example, and few could even think of making their own cars.

These vast and, on the whole, beneficial changes appear to favor the view that industrial life moves us in the direction of Dewey's means-end integrated actions. The appearance, however, is deceptive. Industrial society makes life more comfortable at the cost of a momentous separation between means and ends at the workplace. The tasks we perform in huge organizations are routine and restricted. As the sheet metal worker in the airplane factory, we make small and anonymous contributions to large social products. Our actions constitute the means, or fragments of the means, to ends we have not intended and may not understand. These means may well be 'integrated portions' of the ends, but they are not freely and intelligently chosen by the individuals involved. Even if instruments and products stand in a consummately rational relation in the institution, those who work there cannot easily connect their efforts with the objectives they subserve.

---

* William, James, *Pragmatism* (Cambridge: Harvard Universtiy Press, 1975), 139.

The gulf between means and ends is widened by the fact that necessary specialization makes tasks narrow and repetitive. Competition with others generates internal pressure to work relentlessly, and the demand for productivity causes haste. Under these circumstances, it is difficult to view fragmentary tasks as intrinsically enjoyable ends. Perhaps the work of those who shape metal sheets does have an intrinsic quality that, if only they could focus on it, would give them satisfaction. Their situation at work, however, is not well adapted to promote such focusing. And even if they succeed for a day or two, their need for work will outlive their ability to see it as meaningful or fun.

All of this may, of course, be true only because we are at an intermediate stage of industrialization. In another hundred years, all jobs unworthy of humans, all routine, repetitive and boring tasks, will possibly have been eliminated. This could leave for us only acts, such as love and play, in which everything is both means and end. All the rest of the work of the world may well end up being done by intelligent machines.

If we do not destroy the human race and the planet in the process, this is a plausible scenario. Suppose that it comes about. Would human life then consist only or largely of means-end integrated actions? The likely answer is no. For the mechanization of productive tasks does not substitute pleasurable means for unpleasant ones; instead, it trivializes means or eliminates them altogether. The development from raising, killing and plucking a chicken and then cooking it on a woodburning stove to warming prepackaged microwave fowl makes the point obvious. In reading, we have to move the eyes and turn the page; television requires little more than a grateful stare. We do not have to go to science fiction accounts of electrically stimulated brains in pleasure vats to know that people gladly choose and often dream of passive sensuous delights. The mechanization of the world is propelled by this desire and serves it. The promise and ultimate reward of such a society is to convert much of life into enjoyed ends. This is closer to Aristotle than to Dewey, with the difference that such ends are passivities, not activities. A large additional increase in technology offers, therefore, little of benefit to Dewey's ideal.

It may be better to look for the growth or distribution of means-end integrated actions by starting from the example of professionals and their work. Physicians, presumably, do not have to engage in disagreeable routines. The actions they undertake are freely chosen, and the treatments they administer (especially in preventive medicine) are integral parts of the sustained health of their patients. It appears, therefore, that doctors have the privilege of performing only or mainly those actions that feature both instrumental and consummatory value. Perhaps we could all be like doctors and other professionals and thereby enhance our enjoyment of what we do.

This picture of physicians is, unfortunately, selective and therefore inaccurate. It romanticizes their work by overlooking the everyday context in which they operate. In reality, doctors can enjoy what they do only because they hand over much of what is unpleasant or routine to nurses, orderlies, assistants, bookkeepers, and secretaries. And even with these tasks delegated, it takes a wild stretch of the imagination to see their daily work as similar to making love. Particularly is this true after the fifteenth Pap smear or when examining, late in the afternoon, the fiftieth baby with colic. Even love, I suppose, loses its allure when there are too many customers.

The key, then, is to do what one wants for as long as one wants to do it. This is not a bad, brief account of freedom. Most people know the connection between freedom and pleasure because they find that they tend to enjoy what they choose without constraint. If we keep this in mind, we may conclude that the first criterion a means must meet according to Dewey, namely, that it be freely chosen and used, may be adequate by itself to assure a significant improvement of the human condition. If only all of us could do what we wished, embracing ends and choosing means without external interference and without the demands of necessity, we would be able to experience each means as at once a consummation.

What is there to stop us from growing in this direction? Dewey himself stresses the importance of freedom and sees it as indispensable for a satisfactory moral and political life. What we need here, however, is radical freedom for the individual. Each person must be in a position to decide what he or she wants to do, even if the decision disregards legitimate social needs. Can a society operate with this much liberty? Only if it finds a way to make people want what is needed. This is excessively difficult to accomplish. We can force individuals to do the socially necessary—to pay taxes, for example. We can train people to do what is useful (to take care of their parents, for instance) by creating in them a sense of obligation. Human beings get used to having to do such things and accept them as unavoidable parts of life. But they do not come to like or to enjoy them and they certainly do not seek them out. Socialization has its limits. Although some psychologists claim that they can make anyone like anything, it is clear that no one can make enough people like enough unpleasant things to enable a society to run on the basis of free choice alone.

Friends of Dewey must by now be anxious to set me right. Since the search for large-scale or utopian improvements in human life did not appeal to Dewey, it is unfair, they might assert, to saddle him with a view that requires us to turn most of the actions of the largest number of people into meaningful, means-end integrated acts. This is a good reminder, even though it misses the point of what I have done. Of course, Dewey is a meliorist looking for incremental change. Of course, such change is possible: we can reduce the unpleasantness of means a little here and there by making life more like love, by selective advances in technology, by modeling more jobs on the professions, by expanding the sphere of freedom. Those, however, were not the questions we set out to examine.

Dewey presents his idea of means-end integrated actions as an alternative to Aristotle's notion of activity. As such, the conception articulates an ideal of human conduct in the most general terms: although it does not tell us in detail what to do, it gives precise instructions on how to do it. I have been examining the warrant for this ideal and its scope. I had little trouble identifying its source and instances in experience. Its range, however, gets Dewey in trouble. For he advances it as a condition at which human action in general should aim, bemoans the fact that such action falls short of it, and attributes this failure to current institutional arrangements.* This suggests that there are some strategies we can pursue to bring much of our conduct significantly closer to the ideal. I have explored what these strategies might be, but found none that offers significant relief.

Aristotle was satisfied to note that some things we did were by nature processes, others activities. The Stoics developed this distinction into a technique useful for dealing with the rat race. To maximize satisfaction in life, they admonished, we need simply to convert processes into activities by doing each element of them for its own sake, as an end. This requires only a change in aim or attitude, and that, they believed, is always within our power. If we followed the Stoics, we would perform whatever actions were needed without concern for their ultimate success. Such focus on the present would, pre-

---

* Dewey, *Experience*, 362, 368.

sumably, make our personal lives and social actions meaningful at least for the moment.

Dewey's ideal, more robust and less resigned about the future, provides a better expression of the modern temper. But how can we turn it into a useful strategy for dealing with the pressures and the meaningless necessities of existence? Can we hope to spend our days as though we were making love to life? Having Marx before him as a failed example, Dewey shied away from recommending revolutionary social changes to institutionalize means-end integrated actions. Unfortunately, even if he had wanted to advance such recommendations, my discussion shows that it is not at all clear what they might have been.

There is one sure way in which we can all enjoy the intrinsic qualities of otherwise objectionable means. We can simply perform the acts of which they consist as ends-in-themselves, for their own sake alone. All this takes is a change of attitude or a firm resolve to focus on the immediate. The only trouble is that it is the Stoic gambit, and it converts means-end integrated actions into activities.

CHAPTER 10

Violence as Response to Alienation*

I t is a severe but infrequent error to suppose that all people are nice. Wholesale optimism about human nature rates with pessimism about one's own prospects as among the views least likely to tempt us. But if evidence were needed that human beings are not all prepossessing and wonderful, we can simply look at the record of violence in the world and at terrorists. Or we might observe how children treat animals and, too frequently, one another.

If we suppose that humans are by nature wicked, kindness and love need special explanation. If, on the other hand, we think that the depth of our soul knows only the good, we must provide an account of wickedness and violence. But framing no sweeping view of our tendencies puts us in the most difficult position: we must explain both the good and the evil we do without benefit of supposing that either is in some sense 'natural.' This protects us from broad and insupportable generalities and is therefore, in spite of its difficulty, the soundest course by far. Accordingly, it is the one I shall follow.

We cannot, of course, explain everything at once. I shall restrict my attention to what is generally acknowledged to be our dark side and within that, specifically, to the phenomenon of violence. Violence is particularly interesting because it frequently represents an incongruous and apparently irrational episode in the lives of individuals. Its occurrence is difficult to predict and there is no general theory on the

---

* Although I use the word 'alienation' here, my account of the phenomenon to which it normally refers is framed in terms of the notion of mediation and its costs. See my *Intermediate Man* (Indianapolis: Hackett Publishers, 1981.)

basis of which it can be understood. If it is a reversion to uncivilized instincts, its prevalence in the modern world shows civility to be a thin veneer. If, however, some of its forms are uniquely connected to current conditions, reflection on them might yield unexpected insight into the structural problems of our society.

I shall attempt to sketch the generative conditions of some forms of violence. By 'generative conditions' I mean circumstances that, if people find themselves in them, make violence as a response probable, attractive, or natural. My intention to deal with some but not all types of violence expresses the fact that I have no general theory to offer and my conviction that advancing such is, in this case, altogether inadvisable. The concept of violence unites under one head phenomena as diverse as those gathered together by the notion of shower; although it may be important to understand the mechanics of taking a shower in the morning, the causes of meteorite showers, and the rules that govern giving a shower for a happy bride, these neither require nor foreshadow a more sweeping, general theory of showers.

Violence is the application of great power that results in measurable harm. That it is the application of force suggests that only conscious agents can commit acts of violence, even though they need have no specific intention to damage anything. This means that thunderstorms, however violent, cannot manifest violence, while careless but well-meaning doctors clearly can. The magnitude of the force involved is relative: a flick of my finger must represent overwhelming violence to the crawling ant, though my toughest slap is likely to be deemed below notice by a sumo wrestler. What constitutes harm is itself relative to the nature, condition, and valuations of the persons involved. Applying force to rearrange a face is harmful if done by thugs in accord with how they feel, but not if it is the work of a plastic surgeon complying with her patient's wish. The requirement that the damage be measurable is added to exclude fanciful forms of psychological harm whose existence cannot be reliably ascertained and that leave no behavioral signs. It is not meant to give preference to any particular fashion of gauging harms or to any level of precision in measuring them.

Violence in the sense defined enjoys broad currency in the world today. Great power can be exerted by individuals when they operate alone, in mobs, or organized in institutions. Violence is not restricted to stabbings and fistfights; strip mining, and the destruction of forests, rapes, and bombings, and wars are all qualifying acts. This makes it evident that violence is by no means restricted to the contemporary world. On the contrary, human beings have engaged in it and experienced it in all social contexts throughout history. And if we think of the paradigm of violence as the fury of a wounded or humiliated man, we can readily see that violence, or something very like it, is not even a uniquely human possession. Animals also release their energies in violent and destructive ways; it is, in fact, its similarity to the behavior of brutes that makes violence so distasteful to the civilized mind.

I shall begin my search for the generative conditions of some current violence with the assumption that they grow naturally out of the structure and conditions of modern society. Some violence may be due to social malfunction or atavistic return, but these constitute neither the bulk nor the most interesting forms of the phenomenon. I suspect that much of the violence we see is organically connected to prevailing social conditions and constitutes a portion of their cost. To understand it, therefore, we must try to give an accurate and enlightening account of how our society operates and how its structures and habits of action make violence a natural and attractive form of behavior.

Society consists of mediating structures. These are not realities of an order higher than, or independent of, individuals: they are just the complex connections into which persons enter in the course of social life. Mediating relations are those in which individuals perform actions on behalf of others. Unnamed others built the road on which I drive and the car in which I sit; countless people pumped and refined the oil, transported and sold the gas I burn; others are cooking the lunch to which I go, using ingredients they did not raise, grow, make, preserve, package, or deliver. The road builders, of course, did not have an inkling that I would come this way today, and even those preparing lunch may do it for whoever might happen by with appetite and enough money to pay the price. The identity of the persons who benefit need not be known; the important idea is that without mediating others, they would be reduced to doing these things themselves or else learn to do without.

Viewed from one perspective, mediation is the interposition of others between oneself and certain consequences one seeks to attain. This can be done on a person-to-person basis, such as when I ask a friend to help me cut wood for the winter. In large-scale society, however, permanent service structures tend to take the place of ad hoc personal relations: to keep warm, I tie into the power grid of the gas or electric company. Mediation is, in this way, institutionalized and my relation to others becomes 'official' instead of personal. This means that we touch each others' lives primarily through our roles in various institutions. And however humane the rules that govern these roles may be, they cannot compensate for the loss of the personal element.

Institutions consist of human beings connected in their roles. These mediated chains are centered on the achievement of certain ends. Accordingly, efficacy and efficiency tend to be primary values in such social organizations. The values, in turn, mandate an interest in others not as autonomous human beings endowed with complex subjectivity, but as objects to be converted into manipulable tools. The smooth functioning of mediated chains requires the frictionless intermeshing of their elements; this is accomplished best if, when we go to work, we leave our personalities behind. The concern of the boss with the employee, of the supervisor with the worker is to get the job done; the ideal is to know as little of the other's personal life as possible and not to mix business and pleasure. What little of communicative nicety enters the workplace does so for manipulative purposes: efficiency experts teach that workers do better if they think the boss cares about them as individuals. In fact, of course, the boss just wants to get things done while the worker desires more time off and better pay. Each manipulates the other, if need be, by pretending personal interest, for each is ever ready to do what is necessary to get the other to do what is desired.

The efficiency orientation of mediated chains leads not only to manipulativeness but also to a special sort of frustration. Specialization vastly increases the number of things groups of people can do and the ease with which they can do them. In large-scale industrial society, division of labor reaches exceptional levels. Each person is assigned a minuscule role in the productive process; the work gets done by the exquisite integration of the minute parts. But the fact that everyone performs only an act-fragment leaves all of us in the dark about the nature of what we do. Without knowledge of the larger context of one's acts, it is impossible to understand their meaning and to gauge the significance of one's own contribution. The result is the lived misery of acting in the dark, of feeling that what we do is senseless and unimportant.

The fragmentation of the act is not only a matter of breaking down productive processes into their minute components and assigning each to a different person to do. It is also, and even more devastatingly, the shattering of the natural unity of actions. The normal human act consists of three integrated elements: plan, execution, and enjoyment or suffering of the effects. Mediation separates these functions and assigns the first to legislators, boards of directors, and executives. The second becomes the domain of bureaucrats and white-collar workers and laborers. The third is reserved for citizens regulated by government edicts, for customers and clients. Because mediated chains distance their participants in direct proportion to their size, none of the three groups knows what the others mean, do, or feel. Planners see their intentions frustrated in the execution and rarely have firsthand acquaintance with results. Workers have little understanding of formative purposes and less concern with how those feel who suffer from their acts. In some ways, clients and customers know the least: they stand at the receiving end of the huge machinery of the modern world, baffled or stunned by what betides them.

The special frustration of which I speak comes of feeling that we do not act. Some plan but never do; some do but never mean it; some just have things happen to them without having brought them on. No one is fully active, and no one is in charge. No one feels the satisfaction of having done something, and none assumes responsibility for the result. Indeed, the act that emerges from these separate elements is truly no *one*'s: none can view it as one's own, take credit for it, or call oneself accountable. This escape from responsibility is perfectly understandable precisely because the social act is not of any single person's doing and no one involved with it performs an integrated human act. Yet in another sense, the action belongs to everyone who contributes to it, and only by holding each accountable can we restore responsibility in the mediated world.

The fact that mediated chains do not permit the performance of integrated human acts, of acts whose intention, execution, and consequences all belong to a single individual, makes each member of the chain feel passive. When the mediated structures in which we operate are large and numerous, this passivity is attended by a sense of impotence. "I am but a single individual," each of us thinks, "so, how can I hope to change anything in this vast machine?" Contrary to civics propaganda, average citizens feel that their votes do not really count, that personal boycott of the crooked store leaves it flourishing, that whistleblowers tend to lose their jobs as the bureaucrats closes ranks in the cover-up. We end feeling that nothing we can do makes a difference: the forces against which we must vie so far outstrip our power that our choice is only between voiceless compliance and the certainty of defeat.

Of course, we can do things if we band together, compound our votes and power, and then work for needed change. In the sure knowledge that we can make a difference where no single I can, we create citizens' lobbies and consumer groups. And such organizations can indeed come to wield considerable power. But what they can accomplish is at least partly a function of their size: it appears that only an institution can make significant changes in our institutions. In this way, the curse of impotence follows individuals even when they join others to protest: soon the citizens' lobby becomes as closed to the influence of the single person as the government and the corporations it was created to change had been.

Our roles in mediated chains render us not only manipulative, irresponsible, impotent, and passive. They also have a profound influence on our sensory lives. The omnipresence of experts relieves us of the need to perform, even to witness, sacred and fundamental human acts. Birth and death, sickness and cure, the slaughter of animals for food, the protection of the home against intruders are all relegated to others, who perform their work out of our sight. There are special places where many of the great moments of life occur, and they are supervised by specialists whose language and rules of procedure we do not understand. Ordinary people cannot witness these secret rituals unless they happen to be their object or their focus. But then, as is typically the case in hospitals, one is too drugged or nervous to learn or to attend. The result is a bland, disinfected sensory life and trivialized human experience.

True enough, the machinery of the modern world carries us to distant places, and faraway countries into our living rooms. But the remote corners of the globe look more and more like Iowa, and what we note in Singapore is the trivially different. Television brings us every odd perversion in the world. But our exposure to such things is without context and personal significance; the experience it yields is primarily visual, not fully physical. The result is a generation of people cut off from both animal and spiritual roots, ignorant of the depths and sacraments of personal experience. They neither see death nor deal it; they cover the signs of aging and send their old out of sight; they eat steak unmindful of the steer; they act without knowledge of the profound contingency of everything they do and live unaware of the subjective center of their lives.

The tone of this description may suggest a condemnation of contemporary society. Nothing could be farther from my intention. Although some of my terms carry normative weight, they are not employed to articulate a summary judgment on mediation. I merely stress the costs of large-scale institutions, and since costs are consequences generally deemed undesirable, even a descriptive account of them will naturally sound value-laden. Let me counteract the false impression this may foster by emphasizing that any evaluation of mediated chains must take into account not only their costs but also their benefits. And the benefits of mediation are immense. Industrial society has enabled us to attain an astounding level of control over nature and ourselves. In the highly mediated West, more people live longer, healthier lives than did ever before in the history of the human race. Plentiful food, clean water, excellent medical care, rapid travel and universal communication are all results of intelligent, cooperative interaction. Much as we complain about crime, it is unlikely that life on this earth has ever been safer or more stable.

We must not underrate, therefore, the virtues of extensive mediation. Nor must we overlook, however, the price it exacts. In searching for the generative conditions of violence, we must emphasize the costs; it is, after all, implausible to suppose that people resort to violence to express their happiness. That mediation has costs is neither surprising nor a compelling consideration against it. Everything in life tends to be a mixed bag: whatever produces desirable results also yields unwanted side effects. Perhaps not surprisingly, the patent advantages of mediation overshadow or disguise its costs, which are then naively misinterpreted as the results of some social malfunction. It is of value to see costs and benefits flowing with equal naturalness from mediation, which is the central social fact in the world today.

If we view the individual as the locus of all feeling and the source of all action, we can see why the growth of mediated chains coincides with the decrease of opportunities for autonomy and with sharply diminished attention to the subjective life. At any rate, large-scale mediation curtails the significance of persons as individuals, that is, as they view themselves from their own perspective. Persons are evidently not eliminated, for then all social activity would abruptly cease. But the singularity of individuals, their uniqueness, showing itself in that special irreplaceability I experience when one of my parents or my child dies, is supplanted by their interchangeability in institutional roles. We may then think that persons are just collections of the roles they occupy; we may even come to believe the obscenity that our obligations do not reach beyond what our roles demand.

These, at least, are the beliefs the mediated world fosters. But we do not yet lead only official lives; there is a private person in each of us. And that center of the world, of the world as it exists from one's own perspective, bristles at being overlooked. In quiet rebellion, many of us find harmless ways to create or to affirm our individuality: we refinish furniture, grow radishes, or make a living-room model of the Pacific fleet. In some cases, the rebellion is violent; the self wants to be sure that the world that took little interest in it hears its thunder. This is where we must look for the generative conditions of violence: much of the destructive power applied in our world is the work of individuals reacting against the felt loss of their significance in mediated chains.

We should not be surprised that it is this way. For the mediated world gives persons the sense that as isolated individuals they are powerless. What force they wield is a function of their role in institutions and always remains subject to the rules and limits that define it. In the last analysis, such power is never one's own. And when it comes to a need to transcend the regular procedures of the institution or to a desire to influence processes beyond the confines of one's station, individuals quickly learn that they have no privilege at all. The sense of impotence begets self-affirmation, and violence offers a sure way to make people think that they can affect the course of things, after all.

When the structure of political life makes public officials inaccessible, it is a natural temptation for frustrated people to burst into their offices and pound the desk, to grab and shake them at shopping centers, or simply to shoot them. And when an unwieldy bureaucracy fails to respond to a grievance or to right a wrong, it is understandable if the aggrieved, in desperation, resorts to a spectacular, destructive act. Shooting a police officer or blowing up a bank is not rationally chosen to dramatize one's plight. The motive is anger or hopelessness, which depicts all of society as a single, monstrous machine. Distraught people think they must strike a blow against this evil, mediated system.

Another feature of large-scale societies points to violence as an attractive response. Mediation has made most significant creative acts social in nature. There are relatively few constructive, autonomous actions open to persons who are not writers, doctors, or self-employed professionals. The accomplishment of virtually anything worthwhile requires the cooperation of countless others. Acts of destruction, on the other hand, are among the small number of things a single individual can still do: no one needs assistance in shooting pedestrians from the clock tower or aiming a car at carefree picnickers. The natural desire to do something of moment can, for this reason, be readily channeled toward violence. Given our active nature, it is understandable if we feel it more important that something be done than that what we do be humane or good.

Violence, precisely because it is for the most part an individual act, is paradigmatically something we can do and whose performance leaves us feeling active. It tends not to involve the fragmentation of action so typical of mediated chains: in it, formative intention, execution, and immediate acquaintance with consequences all reside within a single individual. As a result, the sense of passivity and the feeling that whatever I do is not of my own design are transcended; they are replaced by the satisfaction of knowing that what I mean and do and observe as it takes shape are all identical and genuinely mine. Violence perpetrated for ideological reasons on behalf of some systematically promoted cause is different. Organizations in the business of doing such things themselves frequently suffer the problems of excessive mediation. The satisfaction of terrorists told to blow up a target is evidently not that of an autonomous act both conceived and performed by a single person, but one that comes perhaps from the contemplation of the rightness of their cause or from the wild release of anger and resentment. Individuals wreaking havoc on their own, by contrast, tend to take delight in the organic unity and self-possessed nature of their actions. This is shown not only in their accounts of what they did, but also in the readiness with which they take responsibility for their acts. They take pride in their exploits; when they seek privacy, it is mainly to make sure they can continue their violent behavior.

There is a surprising, positive side to the horrors of war. Many people report that great danger leads to an exhilaration that renders experience vibrant. Some say they can never recapture the keen sense of being alive they felt when they were in battle or even when they merely supported the war effort. The sensory dullness of daily life in mediated chains renders such claims believable and natural. The routine of a safe society obliterates the momentousness of life; war reacquaints us with energizing danger, with death, contingency, and finitude. It is plausible to suppose that something quite like this effect obtains in connection with violence. The exercise of great power, especially physical power that threatens damage, vitalizes experience. The predictable triviality of life is gone, and we are suddenly exposed to the sacred depths of existence, the finality and irreversibility of what happens to us.

The desensitized consciousness mediation creates demands escape. Individuals cannot start a war to liven things up. But they can watch one on television, in the wrestling arena, or in the stadium. If they are more adventuresome, they can set themselves at risk by driving too fast or getting into fights. And if their anger issues in action one day, they may learn the pleasure of violence. Gaining pleasure in this way quickly teaches them to end the blandness of sense life through crushing contact with what is tender and important in human existence. Mediated people then counteract one of the effects of mediation by the excitement of destruction, by pain inflicted and the death they deal.

We can clearly connect two other sources of violence with the costs of mediation. The first is relatively rare, involving an attenuated aesthetic motivation. Yet traces even of this exist in ordinary experience, and the motivation should be recognizable to all of us. The goal directedness of mediated chains demands of us a constant adjustment of means to ends. Our interest in anything at hand is, accordingly, utilitarian: we want it not for its own sake but for what it leads to or what it can yield. This official orientation tends to invade our private lives as well, and soon we find it difficult to enjoy the most pleasurable present without concern for the morrow. The ensuing rat race, which exacts exclusive devotion to what is yet to come, makes absorption in the beauty of the immediate impossible.

In an odd or perverse way, violence restores this aesthetic magnificence of the directly present. We can experience something like it in the movies when we overlook the moral horror and the human cost of a shootout and focus, instead, only on the pretty way in which the bodies fall. The person perpetrating violence may be fascinated by the fire and sound of the explosion along with the elegant or comic curves the shattered debris describes. The delight is aesthetic because it centers on sensory appearances irrespective of their meaning or use.

But it is odd and in need of further explanation why these particular sounds and sights attract attention rather than, say, the rush of the wind and the movement of leaves in the fall. And there is a perverse, if not inhuman, element—due perhaps to the compartmentalization fostered by mediated chains—in the ability to abstract the loveliness of looks from the broader, moral context of their cost. In any case, there is little doubt that some people derive such pleasure from performing or observing acts of violence and do so as an unconscious way of gaining respite from the unsatisfying cycle of means and ends.

The second source of violence takes us past individual initiative to the action of mobs. In mediated chains, our sphere of action is limited and our behavior is controlled. Rules must be followed and procedures observed; there is little room for individuality and none for spontaneous release. Role-structured responsibilities define what we do and who we are; our interactions, at least, are governed by an earnest sobriety. The presence of a mob, especially a mob of strangers, eliminates these constraints. Suddenly, we feel safely anonymous and thus set free from control. The playfulness mediation cannot tolerate is what first attracts the crowd; the work of destruction begins only later. But when it does, all the anger, all the frustration, all the energy the system bottled up without release, is unleashed against it in a drunken fury. The violence is felt to be overwhelmingly right, for it strikes a blow against a system that repressed us and made us act in ways we did not choose. We have no reason to suppose that such destruction is somehow a return to what some suppose are our native, violent ways. On the contrary, it is probably a direct result of liberating energies and desires unaccommodated in the world of mediation. Mob violence of this sort is a bitter reaction against the narrow and dehumanizing discipline of our institutions.

I have shown how the frustration, powerlessness, and impoverished sensory life of individuals in mediated chains are breeding grounds of violence. I have also indicated that such other costs of a populous and highly integrated society as the fragmentation of natural acts, the subsequent reduction of autonomy, and the confinement of human interactions within rule-governed roles constitute additional generative conditions of destructive response. Even the need periodically to escape the means-end grind of mediated life tempts us, when mixed with resentment, to take delight in seeing things destroyed. I want now to call attention to three features of the mediated world that, though they may not generate violence, tend to make its perpetration easy and unhindered.

The first is the propensity of mediation, upon which I have already remarked, to support abstraction. Breaking actions into their minute and apparently unconnected elements encourages us to think and to operate without reference to a broader context. Our official roles require that we perform act-fragments without concern for their meaning or consequences. This approach is easily generalized and we soon learn to act, even in our personal lives, with little interest in how what we do fits current circumstances and what its ultimate outcome may be. This psychic distance from the immediate and the long-term context makes it difficult to introduce intelligent moral considerations into the deliberative process. For to abstract from the appropriateness of an act and from its impact on other human beings is to overlook nearly all its ethically relevant properties. The result is that we can contemplate blowing up people without asking a question about their feelings and their hopes, the worth of their lives, the grief of their loved ones, and the suffering of the maimed.

The second feature is connected both with the tendency to abstract from the context and with our lack of sensory immediacy with what we cause. The fragmentation that pervades the mediated world is internalized: our faculties begin to operate in isolation from one another, and we learn to be content with psychological one-sidedness. The well-known problems of coordinating intellect and feeling arise from the independent operation of what should be integrated personal functions. What we know, in the demanding, rational sense favored by the mediated world, tends to be detached from emotion and to engender no action. Feeling, in turn, gives up any claim to legitimation by thought or by reference to how we ought to be.

This separation of organ from organ within the internal life is reinforced by the paucity of our direct experience of the consequences of our acts. Perception is, under normal circumstances, a powerful corrective of actions taken too hastily on the basis of what we think or how we feel. But institutions exact actions from us whose results we never see; without knowledge of what we cause, we have no basis for correcting the excesses, inhumanities, and even horrors brought about by mediated chains. The habits acquired in our official roles carry through to our days of violence. We then act on the basis of how we feel without extensive thought about the appropriateness, advisability, or results of our course. And since we rarely have firsthand acquaintance with consequences, we pay little heed to what our violent acts are likely to bring about. It is not uncommon for people who shoot or bomb others to grieve at the tragedy once they see the pain and death they caused.

The third feature of the mediated world that favors violence is an outcome of its manipulativeness and size. The role-bound, efficiency-oriented nature of mediated chains makes even our coworkers strangers to us. The vast number of intricately connected, gigantic institutions that affect our lives are staffed by myriad faceless strangers. People who do not know me treat me in hospitals, pass judgment on me in the courts, and perhaps decide my fate in the institution where I work. When I, in turn, strike out at this impersonal system, my victims are also strangers. Much as it may feel attractive to harried people to hurt those nearby who may be thought responsible for their misery, it is easiest to fall upon those we have never met. Since we have learned to view our coworkers as tools, not as persons with needs and feelings, it is even easier to see those we do not know as things one may destroy or as flies ripe for the swatter.

Mediation offers too many benefits for us to consider limiting or eliminating it. If the mediated world provides multiple conditions that generate violence and others that make its perpetration particularly easy, must we accept murder, rape, child abuse, the blowing up of planes, and the machine-gunning of innocent bystanders as the unavoidable cost of large-scale society? Few would say so, and I certainly would not. In general, we do not need to obliterate the cause in order to counteract its undesirable side effects. There is no reason to suppose, moreover, that this particular case represents an exception to the rule. We must identify the elements in the complex situation that make for the unwanted results and develop strategies for modifying them.

Swift detection and firm punishment wield considerable deterrent force. But they do not constitute the most desirable social policy: their efficacy is limited, and since they are intrinsically reactive, they presuppose the occurrence of crimes of the sort they are meant to prevent. It is much more effective and appropriate to reduce the incidence of the crime by eliminating the conditions that breed it. In that quest, my analysis, if correct, could be of central importance. For it identifies the generative conditions of violence and relates them to a single feature of contemporary society. And this should at once indicate the general direction in which we must move to gain relief. I shall call it 'the recapture of immediacy,' because its essence is to supply for all of us the direct experience mediation destroys.

We must work to regain immediate contact with human beings far and near in mediated chains, with the nature of the chains in which we act, and with the consequences of the actions to which we contribute. Direct acquaintance with others means knowledge of them not in their roles, but as individual subjects. This reveals them as centers of feeling and choice similar to ourselves. By learning their motives, understanding their view of things and appreciating the constraints under which they operate, we pull them within the orbit of our moral world. Although this does not make disagreements and conflicts of interest disappear, it sets them within parameters where we can, if not resolve them, at least live with them in a humane, accepting way. In this fashion, we can significantly reduce the manipulativeness, unintentional cruelty, and endemic irresponsibility of the mediated world.

Firsthand knowledge of the institutions in which we work and which affect us provides a grasp of the intricate connections between the activities that sustain us. Such understanding, even of a rudimentary sort, explodes the fiction that we are impotent, passive, or helpless in mediated chains. It shows the significance of the contribution of each member of the chain and gives each a sense of worth and participation. Interconnectedness both subjugates and empowers us: in learning its full magnitude, we comprehend our duties and discover our sphere of influence and of free operation. The very grasp of the system has a liberating effect. To know what we do and why is to recognize partnership in the enterprise. And acknowledged partnership makes all of us realize that we have a stake in the success of the whole.

Finally, direct perception of the consequences of the social acts to which we contribute as workers or as paying customers renders it impossible for us to invoke easy excuses. Once we see the result and understand our own contribution to it, we cannot dodge responsibility. Ignorance of the consequences enables us to become contributors to acts we would never knowingly do on our own. Elimination of this protective psychic distance throws all the procedures and aims of mediated chains open to critique. But responsibility is not only for evils perpetrated. If we know what we create, we are also likely to take some credit for the good. If we see the modern world as of our own making, it will not seem so oppressive and alien. And the more we view it as our own, the less we shall be content to blow it up or to see it burn.

This recapture of immediacy must be accompanied by fairness in social procedures and openness in mediated chains. The aim throughout is not to give us a stake in the system, but to help us realize that we already have it: the mediated world is our own creation. Once this recognition achieves full consciousness, our tendency will be to change our lives to make them more humane, instead of destroying them through violence.

CHAPTER 11

Persons and Technology

The natural mind simplifies the world, seeing unity where there is only complex process. In this way, each historical age acquires its name and essence, gravity comes to be seen as a cause, and nationalities are reduced to stereotypes. In this spirit, we speak of technology as a powerful force in the modern world. We endow it (the single reality) with properties, tendencies, dispositions, even a personality. We hold serious discussions about whether it is good or bad, whether we should accelerate its development or learn to do without its benefits.

The sophisticated intellect in us may think it trivial to be told that there is no single being that answers to the name 'technology.' But the natural mind that pulses under the skin of sophistication never ceases to hypostatize; reminders about what constitutes good ontology are, therefore, rarely out of place. Technology is not some impersonal force that causes difficulties for us or else makes life comfortable. It is but a set of skills and activities—skillful activities—of human beings.

Such skilled activity is the application of knowledge aimed at achieving human ends. Science, therefore, is by no means the only body of knowledge that has or can have such practical results. The arts have a technology for the production of plays and paintings: identifiable rules aid in the creation of what is interesting, beautiful, or funny. Religion has a technology consisting of such things as chants, prayer wheels, and the administration of bread and wine. Even philosophy is developing its own application to the world through critical involvement in governmental, business, and medical decision making. The technology employed consists of searching conversation, the analysis of concepts, the exploration of alternative modes of thought. The expected result is a greater sensitivity to the value dimensions in deliberation, and hence better decisions.

One could object that this idea of technology is too broad, for in the current or ordinary sense, technology always involves the use of physical instruments. No doubt it does, as does virtually every human act. But we must not have too narrow a conception of tools and physical instrumentality. Demosthenes was more effective with his words than other persuaders with the sword. In any case, the techniques of convincing people constitute a technology no less than do the techniques of operating on them; whether we transplant ideas through eloquent speech or organs by surgery, we engage in skilled activity with the aid of physical objects.

Admittedly, there are differences between activities whose perfor- mance requires no physical object beyond the organs of the body (such as speech making) and those that require both skilled body parts and external instruments. But these divergences cannot consti- tute the distinction between what is technology and what is not. For if they did, playing music would involve a technology, but singing it would not; listening for the pulse with a stethoscope would be a tech- nological act, but taking it with one's hand would not. From the standpoint of the use of instruments, it makes little difference whether they happen to be made of cells or metal; although using my hands to make scissors cut cloth comprises a double instrumentality, I still use tools if I rip it directly myself.

A more useful distinction emerges if we relate technology to tech- nique. Perhaps all of our actions involve a technique, that is, a proper or expeditious manner of performing them. But no single technique is a technology, not even such an advanced but single industrial oper- ation as imprinting microchips. If we want to be precise, we might say that a technology consists of a set of interconnected techniques and that the 'technology' of which we sometimes speak as though it were a single entity is a system of such interconnected technologies.

But let me say again that this entire system is nothing beyond the skilled activities (or types of activities) that constitute it, along with their complex relations. Yet we find technology an alien force and the world it creates in many ways an uncomfortable home. It is not, of course, that we lack comforts in this world. On the contrary, human life has, on the whole, never been more pampered and secure. But these pleasures seem to come at a cost, even though the cost is ill-defined and little understood. Nevertheless, it is experienced with an intensity matched only by the wide divergence of specific complaints it generates. Some feel frustrated or impotent in a system that appears designed for machines, not sensitive human beings. Others feel manipulated, as though they were machines themselves. Many think that the system itself is the machine that, ill-suited to take account of subjective needs, reduces us to insignificant fragments of its gigantic being. Nearly everyone agrees that in dealing with one another in social institutions, we have ourselves become depersonalized and stiff biological replicas of the machine.

The recurrent theme through all the complaints is the contrast between the machinelike and the human or the technological and the personal. How could technology, our own systematic activity aimed at fulfilling our purposes, come to be viewed as a separate and threatening non-human force? The fact that the application of science has brought us a longer life span, better health, abundant food, and ample leisure, that we can do what prior generations could not even dream, should make technology our proudest possession. To be sure, we are glad to partake of its benefits, though not without the sense that something has gone awry. This feeling is due not to the strangeness or novelty of our tomorrows; under favorable circumstances, the most unusual can become commonplace overnight. It is, rather, a result of the growing, and devastating, suspicion that in this world we made for ourselves, no one of us matters much anymore.

Denouncing technology and smashing the machines would no doubt solve this problem but create in its place intense misery, which would be the harder to bear for the memory of rich and easy days. Returning to some plateau of low technology and small productive units is as impossible—and undesirable—as the more radical solution. Its appeal is the result of the romance of rustic existence combined with the illegitimate assumption of the continuing benefits of large-scale society. Without stable laws, universal commerce, and the economics of scale, most modern improvements in health and nutrition, to say nothing of the optional goods that enhance the quality of life, would evaporate. The momentum of the industrial world makes a reversal of course excessively unlikely; a just assessment of its benefits suggests that any major change would be unwise.

Are we, then, left defenseless against an overwhelmingly powerful, depersonalizing technology? If we put the matter in this way, we will be left without understanding, not defense. Much as we may experience it that way, technology is, as I have said, not an alien or independent force that offers comfort for slavery. Since it is nothing but human activity, to understand it, we must understand ourselves. To counteract its ill effects, we must know what they are, what causes them, and what would cure them. The first step toward accomplishing these tasks is a systematic account of what is wrong with technology.

The most primitive, but emotionally most satisfying, methodological approach here, as elsewhere, is to attribute ill effects to ill will. If we could show that the evils of the industrial world are due to some giant conspiracy, everyone could understand at once. Simple people attempt to do this time and again, with generally laughable results. More sophisticated minds prefer explanations that relate what goes wrong to a single flaw or a small cluster of malfunctions. Single-flaw analyses (such as Marxism) are particularly satisfying because of their simplicity, the unitary vision they provide, and the exhilaration of supposing that we have discovered the secret of the modern world. But such hypotheses lack initial probability, tend to involve tacit value commitments, and frequently end by manipulating the evidence to make it fit.

The most sensible and best methodological hypothesis is that the ill effects of technology, along with its desirable outcomes, are all equally normal consequences of it. If we start with this assumption, it becomes unnecessary to search for some implausible single cause of our problems. We can, instead, view society as a part of the natural order generating regular effects, some of which are seen as costs and some as benefits by those concerned. And this, incidentally, is the only way values function in such a theory: they are important facts to be taken into account. In embracing the hypothesis, we make no tacit or explicit value commitments; what count as costs and what are benefits are determined by looking at what people do and feel, not by reference to the theory or the preferences of the theorist. This means that if people freely and intelligently ever come to place positive value on what now appears to ail us, the attempt to explain the costs of technology will be superfluous. The view I develop in what follows presupposes that there is something wrong with industrial civilization and that there is substantial agreement about the nature of the complaints.

How does technology become the source of a variety of ill effects?

To understand this, we must focus on the use of tools and on the increasing size and complexity of technological tasks. A careful analysis of these two factors will go a long way toward explaining the source of much of our current frustration and unhappiness. In the process, a remarkably divergent collection of phenomena will be seen to have a unitary foundation.

The human body is a sentient tool. When we use it or some part of it to accomplish a task, we gain as much conscious, immediate contact with the world as our frame allows. Under such circumstances, our relation to things and to others is direct, and we know firsthand the feel and disposition of what we encounter. Whatever skeptical objections philosophers may devise, the palate when tasting wine, the doctor's hand on the fevered brow, the total embrace of love all reveal relevant realities and bring us close to the pulse of being.

The introduction of additional tools that intervene between the body and its tasks changes the situation profoundly. The immediacy of the contact between person and world is lost, and we learn to experience things at a remove. When we don gloves to clean the compost heap and poke a stick at the small garden snake that wanders by, we know that the experiential difference between firsthand encounter and distanced or mediated contact is momentous.

The mediating presence of an inanimate third between agent and projected act has obvious advantages. It can greatly enhance safety and convenience, and frequently it multiplies the power of the human arm. The experiential loss differs with the circumstances: it is minimal when the intervening tool, such as eyeglasses, is designed to improve the natural experience, but much more serious where its function is to shield the sense or augment effectiveness. Nevertheless, there is some change in every case, and some of the changes have pernicious side effects.

This is best seen in those instances of tool-use, by far the most numerous, where our purpose is not to improve the quality of our experience, but to effect changes in the world. The human hand is sensitive and thus tends to know what it causes. By contrast, inanimate instruments do not convey adequate information about their effects: the jockey does not know the power of his whip until, by mistake perhaps, he uses it on his own leg. As a result, people who operate with even the simplest tools tend to be unaware of the full consequences of their acts. Of course, they are conscious of much of what they do: they see that when the dog is hit, it quits howling at the moon. But the knowledge is selective; not only does it fail to be centered at the point of the act's impact on the world, it is also focused on the question of whether or not the desired effect is achieved.

Even on this rudimentary level, therefore, interest is in effectiveness and not in its costs. We want to make the dog stop howling so we can sleep; we hit it hard with a stick, unmindful of how it feels to be so whipped. We show children candy to get them away from the comic book shelves. Once out of the store, we claim that candy is bad for the teeth and refuse to deliver, with no awareness of how such deception hurts. When we deal with other sentient creatures, we lose reciprocity; if I whacked the dog with my bare hands, its pain would instantly be measured by my own.

The tendency of inorganic tools to enhance effectiveness at the cost of increased ignorance can be counteracted. But, as all ignorance, this too arrives unannounced, riding at the tail end of the glorious feeling that we are getting things accomplished. And the nescience grows with each increase in the size and complexity of our physical instruments. When tools reach the level of being entire systems, such as that involved in drilling for oil, refining it, and delivering it in the form of gas for use in my car, our understanding of their nature and their costs approaches zero.

Two related factors keep us in touch with the consequences of our tool-mediated actions when our instruments are simple. Single individuals use hammers and sticks and pens to fulfill their own purposes. Since they both plan their activities and execute them, they tend, on the whole, to know what is going on. Since the effects of their actions, moreover, are rarely distant, they can at least observe them, even if direct bodily experience of them is reduced. In this way, planning, physical execution, and acquaintance with results all reside in a single person, and integration of them into an intelligible human act requires relatively little effort.

Increase in the magnitude of technological tasks and of the machines needed to perform them demands cooperation from many individuals. Only when large-scale technology lingers on a primitive level do all the participants do the same thing, for example, square, pull, and stack big stones. It is much more efficient to break down complex tasks into small constituent activities and apportion each to different groups of people. The natural consequence is that some persons design and others coordinate, some perform and others supervise our larger social acts. The physical action itself is severed into fragments: some bend metal, and others bolt pieces of it together, some add plastic parts, others install upholstered seats to make the cars we drive. And if we view the entire production of an automobile as a vastly complex but single social act, typically the effects of it are enjoyed and endured by those who did not participate in it.

The division of the social task into segments, each of which is performed by someone else, destroys the easily intelligible unity of human acts. For now each knows mainly his or her own narrow role in the system, and few understand complex relations between the parts. Planners, doers, and enjoyers/sufferers have little access to one another's work and experience. As a consequence, they fail to understand their interconnectedness in a larger whole, view each other with suspicion, and find their own actions disjointed and without any meaning.

Let me remind us again that technology involves much more than the physical machinery we use in such activities as growing food and going places. The institutions we create for designing, operating, and maintaining the machines are also a part of our technology, if we mean by this a set of interconnected skilled human activities. These institutions consist of chains of mediation—human beings connected to one another by performing actions on each other's behalf. We function in the chains as if we had a tacit contract with one another: each person makes a small contribution to what is of benefit to some or all in return for what is needed for a comfortable life. In a sense, though for the most part without consciousness of it, we use others as tools to make our existence secure and pleasant, and we offer in payment the opportunity of using us.

Primitive humans interposed sticks and rocks between themselves and what was to be done; we thrust an entire system of intermediary agents and machines between ourselves and our actions. The difference is in quantity of mediation, which affects the quality of life. Some effects are benefits but others are costs: the growing mastery over nature must be measured against depersonalization and endemic loss of meaning in life. The important consideration is that both costs and benefits are natural consequences of mediation; only by viewing our problems in this context can we hope to understand them and to make intelligent plans for remediation.

The social shattering of the natural unity of actions, so that purpose, execution, and consequence fall to different people to perform or enjoy, makes it difficult for individuals to see their work as a significant part of a meaningful whole. The size of mediated chains makes tight control over their products impossible; consequently, planners regard workers as people who frustrate their designs. Workers, in turn, have little knowledge of grand plans. They feel restricted by arbitrary rules and moved like pawns in pursuit of purposes they neither share nor understand. Those who enjoy or endure the results are also ignorant; they feel passive in the face of what the huge machinery of the modern world visits upon them, and when what happens does not please them, they feel victimized.

No one quite fathoms the intricacy of the social act. Everyone feels impotent against the weight of the whole: we think there is nothing any one person can do. All of us feel manipulated and valued only for what we can contribute to the social good. And viewing things out of context, all of us feel the insignificance or senselessness of our contribution. When it comes to assuming responsibility for the social act or at least for our part in it, the planners point to their good intentions but frustrated purposes. Those who did the deed claim to have acted on orders and without an understanding of what they advanced.   And the enjoyers and endurers maintain that they have done nothing at all; whatever happened merely befell them.

The result of large-scale mediation is the growth of passivity, manipulativeness, and irresponsibility. Ignorance of the complex world begets ignorance of our own actions in it, and this, in turn, yields a desperate sense of the meaninglessness of it all. As if by a perverse paradox, the larger the social act, the smaller and more insignificant each person's contribution becomes. And the more firmly mediation cements us into a social whole, the less we feel that we belong to a community.

The depersonalization we endure in industrial society is, in this way, clearly the result of technology. For the technology we developed for meeting our needs and wants involves machine-mediated integrated social acts. These acts require large mediated chains in which individuals function merely by filling roles. The interest in persons in this context, moreover, is restricted to those of their features essential to playing their roles. Their responsibilities are defined in terms of their function in the chain and not by reference to what human decency or moral maturity might demand. Their development as persons is held of little account and is at best allowed as an optional activity so long as it does not interfere with reliable social function. We embody the insignificance of persons in the contrast we draw between essential role responsibility and what is "merely" the view or preference of the person: extermination camp guards can, in this way, maintain that they have "nothing personal" against the people they murder in the line of duty.

The increased scope and efficacy of the social act are possible only at the expense of reducing the range of the skilled activity of each individual. This leads to a great growth in narrow specializations and to the rule of the expert. Mediated chains consist of specialists each of whom is competent in a circumscribed area of operations. This slender beam of knowledge is bathed on all sides in a sea of ignorance. We know little of what our fellows do in the same chain, how others live, what skills distant specialties require. Experts tend to extol this ignorance; professionals in our society manage to combine the claim to sovereignty in their chosen field with ostentatious reliance on others everywhere else.

Only now are we beginning to recognize the destructive effects of this institutionalized fragmentation of skills and knowledge on the development of persons. To suggest that certain tendencies in the modern world are depersonalizing is to presuppose that there are persons who may be damaged or debased. There is also a deeper and more distressing point to note: some consequences of our technology make the very creation of persons difficult. Individual personhood is, of course, always an achievement. But it presents a particularly arduous task if the social conditions necessary to foster it are absent. And large-scale mediation tends to undercut the formative conditions of at least three essential structures of personhood.

Persons must be dynamic epistemic centers, sensitive observers, and responsible agents. To be a center of knowledge involves more than being a warehouse of information: it requires the organization of what is known in accordance with general principles. The generality of these axioms leaves room for the indefinite expansion of knowledge, which the person with vigorous inquisitiveness undertakes. Specialization and satisfaction in one's specialty, with attendant reliance on experts everywhere else, eliminate the motive for continued inquiry and for the formulation of autonomous beliefs. Curiosity becomes centered in one field, and the rest of the world drops out as subject of interest and informed critical judgment. This lamentable development is confirmed by the cognitive void in the soul of some of our great experts.

Sensitivity can be learned only by the doing. It is potentially omni-modal, relating the imagination to possibilities everywhere. But the imagination must be sensitized by actual exposure to different ways of thought and divergent forms of life. Immediacy with the suffering and joy of others is an indispensable means of developing the ability to recognize alien goods and to appreciate them. Without this foun-tainhead of sympathy, the equal legitimacy of the different could never achieve plausibility. Yet it is just this immediacy that our medi-ated chains destroy. Confined within roles, denied sense experience of the important skills and the sacraments of life by the encircling ministration of experts, and educated with facts and concepts uncon-nected to practice, we lose contact with the richness of existence and cannot think that things could be otherwise. The human beings this produces do not see the sky: their insensitivity to the world makes it impossible for them to gather stable resources for their soul.

Taking responsibility for one's acts presupposes the ability to appropriate them. Being held responsible for something I cannot think I did engenders charges of unfairness and results in resentment. To appropriate an action, I must stand in an intimate relation to it: I must have done it with intention, or planned it and had it done, or at least made a significant contribution to its possibility. The ideal here, as elsewhere, is the unity in one person of intention, physical perfor-mance, and enjoyed/suffered results. For all who understand how what we do is connected with what we get are likely to choose their actions by their yield and, in turn, accept the consequences of their acts.

Mediated chains destroy this unity of actions. The magnitude of the social act and the sensed fragmentation of its elements make it dif-ficult for us to see it as an action at all. At any rate, it does not look and feel like anyone's act. And since we understand little of its pur-pose, structure and consequences, we cannot locate our own contribu-tion in it, nor can we assign significance to what we do. Because we hold minuscule jobs in colossal institutions, because our roles call for narrow repertoires of routine operations, we simply cannot grasp the purpose we advance. No one plans the social act and no one per-forms it; since we do not see the whole, we cannot regard our work as a part of it. The result is that we do not identify with the social act and cannot embrace it as our own. But without such appropriation we cannot take responsibility for it or its consequences. Our psycho-logically accurate but morally empty disclaimer is that we did not mean it and did not do it and perhaps did not even intend for it to come about.

Creating persons without epistemic autonomy, sensitivity, and responsibility is like making bodies without muscle and backbone. Our mediational technology makes it ever more difficult to raise children so they become self-possessed individuals with the intellectual courage to frame their own opinions and the moral daring to act them out. All of this is, of course, open to the objection that it amounts to a surrender of my initial plan to endorse no values because it presupposes a value-laden conception of personhood. I respond by admitting the facts but rejecting their interpretation. The idea of personhood I use, as all such ideas, involves valuational elements. According to it, a fully developed human individual must possess certain desirable capacities. But I have not arbitrarily determined what these features must be, and the success of my theory does not in any way depend on viewing these, only these, or any traits as good.

My claim is that large-scale mediation undercuts the conditions necessary to foster epistemic autonomy, sensitivity, and responsibility. This relationship between our technology and the sorts of people it raises is a natural one that obtains whether we think that forming our own opinions and taking responsibility for our acts are good or bad. The function of mediation analysis is to note the connections; they would still be there if we came to believe that it is best to act as if we were insensitive blobs. It so happens, however, that judged by our shared ideal of what a person should be, absence of inquisitiveness, failure of courage and lack of accountability are execrable traits. Although I am in personal accord with this ideal, its alteration or decline would not render my theory wrong, only uninteresting or unnecessary. For then we would perhaps not consider these personality features costs of social life and hence might show little concern for understanding how they come about and none for their amelioration.

Not everything in mediated chains, I might remark, makes for sensory impoverishment and desensitization. Impressive technical achievements can be used to counteract some of the tendencies of modern life most damaging to the development of mature persons. High-speed travel opens the world to us, and television brings immediacy with the distant into the living room. The media of communication, if well utilized, exercise enormous educational power by the graphic and virtually instant presentation of the consequences of what we do. And the most basic obstacles to the development of persons, inadequate nutrition and disease, have been largely eliminated in the industrial countries.

Although all of this is true and heartening, there is a dark side even to these benefits of technology. Travel may well lay the world with all its diversity at our feet, but multinational corporations and universal commerce work hard at hammering it into uniformity: we fly to Hong Kong but eat hamburgers at McDonald's there. The immediacy television provides is itself mediated and controlled by others: the presence is primarily visual, not omnimodal, and even our eyes are not allowed to follow their natural instincts but must settle for what the camera presents. The media combat the frustration of mediated life not by helping us understand, but by the escape of entertainment. And the food, physical health, and possessions technology makes possible overrun their humble role as means and usurp the place of higher, final goods.

Is there, then, any way to make peace between persons and those activities of theirs that constitute large-scale mediated technology? I have already indicated that to hope for the removal of mediation is absurd. It is equally wrongheaded to suppose that technology can be left to satisfy our desires without any reference to the essential structures of personhood. Techniques are skilled acts aimed at reaching our ends; the sound ordering of what we need and want is therefore presupposed by the work of technology. Accordingly, we must settle for counteracting the undesirable results of mediation. We have to reestablish the greatest possible immediacy with the world, with one another, and with ourselves. Direct encounter with the world is sensory exposure to its variety, along with a sensitive appreciation of our relation to it as its transforming, yet profoundly dependent parts. Immediacy with others involves sustained contact with a wide range of individuals as persons, that is, outside their official roles in mediated chains. Exposure to ourselves is a resolute reflectiveness on what we do and how we feel, in addition to sincerity about our motives. Such widespread immediacy would be a constant spur to personality development; it would render the atrophied organs of our invisible selves lithe again.

Immediacy without understanding, however, is not enough. We must find ways of learning our precise location in mediated chains, the products they yield and the consequences they cause, and the manner in which our actions contribute to these results. At least three institutional measures would tend to stimulate and advance this quest for understanding. Openness in government, devotion to education in corporations, and stress on the development of epistemic autonomy in the educational system would go a long way toward equipping us with the information necessary to grasp our place in the mediated world and to incline us to accept responsibility for it.

The three levels of government in this country constitute the most extensive and most powerful set of our mediated chains. The government technology for undertaking communal projects and providing social services is so complex and pervasive that passive openness to citizen queries is not enough: most of us would not know where to start the questioning. What we need, instead, is for politicians and civil servants alike to take an educative stance and actively instruct us in the public's business.

Specialization of function and restricted information flow in a hierarchical structure have long been thought essential for efficiency in corporations. But the less workers understand their contribution, the less they care; the result is inefficiency born of disregard. To overcome this, we must short-circuit mediated chains and expose each part to all the others. The free and ample flow of information, along with a generous appreciation of everyone for his or her contribution, would help us become not only better employees but also better persons.

Our educational system stresses familiarity with facts. Even processes and procedures are presented with dead factuality: they represent established skills to be mastered and deployed on demand. In this way, we teach largely results and very little of the dynamic process of uncovering them on our own. This tends to institute habits of repetition and to crush whatever is playful, adventuresome and inquisitive in the mind. A partial change in emphasis designed to give the logic and delight of discovery their due would give students the sense that they are partners in human inquiry instead of empty vessels to be filled. And if we encouraged young people to reach for cognitive integrity by framing their own opinions, the task of forming persons would be eased. For the foundation of personhood is an open and agile mind ever aware that it must make its own decisions.

𝓇

Professional Advertising in an Ignorant World

Our thoroughly commercial world dreams of what escapes the clutches of business and finance. We admire godliness that seems to flourish without self-interest; we delight in excellence achieved without benefit of connections and money; we celebrate an integrity that cannot be bought. We seem to think that virtue, in others at least, ought to be its own reward, but also that the truly fine shines by its own light. Why should professionals, for example, resort to advertising and degrade their art to a marketable skill? If they are good at what they do, they ought to feel fulfilled in that knowledge. But in any case, their fame will spread throughout the community, and people will come flocking to their doors. Can the merchandising of the professions do anything, therefore, but solicit business for incompetents and confer respectability on charlatans?

This fine dream is not different from others: it is in clear conflict with reality. It is not that virtue can no longer flourish in the modern world. And satisfaction with what we do will always remain the foundation of happiness. But virtue and happiness, except perhaps in their rare heroic variety, have identifiable social and economic conditions. Even if some broad generality could capture their timeless 'essence,' their concrete shapes change with the years.

The principle that excellence shines by its own light itself points to a social context in which alone it could be true. In a small community with easy access of people to one another, consciousness of outstanding performance spreads readily. The beneficiaries of remarkable cures can be seen living happily after a close brush with death. The works of architects, builders, even carpenters wear names in the public mind, and these names are connected to people one knows from church or evening strolls. Incompetence is difficult to hide when its effects are palpable. And the open affirmation of one's excellence is redundant and distasteful when everyone knows that we all know it already.

Such information in small communities is, of course, not always accurate. The important consideration is that there are established avenues for obtaining and for correcting it. These avenues are closed in large-scale society. In the big city, there is no shortage of unsuspecting and ignorant people on whom charlatans can prey. Their ignorance is perhaps not totally unavoidable: a thorough inquiry might well have revealed the sordid history of the person to whom they entrusted their fate. But it is a natural ignorance requiring extraordinary effort to overcome. And ordinary people will not and perhaps cannot make such efforts. In large-scale society, then, excellence cannot shine by its own light. The direct presence of the community to itself—the broad network of personal acquaintances and communications fueling that light—falls victim to the growing size of the society.

When excellence no longer shines, we light a candle for it. We invent substitutes for direct communal knowledge of which professionals are reliable. The best known of these are professional certification of practitioners and of the programs that train them. The premise of such certification is that clients/patients are not in a position to find out and to evaluate the quality of professionals. Not only do we lack expertise in what have become highly specialized fields of endeavor, professionals—like the rest of us—have become anonymous strangers in mass society. Certification presumably assures us that these strangers have met peer standards. And professional watchdog bodies, together with the press (which replaces public consciousness), are supposed to make sure that unscrupulous operators are exposed and punished.

Such substitutions and general safeguards obviously often do not work. But it is not the spectacular individual failures that should interest us. Institutionalization itself entails significant costs, many of them ill-understood. It is part of a larger phenomenon, which I have called 'mediation,' one of whose important marks is the replacement of informal and frequently impromptu direct action with organized social structures.

Mediation in its most general form is human cooperativeness. We constantly find ourselves doing things for others and, in turn, relying on others to meet our needs and satisfy our wants. We mediate the actions of others when we act in their stead: we do this frequently to enhance their power, relieve their burdens, or increase their convenience. Parents mediate the actions of their babies; barbers, of their customers; gas company employees, of everyone who wishes to keep warm.

In small social groups, cooperation can take the form of doing the job together. In populous societies, it is impractical or impossible for us to be present at every place where others act on our behalf. Cooperation becomes shared participation in diverse phases of some larger social act—a poorly understood, momentous exchange of services. In this situation, we do not know the precise nature and do not have immediate experience of what others do for us. As social institutions grow, we lose sight even of the fact that others labor on our behalf. The physical and institutional distance at which they operate from us makes them disappear from our ken; we are left in ignorance of the conditions of our life and weal.

Mediation, when it takes the form of large-scale institutions, shatters social acts into their minute fragments. Without the allocation of small interrelated tasks to diverse individuals, there could, of course, be no complex social act; and such collaboration vastly enhances human power. From the social point of view, the individual acts performed interrelate in a rational way and constitute a whole. But viewed from the standpoint of individuals whose lives are exhausted in narrow roles and whose perspectives are local, the collection of acts to which they contribute has neither meaning nor intelligible structure.

The experienced fragmentation is due only partly to the fact that it takes many hands to accomplish any task and that contributors to the social act do divergent things at a distance from one another. In a mediated world, the basic unity of actions is destroyed: those who actually perform act-fragments are neither the planners nor the beneficiaries of what is accomplished. Planning, execution, and enjoyment (or suffering) of the results fall to different individuals in the chain, none of whom is likely to have direct acquaintance with the work of the others.

The result is that the decision makers feel frustrated by what they view as the incompetence of those they command. The individuals who actually perform the required deeds feel put upon and think themselves the powerless instruments of an alien force. Those on the receiving end greet what is visited on them (even if favorable) with suspicion and resentment. Everyone agrees in disclaiming responsibility for communal or institutional acts, though each has a different excuse: some say they did not intend untoward results; others claim they never knew what they were doing; many complain that it all just happened, they did not *do* anything.

As a consequence of large-scale mediation, then, generations are brought up ignorant of their social ties and unable to accept responsibility for their contribution to social acts. Nevertheless, in times of relative stability our institutions manage to function well enough: with a sufficient number of checks, people can be held responsible for their narrow roles. But the more we stress role responsibility, the less room is left for the larger, humane response to other human beings. The individual's life, therefore, is doubly wretched. In the mediated chains of which I am part, I feel hemmed in and manipulated. And in dealing with others, with businesses, with government, with sundry institutions, I cannot transcend the mass role of client, customer, or consumer.

Professional practice and advertising by professionals must be understood in the context of such a mediated world. The vast increase in the sum of social knowledge in our society is accompanied by staggering ignorance on the part of individuals in matters of practical and moral significance. I do not deny that each of us is familiar with a vast collection of facts: virtually any tenth grader today knows more about physics than Newton knew in his prime. But when it comes to even an elementary understanding of social life, economic reality, the interplay of activity and happiness, or the structure and needs of our bodies, most adults grope hopelessly in the dark. Formal education cannot teach them enough about such things, and the mediated world denies them the opportunity to learn by direct experience.

Mediation offers expert advice and specialist intervention on every level of life. The price exacted for this is isolation of the individual from the momentous and sacred activities of life. Despite recent signs of change, birth and death still occur largely in special places out of our sight. Healing, toolmaking, constructing our homes, raising the young, caring for the old, growing food, and slaughtering animals are all done for us by people with special and narrow competencies. It is not just that, as a result, we never develop these skills. Few of us experience, and we rarely even observe, the activities involved. As a result, we know little or nothing of what our mediators do on our behalf, even when their actions are conditions of our survival.

Mediation makes specialization possible and fosters it. Specialists develop their own languages, procedures, and technologies. They establish special places—the garage, the courtroom, the hospital—where only they know the rules and the meaning of what occurs. Nonspecialists become outsiders who understand little and are normally denied admission to where these odd but effective rituals take place. They are permitted in when, as patients, clients, or customers, they themselves play a small part in the proceedings. But that is the wrong time to try to learn: the sick, the sued, persons whose cars have cracked engine blocks are too anxious and vulnerable to attend in a sustained way and to integrate what they observe.

Specialists do not think it is in their interest to let outsiders know a lot about what they do and how they do it. Openness may lead to having to meet external standards and extraneous demands, to lawsuits, regulation, loss of revenue. And even if they have only the highest motives, there is no reason to suppose that experts know how ignorant their clients or patients are. Mediation creates blindness on all sides. Just as patients cannot imagine all that doctors know, so doctors have no true sense of the magnitude of patient ignorance. What to the world around them seems shrouded in mystery is daily commonplace to specialists. Being at a great psychic distance from their clients, they cannot believe that things so obvious could remain unknown.

Ignorance is the natural condition of everyone in the mediated world. The larger the social organism and the more tightly it binds us to one another, the greater our nescience in both scope and depth. This ignorance is of the ultimate form: it is not lack of knowledge about a subject kept in view, but unconsciousness of whole areas of life. In such a world, advertising by professionals should be viewed not as primarily a commercial act designed to increase profit but as a public service whose aim is education.

Advertising by professionals is usually justified by one of two major lines of argument. The first squarely admits that in addition to whatever else they do, professionals run business enterprises. Public announcements of the services they provide are, therefore, amply warranted by their results: the increase in the number of clients and the improvement of the bottom line. The second argument stresses the other side in the professional-client relation. Whatever else clients may be, they are consumers of certain services. Advertising, then, is justified by the improved consumer choices it makes possible.

Each of these arguments makes a valid and valuable point. But both of them present advertising as a merely permissible, at most desirable, option and thereby altogether miss its central importance. The vital function of advertising by professionals is neither to increase profit nor to protect the consumer, but to educate the people of our mediated world. Viewed from this perspective, it becomes neither an expression of individual freedom nor simply a good and useful social strategy, but a positive obligation to be discharged in the public interest.

Such an obligation may be appropriately imposed on the professions. We would not want to make promotion of the public good the obligation of all. But professionals enjoy certain privileges, such as virtual monopoly in their areas of competence, which are granted and guaranteed them by society. We can reasonably exact a price for such monopolies, and it is particularly fitting that a part of the price should be the requirement that protected professionals lift the veil of secrecy shrouding their operations.

This immediately suggests that not any kind of advertising will do. Much is notoriously misleading or uninformative. Some aims to create a mood or an image by using suggestive but cognitively irrelevant materials. Evidently, we cannot measure the quality of an ophthalmologist by the eye-popping cleavage of someone dressed as nurse.

It is not that such hype is undignified; rather, it mocks the need advertising should subserve. The consumer needs to know what professionals do, how well they do it, and for how much. Professional advertising needs to focus on providing the public with useful material concerning the scope and variety of services offered. To make the services intelligible, there must be information about the needs and conditions that might require them. In this way, physicians, for example, may well convey a wealth of information about health and disease, the proper function and limits of medicine, and the specific content of the subspecialties. It is also appropriate to indicate the behavior expected of professionals, the qualifications of individual practitioners, and the attitude of the advertiser to client-professional relations. Disseminating such useful, factual information is, of course, only a small part of the educational obligation of professionals; the process must be broadened and personalized the moment a new client or patient walks in the door.

The last point indicates why the obligation to advertise cannot be adequately met in an institutional way. Educational advertising by national or state professional organizations is perfectly acceptable, but it cannot serve as a substitute for advertising by individual practitioners. There are two reasons for this. First, the public needs to be informed about the differential qualifications and attitudes of competing professionals. And second, education is a personal affair whose success is largely a function of the communicative interaction of individuals. Advertising by a professional, as the solicitation of such interaction, is at once the initial phase of an intimate, in many cases touchingly confidential, relation.

We cannot, of course, hope that educational advertising and the subsequent frank and informative interaction between professionals and laypersons will by themselves take care of all the problems of the mediated world. Manipulativeness, a sense of personal impotence, resentful passivity, and the unwillingness to assume responsibility for our deeds are all consequences of the way large-scale mediated chains structure our lives and limit our horizons. Impoverished direct experience—which, as the source of our ignorance, is the functional heart of the ill effects attending mediation—cannot be adequately enriched by advertising. The presentation of information, open communication, and the imaginative extension of the boundaries of the mind are all value, but they are no substitute for direct sensory encounter. The reason is that in their own way words themselves are interposed between people and the realities for which they stand: they mediate our intentions and our thoughts. Broader immediacy with others and with the world is the only and ultimate solution to the problems of fragmentation from which we all suffer.

Words, and especially the impersonal words of advertising, constitute but a first step in combating the costs of mediation: they invite immediacy. In a mediated world, virtue no longer shines by its own light; that is why professionals have to advertise. But their advertising makes false claims if they have no virtue to announce. It is only a mark to the world that a well-performed service may be obtained, never a substitute for professional competence and the caring personal relation without which professional and client remain, what they tend to be today, cash-connected strangers.

CHAPTER 13

Education and the Power of the State: Reconceiving Some Problems and Their Solutions

with Shirley M. Lachs

The twentieth century has seen a vast increase in the scope of state power. The expectation of government solutions to a broad range of problems has been both a cause and an effect of this development. Through legislation and the activity of the courts, the federal and state governments have come to regulate such previously autonomous interactions as those between employers and workers. They have interposed themselves between interested parties in a variety of hitherto private areas of concern, such as life-and-death treatment decisions that had been the exclusive province of physicians and of patients and their families.

A governmental presence in nearly all areas of life tends to obliterate the realms of what is private and what, though social, used to be immune from the power of the state. As a result, nearly everything becomes a public good, and we lose sight of any clear limits on regulations imposed in the name of the public interest. This entails a significant loss both of freedom and, because not all activities are equally well suited for regulation, of efficiency. Nevertheless, the growth in the number of people and in the complexity of their interactions exerts steady pressure for extensive and uniform rules centrally administered.

Although education in the United States has so far escaped the monolithic state control we find in many European countries, it has become subject to a growing variety of federal demands. To many, it is of special concern that these rules and requirements are aimed at private no less than at public schools. The debate about the appropriateness of such an extension of central power is conducted in terms typically of the right of individuals to raise their children as they see fit and the right of society—and of the government as its agent—to set limits to and place conditions on this liberty.

Reconceiving the Problems

The terms of the discussion are natural and inevitable so long as the issue is primarily the power of one side or the other to do what it desires. But conceiving the problem in this way does little to advance our grasp of the changing conditions of social life that render the conflict acute and frequently fails to provide a generally acceptable solution. For groups that challenge state intervention, the use of this conceptual framework constitutes, moreover, an acceptance through its terms of what they want to reject in substance. For the very language of rights, requiring adjudication in the courts, concedes that government control is a politico-legal issue and thereby invites invocation of the public interest.

We shall altogether sidestep the formulation of the problem of the relation of the state to the schools in the currently popular terms of individual rights and legitimate government power. Political solutions presuppose social problems; only by understanding them can we assess the adequacy of the remedy. We face at least two major problems with respect to education. In general terms, they are the desperate need to improve teaching and learning, and the continuing requirement not to let the schools contribute to injustice and discrimination in our society. We cannot devise effective solutions to these problems without understanding the social conditions that obtain in a populous and thoroughly institutionalized community.

Accordingly, we shall attempt to provide an account of the structural problems that beset our educational systems. Not surprisingly, these difficulties are for the most part the same as the problems we face in society at large. They arise out of the growth of specialization and widespread loss of immediacy that characterizes our interactions. As a result of their ubiquity in our social life, they infect private educational institutions no less than large public school systems. If this analysis is accurate, it has profound implications for how to improve the educational experience of young people. It also bears direct relevance to the socially desirable limits of politico-legal conflict resolution and to the manner in which laws are to be made, interpreted, and administered.

The Nature of Education

Except for sex, education is the most intimate of human contacts. Other than marriage, it is the most loving and momentous of personal relations. The comparison with sex and marriage is not gratuitous. Education is essentially parenting: the begetting of human beings or the transformation of suitable biological organisms into socialized individuals.

This activity, poorly understood even today, displays immense complexities. It includes conveying a certain amount of information, helping to develop necessary skills, fostering important social attitudes, and establishing vital values, among other elements. The means used to accomplish these ends are both deliberate and discursive—as we find in overt attempts to teach—and subtle, unspoken, and surprising—as when young people learn by imitation and example. The ultimate aim of education consists in the development of persons who are both self-determining and respectful of the self-determination of others, both individuals and supportive of a shared social life.

This intensely personal interaction is organized and governed, in the modern world, by large, impersonal institutions. Legislatures have wrested control over and parents have, for the most part, surrendered responsibility for the education of children. Only lately have sperm banks and surrogate motherhood enabled us to have biological offspring by proxy. But the day care center, the school system, and Sunday school have for a long time made it possible for us to raise our children by proxy: to retire from lovingly teaching them ourselves and to delegate the task of endowing them with personality to strangers. These people, presumably experts at the art of person making, operate under the constraints imposed by the institutions that employ them. The creation of the next generation ceases, in this way, to be self-improvement through cultural self-reproduction and becomes, instead, a bureaucratic job.

The Institutional Context

Large institutions inevitably suffer from certain structural problems. They consist of chains of individuals interacting in complex
patterns. The tasks accomplished are broken into their constituent
elements, and each of them is executed by a different person or group
within the chain. In this way, momentous acts can be performed, and
the need for collaboration greatly enhances our social, cooperative
tendencies. But there are also costs, many of them due to the fragmentation of tasks and the attendant growth of specialization.

The natural pattern of an integrated human action includes intention, execution, and enjoyment or suffering of consequences. In
large-scale social acts performed by institutional chains, these functions are separated and assigned to different individuals. Some people plan and administer while others carry out directives or man
operations. People primarily affected by the actions constitute a separate group from either of these two; they are customers or clients or,
in unfortunate cases, victims of the institution. The division of tasks
places the three groups at a psychological, and frequently at a physical, distance from one another. The result is ignorance by each of the
purposes and activities of the others and inability by persons in every
section of the chain to view their own actions as parts of a complete
and significant human act.

A pervasive sense of meaninglessness, lack of control over one's
own contribution, frustration at the insensitivity of the institution,
and fear that all its functionaries are manipulated manipulators con-
spire to create an atmosphere of uncaring irresponsibility. In such
structures, it is natural to retreat within the narrowest parameters of
one's job; since we feel that it is beyond our power to change the system, we tend to disclaim responsibility for what it causes. Surprisingly, even expertise fosters cold indifference: primary allegiance to
professional standards narrows the scope of caring and shifts its focus
from people to the quality of one's performance.

These general problems of large-scale institutions now pervade
education throughout our land. The image of the small country
schoolhouse with a loving teacher beckons only as the symbol of a
simpler and better past. The sheer size of the task of instructing the
next generation presents problems: many teachers see hundreds of
young people in their classes, and school boards deal with tens of
thousands of students. The press of numbers eliminates the possibil-

ity of sustained contact and personal relationships between teachers and students. Education then becomes a product whose uniform quality must be assured by a multitude of rules and regulations. Administrators are the creators and enforcers of these rules, and teachers learn to herd their charges through a body of material in accordance with them. Young people know little of the reason for the regulations and the institution is in no hurry to justify or to explain them. The result is that students view the educational system as an alien machine to which they must submit because of its enormous power.

Students, however, are not alone in regarding the educational Leviathan with suspicion. The initial pleasure of parents in having their children taken off their hands tends to be followed by repeated encounters with an unaccommodating bureaucracy. Teachers themselves feel their autonomy threatened and their lives consumed by the petty demands of functionaries. And school administrators find themselves in a hierarchical system hemmed in by parents, taxpayers, and politicians at the one end and the shoulder-shrugging incompetence of coaches and assistant principals at the other.

This lumbering institution consumes the good intentions and the energy of all who join it for idealistic reasons, without yielding significant improvement in return. Astoundingly, no one who comes in contact with it does what he or she wants: constraint and compromise remove both the joy of learning and the special pleasures of intergenerational communication. The prevailing experience in the educational system is frustration, and the universal reality in it is that anything out of the ordinary requires backbreaking effort. Openness to change and to reason as well as the very spirit of experimentation that we think should characterize the enterprise of spreading knowledge appear to be altogether gone.

This litany of the current ills of education is not meant to deny the efficiency, enthusiasm, and inventiveness of isolated individuals or groups. There is no doubt, moreover, that in spite of its problems the system manages to do a great deal of good by socializing young people, teaching them useful skills, and transmitting vast amounts of information. But the accomplishments of individual teachers and administrators occur too often in spite rather than because of the existing structure. And what education achieves pales by comparison with its ideals and its possibilities.

Not all the problems of education are due to its institutional shape.

But many are, and they are the ones we wish to discuss here. They are not normally seen to be related, much less to have a single cause. Our analysis offers a unitary explanation of widely diverse phenomena and, through identification of the source of the difficulties, promises the possibility of intelligent remedial action.

Loss of Immediacy

The central reality on which we must focus is the loss of immediacy and through that the loss of intimacy in the educational process. There is some forfeiture of immediacy in every institution. But when the social structure is small, the loss is relatively minor or easily counteracted. In a single, small, autonomous school, for example, teachers are in continuing contact with one another, and the administrator can readily acquaint her staff with the constraints under which she operates and the issues she faces. In the small community this small school serves, teachers and parents are neighbors; their direct, daily contact gives each side a living grasp of the concerns and practices of the other. Such communities are, of course, not free of conflict. But whatever difficulties may beset them arise not from suspicion, people's ignorance of one another, and nameless irresponsibility. Teachers see and know their students not only in the classroom but throughout the activities of daily life so that the enterprise of learning is naturally conceived as a necessary and perhaps even exciting partnership.

The growth in the size of institutions is proportional to the decline in them of immediacy. In large schools, there is little educationally significant interaction among teachers. They tend to deal with their classroom problems as best they can in isolation from one another. Sharing difficulties with the administration is considered unwise: the principal may well regard trouble as the result of teacher incompetence rather than welcome its discussion as the salutary effort to bring social experience to bear on its resolution. Administrators, in turn, think it best to keep teachers in the dark about the details and about the procedures of their work. But the issue is even deeper than the intentions of people. The institution requires a division of labor; once individuals develop the narrow skills necessary to occupy specialized roles, others lose sight or fail to see or to understand the precise nature of what they do. Psychic distance from one another, ignorance of the feelings and actions of others, become in this way endemic to the institution.

Immediacy between teachers and students may appear to be unaffected by the size of the educational system. Audiovisual aids, computers and teaching machines have not, after all, replaced the person who enters the classroom to instruct. But this appearance is deceptive: direct contact in classrooms is a sharply circumscribed and relatively impotent affair. Teachers and students are strangers to each other when they meet; their brief time together, focused on the mastery of a body of material, is inadequate to bring them to the point of friendship and sharing and trust. The very roles they fill make a close relation difficult. Education is supposed to be a one-way flow of knowledge that can be turned on at the beginning of the hour and turned off at the end. The asymmetry between the teacher, as a kind of spigot, and the students, expected to be empty bottles ready to be filled, is so great that the group can never constitute itself as a community of inquiry exploring matters of mutual interest.

Moreover, classroom immediacy is meant to be all business. Personal relations are unnecessary for and may, in fact, place obstacles in the way of learning. With large classes and limited teaching time, instructors find that there is no possibility of taking a direct interest in their charges. There is not even time to explore the relevance of what is learned to the students' lives; everything is centered on covering and remembering material, and compliance is assured by the threat of grades. The encounter in the classroom, though it appears to be between persons, lacks all personal elements: it is bereft of unity of purpose, long-term caring, and mutual respect. It should not surprise us that teaching machines can readily replace human instructors in many fields. Once the deeply personal nurturing aspect of teaching is lost, flesh-and-blood instructors themselves become mechanical.

Expertise and Professionalization

The growth of expertise in society and, with it, the professionalization of teaching naturally lead to narrow but exclusive social roles. The jobs that must be done require both specialized knowledge and the freedom to perform them without interference from unskilled outsiders. The educational establishment developed and acquired its monopoly power by insisting on this liberty: professionals, it was frequently affirmed, must not be subjected to the standards and the review of those who are not experts in the field. This understandable, and in some respects even salutary, insistence on professional self-determination has essentially eliminated immediacy between teachers and the society they serve. What happens in the classroom has become in this way a secret, if not mysterious, ritual. Parents feel ill at ease to say anything about it, even when their deepest instincts tell them that their children are poorly served. There is a similar reluctance on the part of the public to deal with bothersome aspects of school administration: ignorance of how things are run and of how they ought to be effectively stills external criticism. Needless to say, parents do not surrender dissatisfaction when they cede the right to object. If anything, their frustration increases with the perception that the system for which they pay appears unintelligible and remains unresponsive to their concerns.

When the sense of parental impotence reaches a peak, the political and the judicial systems are enlisted to bring the educational establishment to heel. Although effective, using these systems further reduces immediacy. For the attempt to resolve problems face to face is then altogether abandoned, and new mediators are interposed between the community and its schools. The intermediaries themselves are in a difficult position: judges and politicians find themselves as ignorant of what goes on in the educational system as the rest of the society whose interests they try to represent. And how best to represent the interests of the community is also not without problems. The educational establishment defends itself by seeking access to courts and legislatures in order to convince them that students will be best served if it is left alone. Legislatures, in particular, are accustomed to being used to consolidate the power of professional educators: they rarely balk even at such absurdities as putting the force of law behind the number of hours students must spend in school.

Parties to conflicts, many of which result from the loss of open and direct contact between the schools and the community, then attempt to resolve their differences by having even less immediacy. Issues may get settled this way, but only because decreed or legislated solutions are supported by the coercive power of the state. The relation of the schools to the community is rarely improved, and the quality of education is not affected much or for very long. In the nature of the case, no distant institution can sensitize or vitalize another. Once a social structure rigidifies and forces its members into narrow roles, nothing less than a threat to its existence can restore its responsiveness and life. The reason for this resides, once again, in the nature of social structures.

Attempts to Revitalize Institutionalized Education

At times of business as usual, no one in the institution actually understands all its work and no one controls it. Superintendents know little of what transpires in their classrooms. Classroom teachers, in turn, have little influence on and even less concrete grasp of management decisions by the leaders. In no single human mind is there a clear and detailed idea of both rules and their implementation, of both design and execution. Location in a complex chain of agents limits everyone's vision; although people in executive positions tend to see more than others, even they do not see it all. Since they utilize established channels of communication, they may come to believe that they know what happens in the far reaches of their institutional world. This is a mistake partly because it is in the interest of employees to inform their superiors selectively and to present events in the best possible light. But even the most accurate report is inadequate by comparison with direct experience, and leaders lack precisely this immediate encounter with how things really work.

To revitalize an institution, someone must actually realize that all is not well. The recognition may come as a result of external criticism or threat, but the ultimate motive power for change must spring from direct acquaintance with ways in which the institution fails. Of course, people do not always make a constructive response to the perception of problems; it is possible to shut one's eyes or to present excuses. But firsthand grasp of a situation offers knowledge that is vivid and detailed and that tends to motivate the will. The palpable experience of cruelty or wickedness is more likely to engage our active parts than a description or distant report of it.

Reestablishing Immediacy

Administration

Immediacy serves not only as a spur to reform but also as a major part of the cure for our ills. Since in institutional contexts direct contact between two parties always occurs on someone's turf or concerning one group's work, there are no less than twelve areas of action in which the unhindered flow of information must be established. The first three areas surround the operation of school boards and school administrators. The school system must find ways to ensure that education is near the center of the public's agenda at all times and not only when the need for increased appropriations becomes intense. To accomplish this, school boards must consist of individuals elected in campaigns that include an informed and detailed public debate of educational problems. The meetings of school boards must be open to the public, and the media must be invited to provide helpful and responsible coverage. School administrators must make extraordinary efforts to acquaint the public, and especially parents, with the rules and procedures and the reasons for the rules and procedures in accordance with which their institutions operate. Such openness through unforced disclosure and the repeated invitation of public comment is admittedly bothersome and time-consuming. But in the long run, schools that adhere to it encounter fewer problems, enjoy greater community support and, in the case of mistakes, receive more ready understanding and forgiveness.

School administrators must supplement such unrestricted flow of information toward the general public with even greater receptivity to the cognitive needs of teachers and students. A secretive, unapproachable principal can have a ruinous effect on the learning environment in an entire school. Arbitrariness and injustice destroy morale. Unless there is forthright communication about administrative decisions, arbitrariness and the appearance of it cannot be distinguished, and students and teachers fall into the habit of suspecting favoritism and skulduggery. An open-door policy is not enough to combat such natural alienation: the power of their position keeps administrators from receiving casual visits, searching questions, and timely complaints.

Leaders must take active steps to learn about problems and to disseminate information: they must initiate contacts with those committed to their care and discuss common concerns in a frank and detailed way. This does not mean that they should engage in a public relations effort to gain approval of their views. Although all of us would like to have things our way, few people are so naive as to suppose that the world will play by their rules. Most of us are perfectly content to let the leaders lead, so long as we understand the reasons for their actions and feel that our voices have been heard. Within the school, this demand for respect, for the sense that what students and teachers think and what they say matter, is best met if the administrator seeks regular, informal contact with each group in its own world. Visiting the teachers' lunchroom and the cafeteria, having impromptu conversations in the hall, and spreading word that ideas on the solution of common problems are welcome from anyone create a sense of community. Principals must be among the first to hear the latest rumors and deal with issues as leaders of a partnership.

Teachers

The same immediacy that needs to pervade the world of school boards and administrators must also surround teachers in their official capacity. That this openness be expected of instructors, and that it become a natural part of their exertions, is of central significance. Some teachers take a personal interest in their students and handle their tasks as if they constituted a calling and not a job. Unfortunately, however, such individuals are rare, and our system, viewing their devotion as something beyond what their job description demands, offers them few rewards. We operate on the assumption that it is enough for employees in large institutions to fulfill their narrow, and impersonal, role responsibilities. This may work well in factories where we deal with metals and plastic, but it can lead to disaster when the primary objects of our activity are young human beings. We must, therefore, revise the very criteria by which we judge teacher performance, to include not only professional competence but also human caring and the readiness to sustain a broad spectrum of personal relations.

This means that, in interacting with students, teachers must be direct and approachable. They must show themselves as stable, predictable, and fair persons, and embed their professional activities in the context of humane relations. They must be sensitive to the fact that we teach more by example than by words and that, for this reason, the instructor's character and attitudes and actions must be worthy of imitation. Accordingly, they need to demonstrate a vivid interest in their students and an abiding readiness to aid in their development. They must, in short, resist the natural tendency to view students as their relatively helpless charges, or as savage strangers, and assume the nurturing activity of parents.

The immediate and friendly contact teachers should seek must extend beyond the classroom. Instructors can take care of the needs of young people only if they establish an effective partnership with their parents. The occasional parent-teacher conference is altogether inadequate to accomplish this goal. Teachers must institute extensive and continuing direct communication with the home, acting as if parents were their primary and immediate employers. They must also achieve daily personal contact with administrators and sufficient identity in the eyes of school board members to permit significant conversations when they seem appropriate. The entire educational system revolves around the work of teachers. What they do, therefore, both in and out of the classroom, carries momentous weight. Their commitment to human caring, open communication, and enhanced immediacy would go a long way toward overcoming the alienation in our schools.

Parents

In its attitudes and actions toward the schools, the community must reciprocate the forthright partnership that should be offered by professional educators. Teachers and principals must be viewed as trusted friends and advisors instead of busy functionaries who are not to be approached. Many adults find it difficult to rid themselves of their childhood perceptions: instead of considering them equals, they look upon teachers with fear. The friendliest gestures by school staff cannot serve as more than an invitation to such people. To develop genuine cooperation, parents must avail themselves of the opportunity to discuss shared problems and to develop mutually satisfactory solutions. They need to spend time in the school and to get to know the teachers of their children as parents themselves or at least as kindred human beings.

One way to foster this exchange is to explode the myth that only certified instructors have anything to teach young people. Today, we make only token gestures in the direction of acknowledging the educational significance of outsiders: doctors and lawyers are sometimes (though in too many places only on career days) brought into the classroom for a brief sojourn. All of us would profit by doing much more along these lines. People whose acquaintance with social conditions, political activities, economic enterprises, or varied professional skills is direct, exude a scent of reality. They have much to teach our children not only because of their fund of learning and experience but also because of their instant credibility with them. An incidental benefit of expanding such programs is that the sharp contrast between school and "real life" tends to disappear. Direct contact with teachers on the basis of equality enables parents to view the task of education as a genuine partnership.

For the partnership to be effective, parents must retain or regain immediacy with their children. The popular distinction between quantity and quality of time spent with the people we brought into the world serves as a transparent self-justification on the part of those who wish to abandon a major parental responsibility. It is always desirable, of course, that the activities parents and children share be of the highest quality. But such richness and diversity develop only with a significant commitment of time. And even the best activities performed at white heat are inadequate to meet the extensive and intensely personal needs of a growing human being. In fact, quiet activities and sustained presence are as important as roaring fun and frequently serve as its indispensable conditions. Intense moments of tenderness and self-revelation cannot be precipitated at will and then quickly pushed aside to meet one's next appointment. We cannot be our children's parents and friends without a vast investment of time, emotion, and energy.

When all is said and done, parents cannot cease being their children's teachers. Bringing young souls into the world has a price in terms of lost liberties and unavoidable obligations. The anguished "All I do with my education is raise children!" can be understood as the sentiment of a woman trapped in early marriage. But on the intellectual side, it represents a profound set of mistakes about the function of education, the value of nurturing children, and the proper priorities in the lives of parents. Education is, after all, not primarily preparation for employment, and it is difficult to conceive an end more worthy of the efforts of an educated person than that of guiding the growth, creating the habits, and shaping the personality of another human being. This should clearly not be the exclusive province or responsibility of the mother. It is a tragic perversion when either parent thinks that keeping books, selling fertilizer, or answering the telephone is a satisfying outcome of, say, sixteen years in school, but making a direct contribution to the improvement of the next generation is not.

Students

The sustained interest of parents in the progress of their children must be matched by a suitable level of helpful exertion on the part of students. In some ways, this may be the most difficult task to accomplish. Young people go through periods of extensive and painful adjustment. Organic changes distract their attention and challenge their precariously established beliefs. Their environment presents opportunities for confusion and disaster that, if left to their own devices, they may be unable to resist. The position of students in the school, moreover, leaves them vulnerable and passive. Viewed as immature and transitional members of the community, they tend to be given little say in its affairs. The resulting asymmetry between the power of school employees and of students is so great that it becomes difficult to see the enterprise of teaching and learning as a partnership.

The initiating steps toward breaking up this system of disempowerment must come from teachers and administrators. Since they hold essentially all the power in the school, only they are in a position to invite others to share it. Here again, immediate and forthright communication with students may convince officials that learning can be mutual. Those in the classroom know more about the quality of teaching than anyone else; they also know, from firsthand experience, the obstacles to learning that exist in certain places in the school. There is not much principals could do to gain a keener insight into their institutions than listen to the perceptive and the articulate among their students. And there is no doubt that the single most significant reform immediately available is selective action on the suggestions and complaints of those being educated. This does not suppose that students are infallible or all-knowing, only that direct perceptions are often accurate and that without taking the experience of clients into account, no service can be meaningfully improved.

Once parents and adults in the schools show their readiness to accept students as partners, young people must reciprocate in kind. They need to establish (or reestablish) a measure of openness with their parents. They must also give school administrators the benefit of the doubt: direct conversations about matters of shared concern presuppose an attitude of nonjudgmental mutuality. Most important, they must reveal themselves to their teachers with artless immediacy. Honesty in displaying one's attitudes, feelings, and problems is the foundation of reciprocal trust and decency. They, in turn, are the necessary heart of dealing with one another as human beings, not as functionaries whose lives touch only in their roles.

Private Schools for All?

What we have said about the need for immediacy may be taken as an argument for the privatization of our entire educational system. Do private schools not already manifest the intimacy in size and human contacts that we think essential? And would the dismantling of large-scale public education, perhaps through a voucher system, not therefore establish the cooperative and open interaction of teachers, students, parents, and administrators?

Those who are inclined to answer such questions in the affirmative tend to take a romantic view of private schools. To them, these institutions are pristine islands in a polluted stream, small enclaves of righteousness and enduring values in a world that has abandoned the good and the true. In fact, no part of society is immune to the problems that beset the whole: the mediation-shaped attitudes and character of people are not left behind at the schoolhouse door. Accordingly, even though system size is not a problem in private schools, they suffer from the lack of certain forms and important conditions of immediacy.

A relatively small number of students in a classroom does not guarantee immediacy. The direct exposure necessary for successful education is personal: it takes the form of sustained interest in each other's perceptions, feelings, problems, and pleasures. This caring beyond the confines of official roles is precisely what standards of professional competence disregard or even discourage. Private day-school teachers have as little contact with the personal lives of their students as their public school colleagues. In residential institutions, where constant interaction is possible, the context is artificially impoverished: distance from family and many of the pressures of social life minimizes opportunities for immediacy about matters of significance to young people.

Some private institutions, especially religious ones, make a great show of taking a personal interest in students. But the concern is quickly recognized as tendentious, aimed at saving souls, establishing approved habits, or assuring proper behavior. This destroys the openness necessary for meaningful and reciprocal immediacy. The lack of mutuality is an endemic problem in private schools. Secrecy, unbending commitment to hierarchical structure, and a general resistance to sharing power render them incapable of offering parents and students genuine partnership. Immediacy cannot thrive in authoritarian settings. Imbalances of power, manipulativeness, and claims of expertise are hallmarks of the mediated world; that is the region where nearly all our institutions, including private schools, belong.

The Reach of the State

Debate about the proper limits of state control over schools is inevitably cast in terms of the conflict of individual rights with the public good. The principle of the power of courts and legislatures over significant aspects of public education is well established. But many people think that private schools should be immune from such interference, for they are an expression of the liberty of individuals to pass on their beliefs, their values, and their way of life to their children. Persons committed to a measure of central control invoke the notion of the public good. Education, they argue, is essential for empowerment that, in turn, is an indispensable condition of equality. And without equality, at least of opportunity, no society can be just and perhaps even universally free.

We have proposed to replace this conceptual framework with one less adversarial and more useful. In our terms, the question is not whether government has a right to impose its will on the private schools, but rather what we must do to enjoy the benefits of immediacy. Without such sustained, open, and mutual contact between segments of the population, it is impossible to have a peaceful democratic society. In accordance with our deepest values, this immediacy is for individuals to achieve and to foster. Only when they fail at the task, and thereby endanger the entire project of our communal life, can government step in.

This perspective sheds new light on the reasons for desegregating the schools. Although the official justification for integration was phrased in terms of justice, rights, and the public good, a major—though perhaps unarticulated—motive was the recognition of the need for immediacy. Peace and justice cannot reign in a pluralistic society, it was thought, unless widely divergent groups of citizens have direct contact with one another. The earlier in the life of young people such immediacy is established, the better the chances for ethnic, class, racial, and religious understanding. It is blatantly false that separate must always be unequal, but it is always uncommunal.

The desperate need for desegregation first became clear to us when a young friend of our children innocently remarked that she thought all blacks were cleaning ladies. Nothing combats such devastating stereotypes better than early exposure to the full humanity of others, with all the friendship, or at least understanding tolerance, that involves. Without it, we cannot even be sure that we can raise wise judges, fair police officers or businesspeople who understand the need for equal opportunity. If individuals will not, the courts—acting on behalf of society—must combat this threat to the welfare of citizens and, in the long run, to the stability of the entire social order. Private schools cannot exempt themselves from such last-resort regulation.

But we must move with great caution here. The idea of such distant mediating agencies as Congress and the courts demanding immediacy appears anomalous. Those who mandate open and direct contact must strive to achieve it themselves. Yet the salutary orders to establish immediacy in the schools have not been matched by the efforts of the courts to attain it in their own operations. Such open interchange is always educational in character and leads, at its best, to action on the basis of consensus. Enforcing the rights of one group involves restricting the freedom of some other. The limitation becomes less odious, may in fact altogether lose its objectionable feel, if it is freely adopted. Convincing people to change their ways retains respect for their autonomy; the application of force not only degrades them to the level of manipulable objects but also engenders resistance and resentment. In spite of this, Congress and our judicial system tend to substitute compulsory solutions for voluntary compliance achieved by persuasion.

This tendency reveals a fundamental misunderstanding of the role of government in a society of free individuals. The central function of government is neither control over the behavior of people nor promotion of their welfare. It is, instead, educational in the broadest and finest sense of the term. That education leads to intelligent adjustments in how people act and promotes human welfare is, of course, true. But these are secondary consequences of the successful pursuit of the primary good, which is the development of fully socialized, yet self-determining, human beings. Such character formation is a lifelong activity: government must envelop the work of the schools in a broader and richer educational effort. The application of force can be only the last resort and a temporary expedient in the enterprise of creating free and mature individuals.

Judges as Leaders

If we view government and law in this light, we recognize that the important question is not whether the courts have the right to mandate varied forms of immediacy in the schools. We must ask, instead, whether the enforcement of such judgments is likely to accomplish the ends at which we aim. This, in turn, is tantamount to examining whether the legal system does its job properly if it employs force before the possibilities of persuasion are exhausted. To be sure, matters that come before the courts are frequently thought to have an element of urgency, making them unsuitable for lengthy educational processes. But in many noncriminal cases, such pressing needs exist only because government and the legal system have failed over the years to exert proper instructional influence. And in any case, in an era of rapid and extensive communication, educational efforts focused on selectively narrow issues need not take up much time.

To educate the public on matters before the bench, judges must emerge from the isolation of their courtrooms. They must gain first-hand acquaintance with the problem whose solution they are asked to address, in just the way Thomas Wiseman, a federal judge in Nashville, rode the bus with children some years ago before formulating his opinion in the school desegregation case. They must also seek immediacy with the larger community or at least with the parties to the conflict so that by sensible conversation a generally acceptable solution can be worked out. In this way, judges can become educators and leaders, though not without losing the effective secrecy that surrounds the specialized work they do in their sheltered courtrooms. The fact that they are judges and therefore have the option of applying force enhances the readiness of litigants to settle their disputes.

This image of the judge as wise arbitrator, as disinterested person who can achieve mutually acceptable solutions to community conflicts, accords with the ideas of an earlier age. It represents a rejection of the notion of judge as technician applying statute and precedent or as expert specialist formulating opinions on the basis of mediating words at a distance from the realities those words describe. The same return to direct contact with people and their problems would render politicians and government officials more sensitive to freedom, which they now readily disregard in the name of such abstractions as justice and the public good. If our leaders realized that the need to apply the power of the state is a measure of the failure of government and decided to become our educators, our educators might, in turn, learn to lead. The immediacy of people with one another would then compensate for the depersonalization of large institutions. We could become a community of individuals with life itself our lifelong education.

Our proposed reconception places education at the center of government action and immediacy at the pivot of education. Immediacy is the frank and cooperative way in which people can be together in a pluralistic democracy. The stress on such direct contact and shared decision making converts schooling into a partnership of the young and the mature. The first great success of education is the conviction that no one in the community can be left out of this partnership.

r

Law and the Importance
of Feelings

Philosophers are paid to think. It is not surprising, therefore, that they see thought everywhere or that they believe that thought is the very model of reality. Some take it so far as to declare that the entire universe aims at the promotion of thought or that the emergence of a collection of ideas sufficiently systematic and broad would signal the maturation or perfection of the world. Such a system of thoughts would not only encompass all of reality, but also displace alternative modes of approach to it. This is certainly what Hegel had in mind when he wrote of how sensation is overcome early in the growth of thought and of the way in which immediacy yields to the mediating work of concepts at every turn.

Hegel believed that all immediacy, being primitive, is transcended. This may explain why the last section of his *Phenomenology*, which presents the tantalizing promise of absolute knowledge, is so devastatingly disappointing. For such absolute understanding turns out to be no more than the sum of prior developments with no additional insight that may be savored by the private mind. According to Hegel's view, individuals capable of higher thought should not need such an immediate feel of things.

Peirce, though he called himself a Hegelian, was fortunately not blind to the reality and importance of immediacy. His categorial scheme testifies to his belief in the irreducibility of direct experience. He calls such immediate feelings and private apprehensions 'firsts' and speaks of them, at least in some places, as necessary conditions of thoughts, laws, or "thirds." With the faithfulness to experience for which he is rightly celebrated, he goes so far as to note that even the most exalted thoughts have a certain inexpressible feel to consciousness—in other words, even thirds have firsts. One is tempted to speculate what the last section of *The Phenomenology of Spirit* would be like had Peirce written it. But, of course, Peirce knew that it could not be written: absolute knowledge would not emerge, he thought, until the completion of infinite inquiry. Was part of his reason for lodging the fulfillment of thought in the indefinite future his realization that no finite mind could accommodate the feel of such omniscience?

Peirce's work in semiotics shows the same respect for irreducible immediacy as we find in his metaphysical speculations. When he discusses signification, he speaks not only of energetic and logical interpretants (seconds and thirds) but also of the emotional interpretant, which is the feeling produced by a sign.* Moreover, when he distinguishes the properties of signs, he is not satisfied to note their pure demonstrative application (their physical connection with their object) and their properly cognitive representative function. He also identifies their "material qualities," which are the characters they possess in themselves or the way they appear when they stand naked in human consciousness.† Direct experiences of this sort, such as the all-pervasive aroma of oranges on Christmas morning, defy analysis, explanation, or even adequate description in words. Yet their reality is undeniable and Peirce accordingly announces that "the Immediate . . . the Unanalyzable, the Inexplicable, the Unintellectual runs in a continuous stream through our lives."‡

In spite of Peirce's commendable focus on the way things feel to us, immediacy continues to receive little attention in the world of thought. In philosophy, in semiotics, in law and the other professions, thirds occupy pride of place. Our interest is in rules and laws, in the intelligible structure of what we do. We seem to think that understanding is possible on the basis of description alone and that living, direct experience is an impediment to thought. In our urge to know the consequences of our acts, are we overlook the question of how they feel. We tend to relegate private experience to the realm of the "merely subjective" and thereby rob it of dignity and significance.

---

* Charles S. Peirce, *Collected Papers*, 8 vols. (Cambridge: Harvard University Press, 1931–58), 5:473.
† Peirce, 5:283.
‡ Peirce, 5:287.

Inadequate attention to firsthand experience penetrates our social practices and makes them less satisfying, less perceptive, and less humane. The result is a world that abounds in abstract goods—it is ever more prosperous, just, and sane—while a pall descends on the concrete, directly lived experience of the everyday.

The loss of immediacy of which I speak becomes, in this way, a serious social and personal problem. The alternative to immediacy is mediation, the interposition of a third something or someone between two otherwise directly related parties. Much of industrial and commercial life consists of the introduction of such mediating agencies. Distributors and sales organizations act as connecting third parties between producers and consumers. Bankers serve as the link between savers and borrowers. Real estate agents build bridges between sellers and buyers. We can think of such thirds as tools in the hands of the people they connect. Given the vast independent power of mediating agencies, however, this view is often inaccurate. Nevertheless, it does call attention to the fact that tools themselves are objects we interpose between ourselves and some result we wish to achieve or to avoid. The knife occupies a central position between the cook and his pot roast, while rubber gloves shield the dishwasher from dishpan hands. Mediating agencies are, therefore, not always other humans; they can be physical objects that range in complexity from a piece of paper to a pulp and paper factory. And the elements they connect need not all be persons either; they can be actions, consequences of actions, and even the multifarious objects our industrial world creates.

So long as human beings stand between humans, such as in buying a house through an agent, or our relation is established through a tool, such as when I call you on the phone, the individual's sense of agency remains. Even when I use an inanimate object to achieve an anonymous result, such as when I trim the bushes by a public road, I retain control over what I do and familiarity with both the process and the product of my action. All of this changes when mediation penetrates agency, as it does in large-scale social acts. Here coworkers stand between me and any meaningful action; without their cooperation, my own small contribution to the complex product would be ineffective or worthless. On an assembly line, for example, the action of producing automobiles is not one I or any *one* can appropriate—performance of the action itself requires that what I do fit in with the labor of others, that we mutually mediate each other's efforts in order to make them whole.

The problem with mediation, with the interposition of a third, is that it shows two faces. On the positive side, it is a connecting activity that creates greater, richer, more complex wholes. In the form of the division of labor and specialized competence, it makes organized social life and industrial production possible. But on the negative side, whatever connects also separates. Any agency that relates me to other things or people also keeps me at a distance from them. The more complex the social act, for example, the more cooperating mediators it requires. And the growth in the number of intermediaries proportionately increases my distance from the ultimate outcome of our joint activity. Distance conceals; its increase, therefore, is at once an increase in ignorance. Humans in the industrialized and institutionalized world show, for this reason, a more stunning ignorance than their unlettered predecessors. They lacked a knowledge of facts about the world; we alas know not what we do.

Hegel rightly identified the tendency of modern life: the proliferation of thirds crowds out our firsts. In plain English, this means that the growth of complexity in our institutions has made it difficult for us to have extensive firsthand experience of them. And without such direct acquaintance, we cannot know them, cannot understand our role in them, and cannot identify even with those of their actions that we helped to create.

An example might make all this clear. The large corporation, one of whose department stores I frequent, employs tens of thousands of people. The command and reporting structures it has in operation restrict each employee to a relatively narrow role. Although things go well only when all the roles are suitably interrelated, it is not thought necessary for this that employees understand the interconnection or any role other than their own. Some of them are planners and others execute limited interlocking portions of the plans. The decision makers ask little input from the workers and reveal little to them of their broader plans. The workers, in turn, disclose few local problems to central management. Neither group has firsthand acquaintance with the other's work. The result is mutual ignorance of what the others mean and do, and an easy excuse when the system fails. Distant managers can sincerely assert that through their policies and regulations they meant only the best. The local salesperson who sells me damaged merchandise and will not take it back, on the other hand, can indignantly announce, "I only work here. I do not make the rules." Ignorance of one anothers' work in an integrated whole is at once ignorance of our own. Moreover, since only the total product renders our small, specialized contributions to it significant, failure to understand it keeps us ignorant of the exact nature of what we do. Such ignorance makes it difficult to appropriate the larger act or take responsibility for our part in it.

Sooner or later all of us become both victims and perpetrators of the irresponsibility that the loss of direct experience begets. Lawyers who work in large corporations are likely to see a great deal of it. But mediation is present everywhere in our society, even in the relatively personal and self-determining realm of the professions. The role of lawyers, in particular, is designed to be a mediating third. They stand between litigants or between society and the criminally charged, attempting to create an environment in which justice and reason can prevail. As a moderating influence working to increase the empire of law, they are thirds in the service of thirds. They convert physical struggle and mindless conflict (seconds) into the rational medium of words.

Both faces of mediation are consciously employed in the institutional design of the legal profession. On the one hand, lawyers are supposed to establish connections between parties whose rational or even civil relations have broken down. This mediated contact is graced by outcomes vastly more satisfying than anything that can be achieved by the feuding sides alone. On the other hand, however, a rule-governed and constructive connection can be sustained only by keeping the parties separated. Part of the lawyer's function, therefore, is to introduce healing—or at least cooling—distance between litigants. Their communication about the pending case is not supposed to be direct: each signal they get from the other side and every message they send is mediated by two attorneys who screen out the personal, emotional, and irrational portions of the conflict.

The mediating distance lawyers provide is normally considered salutary. But each denial of immediacy has its price. In the context of the extensive structures of mediation of which the administration of justice consists, the cost is high and increasing. The reason is that the separation of litigants constitutes but a small part of the loss of immediacy in the legal system.

Mediation shatters the world into varied centers of competence. Exclusive expertise in a field involves the development of special standards and procedures. Even where exclusiveness is not a primary aim, outsiders are naturally shut out: they lack the interest or the time or the ability to master the language and to learn the skills of the expert. Casual or informal acquaintance with what specialists do is possible in small communities, where everything happens in the open or where closeness makes secrets difficult to keep. In a large, populous society, by contrast, each specialized practice commands its special place at a distance from the flow of daily life. Healing and dying occur away from the glance of nonprofessionals in the hospital, law is pursued in secluded offices and courtrooms. Lacking both formal study and informal understanding of the professions, the ordinary person finds their work mysterious.

Physicians delight in telling anecdotes about the ignorance their patients display of their own bodies. The general want of knowledge concerning our rights and duties under the law and of the procedures for safeguarding and enforcing them outstrips even our nescience of biology. Communication with lawyers, moreover, is made more difficult by a powerful effect on them of large-scale mediation. They spend all of their professional and much of their social lives in the company of other lawyers. As a result, they lose contact with the language and the daily experience of many of their clients. In Peirce's useful terms, they move in a world of thirds and rarely stop to ask about the firsts of those thirds, that is, about how their odd customs, strange talk, and alien transactions must feel to those unfamiliar with them.

When lawyers and their clients fail to share experience, when their contact is purely professional, communication on the attorneys' side deteriorates to the level of giving instructions and "holding hands." The clients' situation is even more frustrating: they feel ignorant, passive, unable to ask the right questions, and helpless in the face of their fears. Everything in the legal system is strange and new to them and their vulnerability predisposes them to view their attorneys alternately as omnipotent friends and as a callous traitors. When such experiences become commonplace and suffuse the public mind, lawyers come to be viewed with suspicion. They are denounced as secretive and self-seeking, as devoted to the proliferation of mumbo jumbo in order to make ever more work for themselves and their kind.

The problem is exacerbated by the public notion that judges sequestered in their chambers, without any firsthand knowledge of who we are and what we need, make decisions binding for our lives.

This is, incidentally, not an altogether incorrect conception. Judges are isolated in a world of thirds, of words that constitute the pleadings of litigants and the words of statutes and precedents. In many cases, there is little evidence that they understand the issues on which they write learned opinions from the standpoint of the people whose lives they affect. Sometimes they treat the feelings of litigants as if they were mere impediments to rationality that, accordingly, deserve to be disregarded. Though there is no doubt about their good intentions and competence, some of them seem to lack the quintessential human virtue of sympathy. Such sympathy or firsthand feel for another's point of view is indispensable for sound judgment. For adjudication is not an abstract or mechanical art. In addition to meeting the demands of justice, a good opinion must also have the political merit of being acceptable to all the interested parties. And people do not freely accept a decision unless they feel they received a sympathetic hearing.

Federal Judge Thomas Wiseman must have had an instinctive understanding of the importance of firsts when he undertook to deal with the acrimonious Nashville school desegregation suit. He refused to issue an order on the basis of expert testimony and the voluminous pleadings. He must have felt that something essential to the case was missing from the record, something that words—however eloquent and balanced—cannot hope to capture. He left his courtroom one morning and went to ride the bus with the children to see what it felt like to be shipped across town before the sun rises. His direct experience, combined with the openness of a newly elected school board, enabled him to settle the case to the satisfaction of all.

The same fortuitous result is possible whenever lawyers and judges insist on transcending their narrow roles and ask themselves how the thirds they champion appear to those who experience them as firsts. Such caring for the internal life of others is at once respect for them as feeling persons. It is a commonplace among physicians that many more malpractice suits result from the shabby treatment of people than from negligence or incompetence in treating the disease. The proper response to this is not to manipulate patients so that they think the world of their doctors who can then laugh behind their backs. Instead, the concern to compensate for mediation-borne ignorance must compel every professional to become an educator. Whether in law, in medicine, or in engineering, we must teach the thirds of our profession. Only by making clients and patients understand our arcane procedures can we help them as persons and make them feel at home in our world. But we must also be ready to learn from them, for only they can disclose the shape of their feelings and their human fears.

Part Four

LIFE AND DEATH

CHAPTER 15

Questions of Life
and Death

On a cold night in February, our bitch—part black Labrador, part husky, part German shepherd—gave birth to eleven pup- pies. The litter showed the eclectic taste of our dog: in addi- tion to nine predominantly black pups, we had one beige and one off-white. Eight of the nine black dogs were fine; the ninth seemed smaller, slower, weaker. Within twelve hours, it was also colder than the others, and the bitch rejected it.

Almost automatically we swung into action. We placed the pup in a heated box, fed it milk from a bottle, listened with concern to its every moan. We were deeply into our lifesaving ministrations before my wife and I looked at each other and asked whether we had any business doing what we did. We were interfering in the operation of a process that was cruel perhaps but overwhelmingly natural. What moved us to act in the first place was a deep sense of the unfairness of it all—ten well dogs and one sick, a weakling ready to pass. Why should he not have a chance to run and play? Why should fate have singled him out for pain and early death?

These, of course, are rhetorical questions. There is no universally satisfying answer as to why; what happens to the embryo, what hap- pens in the formative years cannot be tied to what we do or deserve. These things just happen and the honest ones among us simply admit that from the moral point of view there is a mad contingency to the world—an element of sheer chance we can neither explain nor avoid. And just as misfortune is not tied to a being for what it is or does, so our sympathy with the unfortunate is free of any attachment to spe- cific individuals. We did not feel sorry because *this* black dog was dying; it did not much matter *which* dog was dying at all. The sensed injustice is in *some* being well while others suffer and die.

With dogs, at least it is possible to raise the question of the desirability of intervention with some measure of objectivity. With human beings, on the other hand, our minds get clouded by emotion, by a tacit identification with the victim, the force of which is impossible to measure or to resist. We can accept irrational contingency, bitter injustice in nature, but we consider it a defeat if we find it in society. Perhaps we feel that nature is beyond our control. But society is supposed to be our creation so that if it is somehow irrational, we have no one but ourselves to blame.

Our little dog expired within a day despite our substantial exertions. In those twenty-four hours we could reach a measure of peace over the outcome; perhaps it was best this way and, at any rate, we did everything we could to keep it alive. Perhaps the same peace can be reached about humans when they go, especially if everything is tried to keep them here. But what if everything cannot be tried? What if the contingency of being attacked by disease is compounded by the more horrendous contingency of not having enough money to buy the best of care?

There is something abhorrent to many of us that the best surgeons, the best procedures, the best drugs, the best machines may be but a hundred yards away from dying people, and yet they are not available to them. And it is not that the doctors are physically tied up so they cannot come to render aid, nor is there a shortage of drugs or machines. Everyone appears to be in the thrall of an inhuman, disembodied force, of money, which in the end is but bookkeeping entries in a silent book. Persons with renal failure die because they cannot afford the high cost of dialysis; hemophiliacs lead a life of fear or bleed to death because they cannot pay for the clotting factor; children and adults face slow extinction because they cannot bear hospital costs and the fee for lifesaving surgery.

In the face of death, money seems insignificant. Our instant intuition is that all of us have an equal right to health and life. If people do not have the cash on hand, that should not by itself be reason, we think, for denying them treatment. To let a person die when a cure is readily at hand is cruel and morally repulsive. If we cannot equalize natural endowments, we should at least neutralize the social misfortune of being poor. Let us, therefore, provide—we might urge—adequate health care for all, irrespective of the ability to pay.

This is a legitimate perspective and very much in line with one set of our moral intuitions. But it is not the whole story by any means, and it can acquire plausibility only by viewing money in its abstract form as marked paper, as ledger entries or as computer records. But this is not all money is, and the bold intuition demanding equality is not our only one.

Another intuition is less moralistic and more level-headed. Since the moralist in all of us is known more for intensity of feeling than for dispassionate thought, we may find ourselves vilified even for articulating or seriously considering this alternative. But it is a real alternative, nonetheless, and one that has an element of sensible simplicity to commend it. Why not face the music, we sometimes aver, and accept the natural inequities of fortune both in and out of society? People beset by disease are unfortunate. If, in addition to being sick, they lack the money for treatment, that is a double misfortune. This double misfortune may justify multiple lamentations. It may be the occasion of private beneficence on the part of those more fortunate. But it should never be the cause of compulsory social action, taking money from those who have, to pay the medical bills of everyone else.

This alternative, superficially cruel and inhumane, surely has something to be said for it, if for no other reason than at least because it does not take a naive view of what money is and does. It is simply not true that money is a neutral commodity consisting of nothing but bookkeeping entries and paper. Money that is not inflated, and therefore progressively worthless, is a measure of social wealth. And social wealth is created by the hard labor of generations. People who die for lack of money, therefore, expire not for the arbitrary or silly reason of not being appropriately plugged into the bookkeeping machinery of the modern world. They die because they have not managed to accumulate their own share of the wealth of the nation. To save them, society would have to use a part of its wealth. And that use must be the result of a conscious decision in the teeth of conflicting obligations and a variety of worthy causes.

And the moment we reach this stage, this second—initially immoral-sounding—alternative acquires plausibility, even an air of urgency. All the abstract thought and talk favors moralists. Their great rhetorical question about our equal right to health and welfare forces us to agree. Yes, no one has a greater entitlement to live and enjoy life than anyone else. Yes, need must be met wherever it is found and whatever it takes to meet it. From this it is easy to infer that society has an obligation to every individual, an obligation it cannot fulfill without doing everything possible to nurture, protect, and cure us.

This is good abstract thinking, but it is abstract and therefore useless, nonetheless. If our resources were infinite, if social wealth were limitless, we could assume the obligation to create all manner of good. In the delirium of an expanding economy during the 1960s we actually supposed that there was no worthy aim we could fail to achieve, no social program we could not afford. In the best terms of the Protestant ethic, we believed that the only failure was the failure of will. We could accomplish anything we wanted; we just had to set our minds to it. Some theologian or psychiatrist will one day write a remarkable book diagnosing these long past days: the unique combination then of a proud belief in our omnipotence with self-contempt for weakness or wickedness of will invites it.

But there is no obligation to do what one cannot, with the best of will, accomplish. It is simply false that we can do everything. Resources are finite, human energy itself is a fleeting and easily exhausted thing. We cannot combat all the ills of the world; we cannot even combat and overcome all the ills of our own society. We *can* make rational choices, and we can allocate resources in a reasonable way. This may always fall short of what some abstract moral ideal might demand; our being rational does not imply that we can or will overcome the irrational contingency of the world. We should like to push back the limits of misfortune and uncontrolled chance. But we cannot even do this on all fronts. We must make a conscious and rational decision about where to start.

What gives particular poignancy to putting the matter in these terms is the current confluence of several major lines of development. The first is the reality and our growing recognition of the finitude of our resources. The second is the striking development of medical technology, of ever new and ever more expensive ways of prolonging life. The third is the rapidly increasing need for such technologies as the average age of our national population increases. Within the next twenty or thirty years, a historically unprecedented proportion of our population will be in the fifty-years-and-older category. The need for every form of medical intervention, including coronary bypass procedures, renal transplants, dialysis, even heart and liver transplants, along with other expensive procedures as yet in their infancy, will increase dramatically. Conceivably, a substantial portion of the national wealth could be spent on prolonging the lives of the older people in our midst.

Is this what we want to do? The moralist in us, once again, wants to answer with a resounding yes. The egoist in us is also jubilant: many of us cannot afford the lifesaving procedures we may, before long, require. Yet we must be coolheaded about this. What would a society be like in which the bulk of the social wealth was directed at prolonging life, at wringing another few months of breath out of cruel nature for each of us? More important, what conceivable motivation could we have for focusing our energies on prolonging life?

We have long felt that life is somehow sacred, that more of it is better than less, that we must hang on at all costs for fear of what, or that nothing, comes next. These are time-honored beliefs; if intense and prolonged adherence could make convictions true, they would surely be beyond doubt by now. Yet let me suggest that they are misleading beliefs. It is not so much that they are false as that they direct our attention away from important truths and fixate it on some compelling but insignificant thought.

I am an unqualified admirer of medical technology. I enjoy freedom from pain as much as the next person and feel as grateful as I feel proud that we are in a position to do all we can to make life longer and more bearable for all of us. Yet the development of medical procedures, as the development of much of technology, has outstripped the growth of our wisdom. We know how to do things, but we do not always know when it is appropriate to do them. Our ability to prolong life has naturally put the *why* in the shadow of *how*, and many of us feel that in saving lives we have at last found an unquestionable and superior value.

I want to dissent. I want to say that the emphasis is wrong. Life by itself is not a value; it is only a necessary condition of values. The emphasis should not be on who shall live and for how long but on *how* we shall live and why. In the hackneyed phrase, the fundamental question is not of the length of life but of its quality. And even this is widely misunderstood. In the days when selection committees were screening and approving applicants for dialysis and other advanced procedures, they typically looked for persons who could lead socially useful lives. Social usefulness was defined in terms of their value to society, of what they could contribute to the lives of others. To view the life of an individual in these terms is a gross injustice. If there is anything in the world that is an end in itself, a being whose existence requires no justification, it is the human person. To measure the usefulness of human beings is to degrade them to the level of physical objects, of mere things whose only excuse for being is what they can do for us. Our lives and the quality of our lives must be their own justification. The primary question these boards should have asked was concerning the inner life, the emotive, conative, and sensory possibilities of the individual applicant. If people can lead lives satisfying to themselves, irrespective of their usefulness to others, they have the minimum qualifications for lifesaving surgery.

Evidently, the minimum qualification is sometimes not enough. My only point is that this necessary but not sufficient condition for surgery is not social utility but the quality of individual existence. This quality is seasonal. In spite of the progressive denaturalization of human life, there is an element of biological and psychological change, first growth and then decay—seasonality—left in all of us. Prolongation of life makes sense only in this context of the acknowledged and all-pervasive seasons of human life.

Childhood, the adult years, and old age all have their unique charms and satisfactions. Extraordinary medical intervention is more readily justified in the case of children whom we can restore to normal functioning so that they may taste the joys of adulthood and old age than in the case of old people who have already enjoyed a full career. What could be the motive for going all out for older people? Only respect for their own misshapen belief that another month or year might make an important difference. If, by contrast, they viewed their lives the way everyone is ready to view the life of the hibiscus flower, they might well be satisfied with less than extraordinary means to keep them among us. When fall comes, the blooms fall, and there is something magnificently natural about it all. That we cannot accept this reality is perhaps a greater misfortune than disease and the inability to pay.

Before long, we shall have to make some rational decisions about how much of our social wealth is to be spent on extraordinary measures to keep the older members of our population alive. We cannot indefinitely add costly riders to Medicare and to Medicaid. When the time of decision comes, we may well find that the amount of money we can plow into making advanced medical technology available for all is more limited than even the most pessimistic among us fear. Should this be so, one of the most promising avenues to a rational decision is the one I have briefly explored. Routine medical care should be available to all. If we place heavy emphasis on prevention and make broad use of paramedical professionals, this should not be beyond the means even of a modestly endowed society. But extraordinary medical or surgical intervention at social cost should be available only to those who are not in their terminal season. We should do what is necessary for children and young adults; progressively less for those well into their adult years; and very little that is beyond the routine management of disease for those whose seasons are done.

This might appear a cruel abandonment of the old. It would certainly be that if it did not go hand in hand with vigorous national education. Such an educational effort should aim at helping all of us think of life as a seasonal career justified in terms of its own rich contents and perfections. This would enable the old to do something that under current social circumstances only very few can achieve: to accept their old age with dignity and to view death as a natural and appropriate end to a satisfying life. There have been cultures in which old people felt and thought this way. We do not, and I find little to recommend our current way of thought.

CHAPTER 16

Humane Treatment and the Treatment of Humans

W hen should we treat patients and under what circumstances should we refuse them treatment? In the last ten years or more, there has been a tendency to think of these issues as ethical problems. It is not that physicians had failed to take important values into account or had failed to make conscientious decisions about treatment before then. Such problems stare nurses and physicians in the face daily, and on the whole, decisions have always been made on the basis of habit or intuition in a way that was serious and humane. But lately, the process of decision making has become more explicit. Critical attention has been focused on the reasoning that takes us to our commitments or that, even if it did not generate our conviction, would at least be necessary to justify it.

Raising some issue to the dignity of a moral problem is part of the strategy of preparing for difficult decisions we might have to make. But frequently we do not have any clear criterion to differentiate moral problems from problems of other sorts. As a result, we sometimes declare that we face a moral problem when the choice we must make is not a moral one at all. On other occasions, we miss moral issues altogether, thinking that our problems are technical only, or ones that require nothing beyond professional discretion.

Such errors are distressing enough. But there is one sort even more dangerous. Sometimes we tend to designate certain problems as moral ones not in preparation for difficult decisions. On the contrary, our unconscious aim is to avoid making a decision. The best way to do this, our cunning subconscious long ago discovered, is to call attention to the immense problems we face. This entitles us to engage in the process of considering matters at leisure and in detail. The discussion of the problem, the airing of every alternative view, and the lengthy attempt to determine who is to bear the responsibility for what is decided appear then to be ends in themselves. Throughout it all, we make ourselves believe that we are preparing for the decision and are doing it in a particularly circumspect and responsible fashion. But the process of discussion is not meant to lead anywhere. It is a way of occupying time in a manner that clears our consciences. We hope that in the meantime the problem will simply go away.

A classic case of this is the attitude nurses, physicians, and hospital administrators sometimes take to treatment of hydranencephalic infants. It may be generally agreed that such children have no chance of becoming competitive or of gaining even a modicum of independence or intellectual life. Yet such cases are not infrequently dignified with becoming the subject of ethical grand rounds in the hospital, as if there were a significant moral decision to be made. There is reason to suspect that, in fact, such discussions function only as a screen. Nobody wants to assume the responsibility of taking the only steps that make any sense. While discussions continue, we can avoid making a decision or can at least justify the course we chose as but an interim measure. The typical interim measure may well be to refuse extraordinary treatment to the child, though it is quickly agreed that we cannot refuse food and normal care.

The obvious hope, readily admitted by candid health professionals, is that the infant will develop some infection to which, without treatment, it will succumb. In the meantime, in lieu of any positive action, everyone stands back and trusts that nature will take its course. The pusillanimous unwisdom of this course is tested, as if by the perversity of nature, when instead of succumbing to disease, the creature grows and thrives like any normal child. Soon, the discussions of the moral issue lose their protective function. Soon, no one feels justified, and yet no one dares to make a move. The hospital, the parents, and in the final analysis society end up saddled with a sad burden, sometimes for twenty or thirty years.

My suspicion that raising such a problem to the dignity of a moral issue is a strategy designed to avoid a decision is founded on the conviction that there is, in fact, no serious moral problem here at all. I know that we all feel instinctively repelled by this idea. We think of the history of human inhumanity and are plagued by visions of little lives terminated at will. I share this moral repulsion. But I want to resist the paralysis that immobilizes many of us when we come to life and death decisions in the treatment of others.

As a consequence, what I want to say may appear harsh. I believe that moral decisions invariably involve persons, and the only persons involved in such situations as the one I have just described are the physicians, nurses, parents, and siblings of the patient. The child itself (and to make the point more forcefully, I should not even call it a 'child') is not a person, and the fundamental error of our ways consists in thinking that it is one. The problem underlying our natural error is that we trust what we see and not what we know. We know that personhood involves a repertoire of behaviors, habits, and decisions, along with an internal life. All of these depend on a functioning brain. The hydranencephalic child is altogether without the cortical structures that make the development of such personhood possible. We know that this is so; all the evidence of our experience, of science, and of medicine points in this direction. Yet all of this knowledge comes to naught in the face of the visual appearance of the organism before us. We see that it looks like a human being, and it was born of woman. We simply cannot escape the force of what we see. Our eyes carry the day and we find ourselves naturally inclined to treat the being before us not only in a humane way but also as if it were human.

That this should be so is not accidental. Our emotive mechanisms are engaged by our senses far more forcefully and directly than they are by abstract knowledge. This is useful for human cooperation and survival: it may be the biological basis of sociability. It points to the natural dominion of the emotions over human behavior; in the teeth of such overwhelming power, reason appears impotent. But in the case of some of our medical dilemmas, we face disaster because emotional control has gone too far. The very reason that enables us to save lives is then disregarded in the application of the tools it provides for our use.

When I put the matter in this way to a nurse, she readily agreed. "Yes," she said, "we treat on the basis of our feelings and our eyes, and not with our heads." Nurses who deal with hydranencephalic children typically report that they find it difficult to treat these unfortunate organisms differently from the way they treat normal infants. For the most part, this is just as well. We would not want nurses and physicians in whom reason is detached from human decency to patrol, syringe in hand, the corridors of hospitals.

Yet there are special cases when our senses and our emotions mislead. We sometimes find ourselves imprisoned by the ideas of our senses; inability to escape what we see then limits our choices until we think that nothing can be done, even though in the back of our minds we have the nagging sense that something *must* be done. This paralysis of choice is at least a part of the explanation of the 'gardens' that flourish in our major hospitals, of the thousands of human vegetables we sustain on life-preserving machines without any hope for their recovery.

The mistake we make is best stated perhaps in terms of the confusion between humane treatment and the treatment of humans. We have an obligation to treat all sentient creatures in a humane way. If we have a choice in the matter, we should not cause them pain; if they are in pain, we should do all we reasonably can to still their suffering. Yet this obligation to treat animals in a humane way is not conceived by most of us as tantamount to the obligation to treat them as though they were humans.

A distinguished surgeon once performed an experiment on a dog, as it later turned out, for the sole benefit of my ethics class. The experiment resulted in the death of the dog. When I expressed shock at his action, the surgeon assured me that it was all done very humanely. I prefer to believe that it would never have occurred to him to perform such a wanton and useless experiment on a human being, no matter how humanely it might be carried out.

To treat a being as though it were human is not only to do what we can to minimize its pain but also never voluntarily to cause its death. The fundamental error our senses and emotions cause is to demand that we treat all who look and used to act like human beings as though they continued to be human to the last. Thus human-looking shapes are treated as if they were human, even though they lack the least vestige of human behavior, intellection, or feeling. When we do this, we overlook the fact that the only way to treat such beings humanely is not to treat them as humans. This is but a relatively neutral way of saying what sounds abhorrent to the ear and what I myself shudder to put on paper: they must be mercifully put to death.

I shudder in writing this for four important and valid reasons. The first is that my emotions rebel at the idea of failing to accord full respect to human-looking shapes. This emotional response is easily overruled when I think about the matter in the abstract. But if I imagine myself wielding the deadly needle, my rational conviction wanes and the repulsion is so intense as to make me fear permanent retribution from my conscience.

Second, there is reason to fear that if we permit physicians or nurses to put anyone to death, we may find that the practice quickly develops into a habit. It is perhaps better to bear the cost of thousands of nonpersons indefinitely sustained, if the alternative is to face a growing, gnawing habit on the part of those who should save lives to take them instead, even in the name of mercy.

Third, I dread, no less than anyone else, the possibility of abuse. In the last twenty years we have grown sensitive to how social decisions vary with the status of those they are meant to affect. If we had a system of euthanasia, would decisions be made on a just and uniform basis? Would we not find ourselves tempted to dispose more hastily of indigents, drug addicts and prostitutes than of the stalwart and well-to-do members of the community?

Last, it is horrifying to contemplate the possibility of error. Admittedly, the probability that someone who has been in a coma without significant cortical function for ten years might come around approaches zero. Yet one can say with some conviction that in this context no finite probability is negligible. If there is any chance at all that the human shape can recover its personality, we should perhaps suffer the cost instead of robbing it of this precious possibility.

I write of the importance of merciful euthanasia, nevertheless, because in the end I cannot make myself believe that the unconscious vegetables in our hospitals are in any significant sense human. In the end, I must trust my mind and not my eyes. Admittedly, there is a problem in determining which among the human forms has a continuing potentiality to regain significant human life. This is a hard task, and when in doubt, we should always err on the side of humanity. But there are some cases, such as that of the hydranencephalic child, in which there is and there can be no doubt. With its head full of water, there is no reasonable basis for hope of human life. Pigeons have more personality, the indigo bunting more intellect than this unfortunate mooncalf in our midst.

Our society takes on the burden of its sustained support as though it had no cost. The pain of the parents, the social cost in terms of goods and services, the opportunity cost of what else the services it uses could procure are all disregarded as insignificant. Our fundamental aim appears to be to keep this creature breathing and growing to no end.

I cannot but think that the only humane treatment of such an organism is to refuse to treat it as though it were human. I am not unmindful of the danger of developing the habit to kill. But we foster that habit routinely in the army and in the CIA. Shall we trust our physicians and ourselves less than we trust our soldiers?

And surely, no human practice is free from the potential for abuse. Rules are formulated and agencies are established for their enforcement precisely because we want to minimize abuse and to make it costly to those who seek their own advantage. There is no reason to suppose that adequate safeguards could not be devised to protect all of us from the needle administered too hastily or against our will. It is just that we have never set our minds to devising such controls because we cannot think that it is ever legitimate to terminate a life.

Yet euthanasia is widely practiced in our hospitals. Physicians unplug life-supporting machines routinely. "It's just that we don't enter it as the cause of death on the official papers," a physician friend told me recently. Our current choice is between such uncontrolled, discretionary euthanasia and the occasional paralysis of decision making I have discussed. A formalized system of easing death, predicated on the idea that biological life need not be prolonged indefinitely but incorporating safeguards from abuse, could enable us to choose humane treatment for all. This would indubitably mean the termination of life for some. But the system, if rightly conceived, would not condone murder. For those humanely put to death would not be human beings, only human forms.

CHAPTER 17

Resuscitation

R ené Descartes, writing in the seventeenth century, developed a remarkable view of the nature of time. He thought that time consisted of very small, self-contained units, which one might call 'moments.' These moments come into being and then lapse in individual succession; their isolation from one another makes it impossible for any of them to generate the next. The world exists in some state at any given time, yet that entire state of the world—the world itself—disappears when the moment lapses. All existence is thus discontinuous or granular, and all of us are constantly on the brink of nonbeing.

The notorious fact that things continue to exist—sometimes for far too long—did not escape Descartes. But this persistence of finite, contingent beings is not, he maintained, due to anything they do on their own. For each moment lapses into nothingness, and the distance between nothing and something is infinite. It takes infinite power, therefore, to restore the world to existence for another moment, and such limitless force is the sole property of God. The dependence of the world on God is not, as is often supposed, a one-time affair that leads us back to creation. On the contrary, creation and continued regeneration are indistinguishable: the world is perpetually indebted to God for its life. If God did not resuscitate us all each moment of every day, we simply would not be. We have no independent life. For existence perpetually ceases; it needs the ceaseless efforts of a benevolent being to make it flow.

I start with this fascinating theory not because I wish to resuscitate Descartes long after God failed to see the point of doing so, but in order to use Descartes's theory of dependent world existence as a conceptual model for understanding the relation of patients in certain circumstances to the health team ministering to their needs. It is unnecessary to spend time arguing how very much depends on proper conceptualization. Clearly, diagnosis in morality, no less than in medicine, is altogether a matter of reading what the symptoms mean or recognizing what something is, that is, bringing the right concepts to bear on a problematic situation.

Now contrast the theory of dependent existence with a view of the independence of human operations. Aristotle maintained that each human being is a substance. Substances are self-complete, one might say ultimate, units of existence. Each is a source and locus of activity and bears unactualized, sometimes unpredictable, promise. They are fully real and continue to exist without external aid. It is not that Aristotle thought humans never die. They clearly do, but in the meantime they are spinning tops moving of their own momentum to fulfill their own purposes. If a substance needs help, it is only to change or improve its circumstances; its life is a continuous fire for which it knows how to gather wood.

Although this description may appear abstract, it represents clearly enough our ordinary view of daily life. Under normal circumstances, each of us operates as an independent individual. However closely our lives intersect in the economic and the social spheres, biologically at least we are nearly substances. We rely on no one to move or to eat; our dependence on others is optional or tangential, or at least nonessential and passing. The critical distinction between doing and suffering change, activity and passivity, so neatly reflected in our language by the quality called voice, active and passive, is itself grounded in the notion of an independent agent trading blows with the world.

The moral distinctions we draw between doing and letting happen and between commission and omission make sense only in the context of viewing individuals as self-sustaining agents. Active intervention and forbearance are different, and morally different, because of the way they relate us to an autonomous other, to someone who invites our efforts or insists on being left alone. The difference in moral coloration between providing food and standing by while another forages is at least partly a matter defined by the other's choice and need. But unless one thinks of others as beings capable of getting their own nourishment, the distinction becomes senseless or impossible.

We can either give people money or let them earn it themselves. But this once again presupposes that they can, at least in principle, get some by their own efforts; the moral situation is altogether different if they cannot get it on their own, no matter what they do. The same is true in the case when physicians choose to intervene or withhold treatment. The very presence of the alternatives as potentially moral courses of conduct presupposes a relatively intact organism, one that can—at least in principle—pull through on its own. The situation is vastly different when the patient is completely helpless.

The classic case of the person who has lost independent, self-sustaining status is that of the patient suffering cardiac arrest. Here the physician's role approximates that of Descartes's God. The patient's life has already lapsed; without resuscitation, death is permanent. Is there a moral difference here between doing and permitting to happen? Imagine Descartes's God attempting to justify His decision not to recreate the world by claiming that He was simply letting the world do it on its own. Since it is well known, and particularly well known to God, that the world cannot do it alone, would we not hold Him responsible for the darkness that ensued?

The moral situation between two individuals is critically affected by their dependence-relations to each other. In the case of two independent, interacting agents, normally neither can be held responsible for what he or she did not cause. But when an individual is totally dependent on the other, to cause and to condone become indistinguishable. It is not an adequate defense against the charge of starving an infant that one was permitting it dietary freedom. Similarly, no one remains blameless for failing to remove his quadriplegic mother from a burning house if his only excuse is that he did not cause the fire, and once it spread, he made room for her to get out rapidly. The point is stronger than that dependence generates special responsibilities. It obliterates moral distinctions that are valid in other contexts, and we find ourselves equally blameworthy whether we bring about or just fail to prevent.

Patients in need of resuscitation are in circumstances best conceptualized in terms of Descartes's world-recreative God. Their lapsed existence places them totally at the mercy of the health care team. As a result, its members have special obligations to them and confront a situation in which they are morally responsible for death (if allowed to become permanent without countervailing efforts), even though they did not directly kill anyone. Where resuscitation is possible, killing and letting die are morally equivalent, and this equivalence derives from the utter existential dependence built into the relationship. In this context, killing and letting die accomplish the same end; only the amount of effort required may differ. For it may appear that killing people takes positive effort, whereas not resuscitating them is a matter simply of standing by. Although to those of underdeveloped sensitivity the felt effort of the murder may suggest a deeper difference, variability of motor output is morally irrelevant.

The patient to be resuscitated is only one, no doubt a particularly poignant one, among many cases of extreme existential dependence. If we take this as our paradigm, a broad spectrum of situations resembling it emerges. Typically, the circumstances of individuals in comas, of patients in intensive care units or under anesthesia in the operating room, of persons suffering from some form of severe mental dysfunction, and of older people in advanced stages of psychophysical deterioration are best conceptualized in terms of Cartesian total dependency. To think of them on the Aristotelian model as self-sustaining agents is inaccurate and invites misapprehension about our moral relations to them. Their complete dependence combined with their helpless reliance on those professionally committed to their care places members of the health care team in a precarious moral position.

Now something truly remarkable emerges. Physicians do not normally find it difficult to write orders not to resuscitate. But they frequently report inability or unwillingness to take positive steps to terminate life. This peculiar juxtaposition is reflected on the level of theory: there appears little difficulty in formulating generally acceptable criteria and guidelines for orders not to resuscitate,* while there is widespread condemnation even of the suggestion that active euthanasia is, on occasion, an appropriate course to follow.

If my argument concerning the conceptualization of the circumstances of dependent patients is correct, this discrepancy is irrational. The illusion that there is a difference between killing dependent patients entrusted to one's care and merely permitting them to expire is fostered by the error of thinking of them in terms of Aristotelian, self-moving substances. If they were such agents, killing them would

---

* Mitchell B. Rabkin, Gerald Gillerman, and Nancy R. Rice, "Orders not to Resuscitate," *New England Journal of Medicine* 295 (1976): 364-66.

indeed constitute an unjustifiable intervention. By contrast, letting them die may be defensible as respectful forbearance from interfering in the life processes of another.

But the moral facts will not bear this interpretation. The helpless dependence of one's charges renders active euthanasia indistinguishable from its passive variety. Consequently, if we know when not to resuscitate, we also know when active euthanasia is appropriate. If we have clear criteria for when to write orders not to resuscitate, we also have, tacitly at least, clear criteria for when to initiate the termination of patients. And finally, if we can develop socially acceptable rules for nonresuscitation, then we can also develop morally and socially defensible rules for mercy killing.

The view that reasons for nonresuscitation are at once reasons for mercy killing may be interpreted as supporting indiscriminate resuscitation. For if we think that euthanasia is never justified, we are simultaneously committed to the belief that orders not to resuscitate are always wrong. The opposite view appears more defensible to me partly because I think it possible to establish on independent grounds that, under certain limited circumstances, euthanasia is not only permissible but obligatory. In addition, I have a deep respect for natural and established human practice. The ease and good conscience with which orders not to resuscitate are handled reveal the good sense of people unconfused by moralistic scruples.

But whichever way one uses the moral identity of nonresuscitation and murder, its discovery demonstrates a curious halfheartedness in the practice of many physicians. Incomplete reflection on their principles has led these persons to believe that there is no rational objection to writing orders not to resuscitate while refusing to participate in active forms of euthanasia. The positive outcome of seeing that the two are of one piece may be the realization that, in the principles governing nonresuscitation, we already have everything needed to articulate a defensible system of mercy killing.

CHAPTER 18

Active Euthanasia

There are times when we understand something full well, yet our feelings do not permit us to act on what we know. Love, for example, clouds the rational faculty and makes it difficult to treat adorable scoundrels in the way they deserve. Similarly, when winds of jealousy drive us to horrendous deeds, we know better, yet our knowledge is ineffectual.

The impotence of intelligence may not be surprising in the sphere of private emotions. But it should evoke amazement and concern when cases of it invade institutional life and establish dominance over some of our practices. Yet that is precisely what has happened with our treatment of certain categories of severely impaired infants and of some groups of adults at the distant edge of life.

Consider the condition of hydranencephaly. This tragic congenital abnormality affects a relatively small number of infants, but those suffering from it bear the burden of being born without their cerebral hemispheres. The appearance and behavior of many of these newborns mock our feelings: they look normal and display the natural reflexes of children of their age. But they never grow into people who can take their place in the human community. An intact cerebellum and brain stem enable them to fulfill basic biological functions and to experience pain. Yet the absence of a cortex and associated structures makes it impossible for them to mature into anything we recognize as human. They cannot even reach the level of self-sustaining and independently operating animals. A light behind the head shows only water where the brain should be. Without this instrument of perception and response, they cannot think, cannot learn, cannot communicate. To break a mother's heart, they grow and show a fleeting smile. But the smile *means* nothing, and their lives, measured in months and sometimes years, bring them more than their share of misery.

Consider next the condition of deep coma caused by irreversible damage to the brain. People who have been in a persistent vegetative state for, say, twenty years, are totally unresponsive to stimuli. It is difficult to think that anything other than fundamental biological processes go on in their bodies. They lie in bed without perception and purposive motion. Their expressionless eyes, their frozen faces, their unnatural calm belie their human appearance; because these people lack the spontaneous movement we associate with life, the Ancients would say that their souls have fled. Their vital organs slowly atrophy, and their brains shrivels to the size of an English walnut.

In both cases, we *know* something . Although professional skeptics can always raise questions about the warrant for our certainty, it is fair to say that if we know anything at all, we know this: that people suffering from such grievous afflictions have neither present nor future. There is no significant doubt that a functioning brain is the biological ground of personality, of satisfaction, of a human life. We know that the hydranencephalic child has no chance of growing a cortex in its cranium. We know that after twenty years in a coma, no one gets out of bed, dusts himself off, and calls a friend for lunch. We know not only that such things have never happened but also that if there is anything to the idea that nature is governed by laws, they never will.*

We *know* all these things with such assurance that in any other sphere of life, we would not hesitate to act on them. What astounds is that in our treatment of these unfortunate people, our knowledge appears to make no difference to our practice. By an elaborate charade, we deal with them as though they were full-fledged human beings whose future imposes pressing obligations on us. We serve and sustain them the way children do their dolls, believing perhaps in the darkest recesses of our fancy that they have thoughts and wishes and human needs. Moreover, we think that in doing this, we do what is right and good, and we justify this idea by refusing to acknowledge that there can be a distinction between those that merely look human

---

* It is, of course, not impossible for them to happen, but no one jumps out the window on the basis that it is not impossible for her to fly.

and those who are.

Such irrationalities in our behavior could be justified as discretionary aberrations if they caused no harm. But they do immeasurable damage. The hydranencephalic child can suffer pain, and often does. It is not the pain we undergo in the process of experience, which may be justified by the maturation to which it leads. It is unredeemed and useless pain that does no one any good. The parents suffer also: their lot is the devastation that comes of having to reconcile the contradiction between promise and hopelessness their baby represents. Members of the health care team suffer when their natural sympathy for the infant is combined with the recognition that nothing they can do is of any use. The entire community is injured by this tragic misallocation of resources that channels hundreds of thousands of dollars away from meeting the needs of the living to the care of the living dead.

The situation is not very different with those in a persistent vegetative state. Although we presume that they suffer little pain, the people around them pay a high price. Their families are particularly deeply affected, exhausting their emotional and financial resources in caring for a relative they cannot benefit. The fictive obligation to support the biological remnants of their loved ones has nearly destroyed many spouses and parents and children. And the nurses and assistants in daily contact with the comatose find themselves depressed or else become callous to the grotesque horror of the 'gardens' they tend.

Despite the vast harm our actions cause, we persist in maintaining a significant number of biological remnants not just past the point of appropriateness or decency but indefinitely. This is all the more remarkable because there are no intellectually respectable arguments for such an unqualified and uncritical commitment. Of course, we do not lack causes for our behavior. It is only that these fail to add up to good reasons for what we do.

Faced with the blatant senselessness of our practices, some philosophers have developed a strategy for chipping away at them indirectly. Noting that we have relatively little trouble with passive euthanasia, thinkers such as James Rachels have attempted to argue that there is no moral difference between letting people die and killing them. If we are prepared at a certain point to withhold further treatment, they imply, we should also be ready to take positive steps to hasten death. Understanding the moral equivalence of passive and active euthanasia should, in this way, expose the inconsistency of our beliefs and nudge us in the direction of a more rational policy in dealing with the bodies of people who lack consciousness and are not likely to regain it.

This indirect strategy suffers from a fatal flaw. In the context we have been considering, passive euthanasia is wrong and active euthanasia right, and this surely amounts to a significant moral difference. To cling indefinitely to the sad remnants of human life is a grotesque ritual. When this exercise, bought at a high price in suffering, secures no present or future good for those it is supposed to benefit, it is clearly wrong. Abhorrent as it may seem to terminate the biological existence of human-appearing forms, it is a far less evil alternative than to let the suffering go on. There is something callous and cowardly about prolonging the agony of a helpless infant and of everyone around it while we wait for an infection to take its life.

In this respect, the hydranencephalic child is instructively different from one with short-gut syndrome. Many young people suffering from the latter tragic condition are otherwise perfectly normal. Although their lives with their parents are saturated by the sadness of an early and inevitable parting, they can in the meantime enjoy the natural pleasures of childhood. One may, accordingly, argue that prolonging their existence benefits them and is, on balance, unlikely to harm their parents. By obvious contrast, nothing in the lives of hydranencephalics is worth preserving: the absence of sustained consciousness and of intelligence removes the foundation, the very possibility, of value.

There is a similar difference between those in an irreversible vegetative state and old people suffering from a terminal disease. Although neither has a significant future, the latter can at least enjoy some elements of the present and look with satisfaction on the past. I acknowledge that the time may come when even such conscious and intelligent lives cease to be worth their price in suffering. But that is a decision only the concerned individual can make. The point about those in a persistent vegetative state is precisely that they are unable to make the choice, and this very inability reveals that when their biological functioning ceases, nothing is lost. The human element in them, whatever renders us worthy of being treated as ends, has long slipped away.

This last comment underscores the fact that active euthanasia of those without mental life is morally right not only on the basis of utilitarian calculations. Even if the foundation of morality is respect for persons, the biological remnants of human life should be cleared away. Organisms without intelligence and consciousness are persons or the bodies of persons no more than are figures in a wax museum. To be sure, biological function is important, but only because it is a natural condition of higher activities, while wax compressed into human shapes is not. When an organism is unable to ground personality or other significant conscious activities, its biological processes become morally neutral. In terminating them, we do not destroy a person. Instead, we show due respect for the condition and concerns of connected living people.

I want to stress that this principle of actively removing biological remnants cannot and should not be extended to cases where there is significant doubt or significant life. For example, many human beings who remain in a coma for months eventually regain consciousness. It would be unforgivable to deny them the opportunity for renewed life by some hasty action. Similarly, people whose existence—though short and painful—is acceptable to them must be left to enjoy it as best they can. My argument justifies, accordingly, no large-scale system of exterminations in the name of mercy.

Yet the imperative to reject active euthanasia if there is a reasonable chance of error does not imply that we can never act. And the moral requirement that we leave those who are conscious and self-possessed to make their own decisions is perfectly compatible with the periodic need to help some bodies speedily reach the state where nature carries them in a halting but inevitable way. Caution in deciding when action is appropriate is best combined with decisiveness and good conscience once the choice is made. Obviously, no one person should be in a position to decide such matters. Relatives, other interested persons, and the entire health care team must be canvassed over a period of days or weeks to eliminate the possibility of haste and abuse.

A system of such carefully limited active euthanasia offers numerous benefits. I select only four for brief attention. First, instituting it would involve a significant reduction of suffering. I have already discussed this and will add nothing further at the present time.

Second, it would enhance our honesty by bringing an existing but irregular practice out of the closet. That a significant number of physicians now condone or engage in active euthanasia is an open secret. But for legal and other reasons, a cloak of secrecy surrounds such activities, casting moral disrepute on them, making them unavailable when most needed, and rendering selective criticism of them impossible.

Third, the system would take decision making out of the power of individuals who now singlehandedly practice it. It would establish reliable, public procedures and public accountability for our choices and render a sad but occasionally necessary service generally available.

Last and most important, it could constitute the long overdue first step in reassessing our ideas concerning the value of purely biological existence. Reflective people generally agree that the growth of our moral ideas has not kept pace with the rapid development of the instruments that enable us to keep organisms functioning for long periods after their properly human activities cease. Unfortunately, however, not many understand that an important part of the reason for this is our failure to realize that ethical principles themselves constitute tools for the solution of problems. They are a sort of technology that is, accordingly, as much in need of development as our life-sustaining machines and our lab equipment. The time has come to devote substantial energy to sharpening and upgrading these moral and conceptual instruments so that we may be able to deal with our pressing problems in a more humane and more rational way.

We find absolute prohibitions, such as that against taking life, in important and revealing places in the human world. They express the dread primitive people felt toward certain actions, their dim perception of the danger of allowing any exceptions to certain rules. They occupy, accordingly, a position near the center of what makes for civilized life; they limit or govern sexual practices, the interaction of members in a family and our treatment of the sick and the disabled, along with our behavior toward the dying and the living dead.

In the course of time, appropriate emotions come to surround such absolute prohibitions. These feelings make it virtually impossible for us to do what good sense, reason, morality, or even minimal decency demand in certain situations if the required action is in violation of the unconditional rule. This may well explain persisting irrational behavior—why in some spheres we act in ways that fly in the face of what we know.

Absolute rules are useful, maybe even essential, in directing behavior within primitive societies where reason has not as yet succeeded in organizing life, where knowledge of nature is lacking, and where constructive moral reflection has not settled into a social habit. But ours is not such a world. In our institutional life, we have managed to isolate reason from the vagaries of the emotions and the imagination. We prize intelligence and look for hard knowledge to solve the problems of the world. Public education and effective media of communication assure that our beliefs are critically examined and that new findings are widely disseminated. Medicine, in particular, insists on objectivity: even those who see our society as pervaded by ancient, irrational rituals must admit that the way we deal with sickness constitutes a modern, enlightened, rational corner of it.

In our world, at least, absolute rules are neither necessary nor useful. On the contrary, they tend to obstruct the progress of morality and sometimes forbid the very actions basic decency demands. That is precisely where we stand with the unconditional prohibition of active euthanasia. It would be a cruel irony if the most rational profession in an enlightened society were not allowed to make decisions about sustaining and terminating life on a case-by-case basis.

CHAPTER 19

When Abstract Moralizing
Runs Amok

Moral reasoning is more objectionable when it is abstract than when it is merely wrong. For abstractness all but guarantees error by missing the human predicament that needs to be addressed, and worse, it is a sign that thought has failed to keep faith with its mission. The function of moral reflection is to shed light on the difficult problems we face; it cannot perform its job without a clear understanding of how and why certain of our practices come to seem no longer satisfactory.

This grasp of the problem is conspicuously lacking in Daniel Callahan's assault on euthanasia in "Self-Determination Run Amok."* The rhetoric unleashed on euthanasia and assisted suicide gives not even a hint of the grave contemporary moral problems these practices, a growing number of people now think, promise to resolve.

Instead, we are offered a set of abstract distinctions calculated to discredit euthanasia rather than to contribute to a sound assessment of its value. Thus Callahan informs us that suffering "brought on by illness and dying as biological phenomena"† is to be contrasted with suffering that comes from "anguish or despair at the human condition." The former constitutes the proper concern of medicine (so much for psychiatry!), the latter of religion and philosophy. Medication is the answer to physical pain; euthanasia can, therefore, be only a misconceived response to worries about the meaning of existence.

---

* Daniel Callahan, "Self-Determination Run Amok," *Hastings Center Report* 22 (March-April 1992): 52–55.
  † Callahan, 55.

Those who believe in it offer a "swift lethal injection" as the "answer to the riddle of life."

This way of putting the matter will come as a surprise to people who suffer from terrible diseases and who no longer find life worth living. It is grotesque to suppose that they are looking for the meaning of existence and find it, absurdly, in a lethal injection. Their predicament is not intellectual but existential. They are interested not in seeking the meaning of life but in acting on their belief that their own continued existence is, on balance, of no further benefit to them.

Euthanasia and assisted suicide are proposed answers to a serious and growing social problem. We now have the power to sustain the biological existence of large numbers of very sick people, and we use this power freely. Accordingly, individuals suffering from painful terminal diseases, Alzheimer's patients, and those in a permanent vegetative state are routinely kept alive long past the point where they can function as human beings. They must bear the pain of existence without the ability to perform the activities that give life meaning. Some of these people feel intensely that they are a burden to others as well as to themselves and that their speedy and relatively dignified departure would be a relief to all concerned. Many sensitive and thoughtful observers agree that the plight of these patients is severe enough to justify such desires.

Some of these sufferers are physically not in a position to end their lives. Others could do so if they had the necessary instruments. In our culture, however, few have a taste for blowing out their brains or jumping from high places. That leaves drugs, which almost everyone is accustomed to taking, and which everyone knows can ease one peacefully to the other side.

The medical profession has, however, acquired monopoly power over drugs. And the danger of legal entanglement has made physicians wary of helping patients speed their death in the discreet, humane way that has been customary for centuries. The result is that people who want to die and for whom death has long ceased to be an evil can find no way out of their misery. Current and growing pressures on medicine to help such sufferers are, therefore, due at least partly to medicine itself. People want physicians to aid in their suicides because without such help they cannot end their lives. This restriction of human autonomy is due to the social power of medicine; it is neither surprising nor morally wrong, therefore, to ask those responsible for this limitation to undo some of its most noxious effects. If medicine relinquished its hold on drugs, people could make effective choices about their future without the assistance of physicians. Even limited access to deadly drugs, restricted to single doses for those who desire them and who are certified to be of sound mind and near the end of life, would keep medicine away from dealing death.

Unfortunately, however, there is little sensible public discussion of such policy alternatives. And they may, in any case, not satisfy Callahan, who appears to believe that something is radically wrong with anyone terminating a human life. Because he plays coy, his actual beliefs are difficult to make out. He says the notion that self-determination extends to suicide "might be pertinent, at least for debate."* But his argument against euthanasia sidesteps this issue: he maintains that even if there is a right to kill oneself, it is not one that can be transferred. The reason for this is that doing so would lead to "a fundamental moral wrong," that of one person giving over "his life and fate to another."

One might wonder how we know that transferring power over oneself is a fundamental moral wrong. Callahan appears to entertain the idea with intuitive certainty, which gives him the moral and the logical high ground and entitles him to demand a justification from whoever disagrees. But such intuitions are problematic themselves: is fervent embrace of them enough to guarantee their truth? Morality would be very distant from the concerns of life if it depended on such guideposts placed here and there in the desert of facts, unrelated to one another or to anything else. Their message, moreover, makes the guideposts suspect: it comes closer to being an echo of tradition or an expression of current views than a revelation of eternal moral truths.

Most important, the very idea of a right that intrinsically *cannot* be handed on is difficult to grasp. Under normal circumstances, to have a right is to be free or to be entitled to have or to do something. I have a right, for example, to clean my teeth. No one else has the right to do that without my consent. But I can authorize another, say, my sweetheart or my dental hygienist, to do it for me. Similarly, I can assign my right to my house, to my left kidney, to raising my children, to deciding when I rise, when I go to sleep, and what I do in between (by joining the army), and by a power of attorney even to pursuing my own interest.

* Callahan, 52.

To be sure, the transfer of rights is not without limits. For example, my wife and I can give over our right to our children, though we cannot do so for money. I can contract to slave away for ten hours a day cooking hamburgers, but I cannot sell myself to be, once and for all, a slave. This does not mean, however, that some rights are intrinsically nontransferable. If my right to my left kidney were such, I could neither sell it nor give it away. But I can give it away, and the only reason I cannot sell it is that sales of this sort were declared, at some point, to be against public policy. We cannot sell ourselves into slavery for the same reason: human societies set limits to this transfer of rights on account of its unacceptable costs.

The case is no different with respect to authorizing another to end my life. If I have a right to one of my kidneys, I have a right to both. And if I can tell a needy person to take one of them, I can tell two needy people to take one each. There is nothing *intrinsically* immoral about this, even though when the second helps himself, I die. Yet by dying too soon, I may leave opportunities unexplored and obligations unmet. Unscrupulous operators may take advantage of my goodwill or naiveté. The very possibility of such acts invites abuse. For these or similar reasons, we may decide that giving the first kidney is morally acceptable, but giving the second is not. The difference between the two acts, however, is not that the first is generous while the second is "a fundamental moral wrong," but that the second occurs in a context and has consequences and costs that the first does not.

Only in terms of context and cost, therefore, can we sensibly consider the issue of the morality of euthanasia. Moving on the level of abstract maxims, Callahan misses this point altogether. He declares that "there are no good moral reasons to limit euthanasia once the principle of taking life . . . has been legitimated."* Serious moral reflection, though it takes principles into account, is little interested in legitimating *them*. Its focus is on determining the moral acceptability of certain sorts of actions performed in complex contexts of life. Consideration of the circumstances is always essential: it is fatuous, therefore, to argue that if euthanasia is ever permissible, then "any competent person should have a right to be killed by a doctor for any reason that suits him."†

We can achieve little progress in moral philosophy without the

---

* Callahan, 54.   † Callahan.

ability and readiness to make relevant distinctions. Why, then, does Callahan refuse to acknowledge that there are important differences between the situation of a terminal patient in grave pain who wants to die and that of a young father in the dental chair who wishes, for a moment, that he were dead? His reason is that he thinks all judgments about the unbearability of suffering and the worthlessness of one's existence are subjective and, as such, parts of a "private, idiosyncratic view of the good life."* The amount of our suffering "has very little directly to do" with our physical condition, and so the desire to end life is capricious and unreliable. If medicine honored such desires, it would "put its own vocation at risk" by serving "the private interests" of individuals.

I cannot imagine what the vocation of medicine might be if it is not to serve the private interests of individuals. It is, after all, my vision of the good life that accounts for my wish not to perish in a diabetic coma. And surgeons certainly pursue the private interests of their patients in removing cancerous growths and in providing face-lifts. Medicine does not surrender its vocation in serving the desires of individuals: since health and continued life are among our primary wishes, its career consists in just this service.

Nevertheless, Callahan is right that our judgments about the quality of our lives and about the level of our suffering have a subjective component. But so do the opinions of patients about their health and illness, yet physicians have little difficulty in placing these perceptions in a broader, objective context. Similarly, it is both possible and proper to take into account the objective circumstances surrounding desires to terminate life. Physicians have developed considerable skill in relating subjective complaints to objective conditions; only by absurd exaggeration can we say that the doctor must accept either every claim of the patient or none. The context of the young father in the dental chair makes it clear that only a madman would think of switching from Novocain to cyanide when he moans that he wants to be dead. Even people of ordinary sensitivity understand that the situation of an old person all of whose friends have died and who now suffers the excruciating pain of terminal cancer is morally different.

The question of the justifiability of euthanasia, as all difficult moral questions, cannot be asked without specifying the details of context. Dire warnings of slippery slopes and of future large-scale, quietly

* Callahan, 52.

conducted exterminations trade on overlooking differences of circumstance. They insult our sensitivity by the suggestion that a society of
individuals of goodwill cannot recognize situations in which their fellows want and need help and tell them apart from those in which the
desire for death is rhetorical, misguided, temporary, or idiotic. It
would, indeed, be tragic if medicine leapt to the aid of lovelorn
teenagers whenever they feel life is too much to bear. But it is just as
lamentable to stand idly by and watch unwanted lives fill up with
unproductive pain.

Callahan is correct in pointing out that in euthanasia and in
assisted suicide, the physician and the patient must have separate justifications for action. The patient's wish is defensible if it is the outcome of a sound reflective judgment. Such judgments take into
account the current condition, pending projects, and long-term
prospects of individuals and relate them to their permanent interests
and established values. As all assessments, these can be in error.
Consequently, persons soliciting help in dying must be ready to
demonstrate that they are of sound mind and thus capable of making
such choices, that their desire is enduring, and that both their subjective and their objective conditions render their wish sensible.

Physicians must first decide whether their personal values permit
them to participate in such activities. If they do, they must diligently
examine the justifiability of the patient's desire to die. Diagnosis and
prognosis are often relatively easy to ascertain. But we are not without resources for a sound determination of the internal condition of
individuals either: extensive questioning on multiple occasions, inter-
views with friends and loved ones, exploration of the life history and
values of people contribute mightily to understanding their state of
mind. Physicians who are prepared to aid individuals with this last
need of their lives are not, therefore, in a position where they have to
believe everything they hear and act on every request. They must
make independent judgments instead of subordinating themselves as
unthinking tools to the passing desires of those they wish to help.
This does not attribute to doctors "the powers of the gods"; it only
requires that they be flexible in how they aid their patients and that
they do so with due caution and on the basis of sound evaluation.

Callahan is once again right to be concerned that if allowed,
euthanasia will "take place within the boundaries of the private and
confidential doctor-patient relationship."* This does, indeed, invite
abuse and permit callous physicians to take a casual attitude to a

momentous decision. But Callahan is wrong in supposing that it constitutes an argument against euthanasia. It is only a reason not to keep euthanasia secret, to shed on it the wholesome light of publicity. Though the decision to terminate life is intensely private, no moral consideration demands that it be kept the confidential possession of two individuals. To the contrary, the only way we can minimize wrong decisions and abuse is to require scrutiny of the decision, prior to action on it, by a suitable social body. Such examination, including at least one personal interview with the patient, should go a long distance toward relieving Callahan's concern that any law governing euthanasia would have "a low enforcement priority in the criminal justice system." With formal social controls in place, there should be very little need for the involvement of courts and prosecutors.

To suppose, as Callahan does, that the principle of autonomy calls for us to stand idly by, or even to assist, whenever and for whatever reason people want to end their lives is calculated to discredit both euthanasia and autonomy. No serious moralist has ever argued that self-determination must be absolute. It cannot hold unlimited sway, as Mill and other advocates of the principle readily admit, if humans are to live in a society. And morally, it would cut no ice if murderers and rapists argued for the legitimacy of their actions by claiming that they flow naturally and solely from who they are.

The function of the principle is to affirm *a* value and to shift the burden of justifying infringements of individual liberty to established social and governmental powers. The value it affirms is that of individual agency: the belief that through action and suffering and death, the life of each person enjoys a sort of private integrity. This means that in the end our lives belong to no one but ourselves. The limits to such self-determination or self-possession are set by the demands of social life. They can be discovered or decided upon in the process of moral reflection. A sensible approach to euthanasia can disclose how much weight autonomy carries in that context and how it can be balanced against other, equally legitimate but competing values.

In the hands of its friends, the principle of self-determination does not run amok. What runs amok in Callahan's version of autonomy and euthanasia is the sort of abstract moralizing that forgets the problem it sets out to address and shuts its eyes to need and suffering.

* Callahan, 54.

CHAPTER 20

On Selling Organs

To persons with a diagnostic ear, the question "Should people be allowed to sell one of their kidneys?" is oddly reminiscent of questions like "Should ten-year-old girls be allowed to wear lipstick?" Questions of this latter sort, it is good to remind ourselves, used to be asked and debated seriously not so many years ago. Paternalism in government and paternalism in the home are intimately connected. In fact, the growth of parental permissiveness may well be a result of the growing dominance of the public sector: if we let government set our goals and provide our education, why should we not surrender to it the task of defining what is proper and of determining the standards of child behavior?

Yet people who would sell or lease an organ are not ten-year-olds who stay out, ready to be corrupted, after dark. Whose business is it if they freely and knowingly contract to have an eye removed in return for a house or a car or a trip to Rio? Such agreements, as all contracts that involve harm only to the free, intelligent, adult contracting parties, should be in the sacred domain of private decision making. Yet increasing government interference in all spheres of life has prepared us to accept any stricture and any ban as legitimate if only it is justified by reference to a compelling state or public interest.

How do we know what is in the public interest? We place politicians and judges on the public payroll to help us decide. One could present a plausible argument that many of these individuals do everything in their power to come up with reasonable and defensible results. But there are two problems. Too often, there are clear limits to the intellectual power of many of these officials. The pressures are great and time is limited: without a crystal clear conception of constitutional principles and of the proper limits of the law, even the most circumspect of persons can become party to silly or oppressive legislation.

Second, the very notion of a public interest is general and nebulous. There are, to be sure, relatively uncontroversial parts to it: people tend to agree, for example, that individuals must be protected from criminal interference in their affairs and that society as a whole must be protected from external aggression. But it is by no means clear whether tax-financed abortions for welfare mothers are or are not in the public interest. In contested cases, we develop our position by resorting to our ideas of what human nature is or ought to be, or perhaps of what our society was meant to be or may yet become. In this way, there is a real danger that the definition of the public interest may be deeply influenced by the unexamined value commitments of politicians and judges.

Why should we think that it is against the public interest to permit sale or lease of the body? Let us make no mistake about it: all we can ever lease or sell in order to earn a living is a part or a function or a skill of the body. Lecturers rent a trained larynx properly hooked to a brain, dentists skilled hands, unskilled laborers the power of their muscles. In addition to such short-term rentals of a dentist's skill as is involved in filling a cavity, we permit long-term leasing of certain body functions. Exxon provides contracts to researchers, Harvard to university professors, and the local country club to its golf pro on the basis of the special skills of special portions of their bodies. The law is completely irrational in permitting the long-term lease of private parts as an element in the contract of marriage while forbidding their short-term rental in prostitution.

Those who claim to have direct access to the public interest argue that legalizing prostitution would place the lower classes at an unfair disadvantage. For, they tell us, it would make it too tempting for too many of the uneducated to choose lives of degradation. But this is an incredibly bad argument. It assumes, contrary to fact, that the desire for easy money through fun is restricted to the poor. Moreover, it falls prey to the danger I noted above, of defining the public interest by reference to pre-existing and unexamined private value commitments. There is little reason to believe that a deliberately chosen life of whoredom is any more degrading than, say, a life of begging for money or of pumping septic tanks. At least the activities in which prostitutes engage are naturally enjoyable; by contrast, few derive orgiastic pleasure from sorting Amtrak tickets.

Not only would legalizing prostitution not harm the poor, it is precisely its proscription that puts them at a competitive disadvantage. The current ban denies the poor and the relatively unskilled the use of possibly their only asset that commands a premium. We permit singers and tree surgeons to collect fees for exercising their skilled parts. But we forbid the uneducated to use the skills and organs that could provide them with a comfortable living and perhaps help them escape the treadmill of poverty. My point is not whimsical: the poor do not wish to be saved for morality. They consider it oppressive that the only route to affluence open to some of them is at once the road to jail.

Perhaps the reason why the sale of body organs is said to be against the public interest is that it involves individuals doing harm to themselves, or at least permitting or inviting that such harm be done. But if this principle were consistently applied, it would require us to ban auto racing, football, and the Marine Corps. Yet one might reply that in these professions all one incurs is the risk of bodily injury, not its certainty. But in professional boxing and in wrestling, this risk amounts to a certainty; only the magnitude of the damage is at stake.

What is the magnitude of the damage in selling organs? It clearly depends on the organ sold and on the quality of the medical care employed in the necessary procedures. In recognition of the realities, we used to have blood banks that paid an agreed fee per pint of blood. When moralistic legislation outlawed such honest contracts, buyers of blood continued their activity but relabeled it as the purchase of plasma. We also pay donors for their sperm. There is no pain involved in the sale of sperm; to sell blood is at most an inconvenience. To sell a kidney is very much more cosmic, yet most of those who freely give one to a child or to a sibling have survived the operation and lead healthy lives.

Does the state have the right to deny people the opportunity to benefit from the sale of their most or only salable asset? The answer must be no. To deny individuals the opportunity to trade on whatever assets they have is to discriminate against them unfairly. The moralistic point that this would place a dollar value on human health and life is at best naive. As insurance and workmen's compensation adjusters well know, there are socially acceptable schedules of the financial equivalent of each sort of damage and every organ.

The emotional point that organ sales would enable the rich to survive by buying life from the poor is also without force. The rich

already buy life from the poor by hiring private physicians and
nurses, by employing bodyguards and chauffeurs and security per-
sonnel. This may be unfortunate. But it is no more unjust than that
no one had an opportunity equal to mine to marry the woman I did,
even though many would have been happy with her and some will
never be happy without.

But what about the poor when they need organs and cannot afford
them? The answer has to depend on what organs they need and how
desperately. If the need is serious and there is a supply of necessary
organs, the state may well help those less fortunate to pay for the
body parts they must have. The food stamp program and federal
funds for kidney dialysis show that such government activities may,
within limits, be both practicable and humane. Yet probably there
will always be sharp limits to what the government can do to help.
Legalizing the sale of organs is not likely to create a flood of transactions. Dismemberment of self will always be an unpleasant and unat-
tractive way to make a living. As a result, the supply of organs is
likely to remain permanently low. And this, in turn, means that
prices will likely be quite high, a good bit above what legislators will
find it in their hearts to fund with tax money. My argument is not
that people should give or sell parts of their bodies to others. Under
certain circumstances, it may be foolish or even immoral to do so. But
we must recognize that people have a right to sell their organs or portions of their bodies, as a minimum because they are theirs and certainly because no one has the right to stop them from disposing of
their assets as they will. We used to think that our bodies belonged to
God; this sacred notion has now been replaced by its secular variant,
according to which we belong to one another or to the state. One day
we may break through to the radical insight that each adult's body is
his or hers alone.

Government has a legitimate role to play in these matters, though
it is not to forbid people to do what they choose, even if such bans are
justified by high ideals of what is in the public interest. It must protect all of us from unscrupulous profiteers. In the sale of organs, government should look over the shoulders of the contracting parties not
to stop them from doing what they want but to be sure that no one is
defrauded, that consent is truly informed, that lawyers and physicians do not deceive. The message is so simple and so right that I am
embarrassed to say it: the sacred trust of government is to protect us
from one another, not from ourselves.

CHAPTER 21

Personal Relations Between Physicians and Patients

Anyone who has ever dealt with a child, a car salesman, or an IRS agent knows that good personal relations can be difficult to attain. They are especially problematic and difficult between physicians and their patients for at least two reasons unique to the context of healing and caring.

The first is the inequality inherent in the relation. At least in our system of sick care, patients bring to the encounter symptoms they can neither understand nor manage. The physician, by contrast, offers healing knowledge and lifesaving or at least life-enhancing activity.

The second reason is that the encounter is often saturated with the urgency of disease or at the very least the worry and vulnerability of the patient. The time, the mood, the conditions, even the desire for a personal relationship are absent. To the physician, the patient is necessarily a body—an object. From his or her standpoint, however, the patient is a feeling, suffering being—nearly the only, certainly the most important, subject.

But we must be careful here. When we speak of personal relations, we might mean either one of two things. In one sense, personal relations are those of friendship and intimacy reserved for a few people dear to us. Professional and cash-based and casual connectedness contrast with this sense of what is personal and close.

In another sense, however, personal relations are simply relations between persons, and specifically relations in which we acknowledge that we are related to *persons*, to individual human beings and not to fruit flies, kidneys, or the Pyramids. Although we sometimes treat

199

people as though they were dogs, the proper contrast of personal relations in this sense is with the impersonal treatment we accord to socks, disposable syringes, and cigars.

In analyzing the proper relationship between physicians and patients, I do not find the notion of personal, in the sense of intimate, relations helpful. For there is a fundamental divergence in aim and expectation between physicians and patients on this point: doctors typically seek a professional relation of care without closeness, while many patients want friendship and support in addition to competent advice. As a consequence, neither side is fully satisfied. The physician may believe that friendship and intimacy interfere with a professional relation; the patient, on the other hand, feels that without personal support as its content the professional relation remains cold and empty.

We shall make more headway if we work with the other, relatively modest notion of personal relation, that is, with the idea that the connection between physician and patient is one between thinking and feeling persons. On the face of it, this seems an obvious, if not trivial, starting point. Everyone knows that patients are people and it is clear that even surgeons are not gods. Even though we know this, however, we tend to forget it. One of the points I particularly want to stress is that if we kept it uppermost in mind, our attitudes and our behavior would be profoundly affected.

What, then, is the proper relationship between physicians and their patients? The moment the question is put this boldly, I find myself tempted to frame a sweeping answer. This temptation is part of a professional disease of philosophers. We love elegant theories, cosmic generalizations, universal truths. In the process of enunciating them, we tend, unfortunately, to lose sight of the rich and irreducible diversity of facts. The developing dialogue between philosophy and such professions as medicine is so promising because the sciences and the professions powerfully remind philosophers to attend to facts and to remain humble in their presence. Philosophy, in turn, can help the professions by providing the tools to face courageously and to deal rationally with intractable, ultimate human problems.

Let me, therefore, resist the temptation to give too simple an answer to a difficult question. There is not, there cannot be, a *single* right relation between physicians and patients. Individuals and circumstances differ, and morality consists not in uniformity or even in universal rules, but in the conscientious application of principles to facts. And the facts are intrinsically diverse.

The relation of emergency room doctors to unconscious accident victims, of house staff to people in deep comas, of tertiary care specialists to the persons about whom they are consulted, cannot be assimilated to the relation of family physicians to their lifelong patients. We cannot find compelling similarities between the relation of a surgeon to the person who needs a routine appendectomy and the complex interaction of physician and patient in a chronic disease such as diabetes.

Nothing is lost and much gained if we admit that any model of the physician-patient relationship is just that—an ideal pattern broadly but not universally applicable. The value of such a model is twofold: it provides guidance in the conduct of our affairs, and it requires that deviations from it be justified.

There are three great models of the relation of physicians to patients. All three are, no doubt, of ancient origin. All three are present in our society. I shall discuss each and argue that the first two are inadequate. Only the third, relatively neglected model does justice to the special nature of the healing and caring relation and to the fact that it is a relation between persons.

The expert-ignoramus model

In an important sense, the relation between physicians and patients is one between unequals. Doctors embody knowledge in the fullest signification: they understand disease processes and can engage in preventive, curative, or ameliorative actions on the basis of this understanding. They cannot, of course, reverse every condition. But there is little doubt that medicine is a classic instance of the coincidence of knowledge and action, a field in which cognitive grasp enlightens what we do and successful practices contribute to the expansion of our understanding.

By contrast, patients are essentially ignorant. It is risky to speculate about the level of human ignorance, but I cannot be far from the truth in saying that many people know about as much regarding their bodies as they do concerning the constitution of the stars. As a result, patients are unreliable; frequently, doctors have to bypass them altogether and go for help in healing directly to their more intelligent bodies.

One would like to think that such inequality between physicians and patients is morally irrelevant to their interaction. But this, in fact, is not the way things have been perceived. Knowledge is frequently conceived as the foundation of authority; accordingly, the expertise of physicians has often been thought to confer special rights on them. The prescription of drugs and the performance of complex surgical procedures are exclusive rights granted to doctors, presumably in recognition of their special knowledge and skills. Physicians themselves sometimes suppose that their superior knowledge entitles them to make critical decisions for patients, decisions the patients cannot be expected, trusted, or permitted to make.

Sometimes the special rights are thought to be justified simply by greater wisdom or more information. More often, however, the justification is cast in terms of desirable consequences to be achieved. For the primary responsibility of physicians is to the health and welfare of their patients: if a patient's desires represent an impediment to getting well, the physician is thought fully warranted in disregarding them.

The important notion here is that the doctor becomes the primary decision maker. Patients come to be viewed paternalistically, as though they were children to be humored to a point, but beyond that lectured and overruled. "I want you in the hospital next week," the physician says, while the assistant makes the reservation. On this model, physicians issue edicts in the imperative mood, and the attempts of patients to exercise autonomy is but the recalcitrance of those who do not understand.

Many, though by no means all, physicians have this model in the back of their minds when they deal with their patients. That this is a natural mode of thought is further evidenced by the frustration even those doctors who leave more room for patient autonomy feel when the persons they treat fail to adhere to their regimen or make choices known to be injurious. But in spite of the understandable naturalness of this attitude, the expert-ignoramus model that stands behind it is an inadequate way of conceiving the physician-patient relation.

The reason for this is profoundly important because it resides in human nature. Knowledge has no claim over self-determination. The fact that I possess knowledge may well give me power, but it cannot provide the right to use it without consent to direct the lives of others. We feel comfortable in supposing that what we do is in the best interest of others. But it is crucial to remember that sometimes people prefer not to have what is, in some objective sense, in their best interest. Thus, human welfare and happiness are not exclusively objective affairs; without the subjective element of choice, the most objectively useful things may appear noxious.

Let me make my point with unceremonious simplicity. The opinions of people cannot be left out when we determine what is good for them. In disregarding their views, we do more than affirm the ignorance of patients—we deny their autonomy. To deny autonomy is to disallow the right to make choices, even foolish and wrong ones. And to view others as unworthy or incapable of making choices is to cast their humanity aside.

You can see, then, that this model violates our initial premise that the physician-patient relation is one that obtains between persons. Inequality of knowledge is rendered irrelevant by the equality of the parties as persons. It is worth remarking that God, who knew even more than the average internist, permitted Adam, who, being afflicted with love, knew even less than the average patient, to make his own choices—and that meant his own mistakes.

The physician-as-tool model

Those who take patient autonomy seriously enjoy the vigorous support of consumer advocates in health care. The model of physician-patient interaction in the minds of both groups is rarely articulated, even though it is gaining credibility, if not wholehearted acceptance. This model is the mirror image of the previous one. It stresses the ultimate right of patients to determine their own fate. The right is thought to be grounded in the individuality, the independence, and the self-activity of the human person.

There is growing concern that being a patient naturally entails loss of control on the part of the individual and encourages, if it does not require, passivity. The physician-as-tool model is used to reaffirm control and to counteract passivity. Patients are represented as engaged in the activity of curing themselves; physicians are merely instruments used to accomplish this end. In this view, doctors might just as well be computers: they are consulted to make a diagnosis and to outline alternative courses of action to deal with the disease. But they are on a short leash: they make no treatment decisions, and the patents must authorize each new line of action. Physicians have no blanket or even broad permission to proceed: their role is best described as advisor to the king. They are to appear when called, speak when asked, do when told.

Evidently, this relationship exists rarely, if ever, in its purity. And under certain conditions, such as obtain in complex surgical proce-

dures and in emergency rooms, it cannot exist at all. Yet some physicians feel comfortable with it, and in an odd sort of way, the entire
system of fee-for-service invites or at least supports it. For in paying
for the work of doctors, patients are customers, and we all know that
the customer is always right. In buying health services, consumers
need to choose what they want and get what they pay for.

Despite the useful reminder it provides of the importance of
patient autonomy, the physician-as-tool model fails on a variety of
counts. First and foremost, it is altogether unrealistic. For the most
part, patients and their physicians do not and probably cannot relate
in this way. Moreover, even if they could, it is unlikely that the relation would be productive or satisfying to either side.

But most important, the model is morally flawed. It fails to capture
the peculiar intimacy of a relation in which physical and psychological privacy are surrendered and in which two human beings strive in
partnership to reverse the processes of disease and decay. The fact
that this model downgrades the physician to the level of a mere tool is
a clear demonstration that, according to it, the healing and caring
relation is not social involving persons, but masturbatory, limited to
one person and an instrument.

The partnership model

The third model lacks the obvious inadequacies of the prior two. It
gives proper weight to the requirement that the physician-patient
relation be conceived as one between autonomous persons. The
notion of partnership is particularly useful in the attempt to articulate
the structure of the interaction. Partners are independent individuals
temporarily united in quest of a common goal. Each partner brings
divergent talents to the union, and each makes a different contribution. Neither is passive or inferior: the free agreement to pool
resources implies equality and therefore equal rights.

This appears to me to be a useful way of understanding the ideal
relation of physician and patient. They are engaged in a joint enterprise: their aim is shared, and neither can accomplish it without the
participation of the other. In moments of optimism about the
prospects of scientific medicine, we might believe that a surgical procedure or some pills are adequate to restore health; all patients need
to do is give doctors access to their bodies. Such cases clearly do
occur, but it is misleading to take them as our standard. The quest for
health is a lifelong endeavor; in it, the patient is no less active and

involved than the physician. The proper paradigm is the situation that exists in chronic, not in acute, disease. There health is a goal never certainly and never for long achieved. Even to come near it requires the concerted efforts of physician and patient. Without this partnership of equals in the management of chronic disease, no healing or even caring can take place.

In acknowledging each other as partners, patient and physician must respect each other as independent individuals and for what each can do. Decisions are likely to be made in concert, even if not always in unison. Respect and cooperation require full disclosure: informed consent, meaningless apart from the ongoing educational efforts of the physician, is the natural outcome of such sustained partnership. Honesty tempered by care sets the tone for the relationship; there is no room for paternalism or dissembling when equal partners communicate.

Obviously, such partnership cannot always be attained. The condition, the intelligence, and the circumstances of patients may make it altogether impossible to view them or to expect them to act as partners. That does not tend to weaken the partnership model as a proper ideal of physician-patient interaction. Such partnership should be our aim. I am convinced that many more patients can respond to the call to this relation and more can develop it to its full potential than we now expect. Admittedly, this means that physicians have to take the lead in fostering the partnership. But that is neither difficult nor unnatural. I want to leave you with three good reasons for doing it.

The first is that education in health care and in self-respect is a central part of the task of doctoring. The role of physician as educator is too often forgotten; it is time to start stressing the total human, and that means educational, context of healing. The second reason is that frequently, though not always, partnership in the quest for health yields better results than any alternative relation. Finally, let me appeal to self-interest. Litigation among partners is not unknown. But patients who view themselves as equal participants in a difficult and uncertain undertaking are much less likely to sue than people who think they are buying services or who expect wise and charismatic Dr. Welby to save them from everything.

Part Five

HUMAN NATURES

CHAPTER 22

The Element of Choice
in Criteria of Death

D eath is easier to undergo than to understand. It comes unbid-
den, or we can attain it with minimal effort. Yet the willful-
ness of human nature makes it difficult for us to settle for the
easy; we want understanding of it, not the experience.

Thought begins with the silent assumption that words reveal the
world; the unitary noun 'death' must, therefore, be the name of a single phenomenon. Since we can readily distinguish living persons
from decomposing bodies, it is natural to suppose that death is something interposed between these two, a happening that rends the smile
of life and reduces us to a heap of cooling cells. But if 'death' denotes
such an event, it must occur at some precise moment between the
time we still thrive and the hour our remains are interred. Lives terminate at some point, we all seem to agree; there must, therefore, be a
simple and correct answer at any time to the question of whether
given people are then alive. If they had been born and have not died,
they are still with us; if they died, we should be able to determine
how long they have been gone. Death, then, appears to be a
point-event that separates us from the dark. It is a single, simple, irreversible happening that has temporal location but no temporal
dimension: it occurs at a time, yet it takes up no time in occurring. It
is an instantaneous affair.

This is not only where thought begins; it is also where it ends for
many earnest people. Physicians tend to conceptualize death in this
way and find support for their view (when they think confirmation is
needed) among certain philosophers. Even the President's Commis-

sion for the Study of Ethical Problems in Medicine and Biomedical and Behavioral Research endorses this idea in drawing a distinction between the temporal process of dying and death as an instantaneous event. It quotes with approval the view of Bernat, Culver and Gert that "death should be viewed not as a process but as the event that separates the process of dying from the process of disintegration."* I readily acknowledge the attractiveness of this approach. We are, after all, either dead or alive, and which of the two appears to be a matter of empirical fact. If so, it should be possible to articulate the correct criteria of death, which the President's Commission promptly undertakes to do.

We should note, however, that such simple and attractive views carry a danger. They seem so right, they tend to paralyze the mind. They stunt critical inquiry and thereby make it difficult to uncover their hidden commitments. Since even the simplest views are based on assumptions, the result is inadequate self-understanding on the part of those committed to them and general inability to give them a just appraisal.

The theory that death is simply an event in nature has its own central assumptions. For if it is a purely biological phenomenon, our proper cognitive relation to it is that of discovery. Its status then resembles that of America before Columbus's arrival: it is there ready for the light of knowledge to fall on it, ready to be detected and explored. To be sure, our continent was not called America before the Europeans arrived. But discoverers add only the name; they do not create the lands. So it seems to be with death also: it is a natural phenomenon we discover and then name. We contribute nothing to its existence; on the contrary, its prior reality makes our inquiry possible and useful. Our initial, natural view commits us in this way to a realist ontology concerning death.

Three Sorts of Cases

To see how much of an unjustified presumption is involved here, we need to distinguish three different sorts of cases. There are some instances, such as that of the Pacific before Balboa beheld it, in which

---

* President's Commission for the Study of Ethical Problems in Medicine and Biomedical and Behavioral Research, *Defining Death* (Washington, D.C.: Government Printing Office, 1981), 77.

objects enjoy existence independently of any cognitive or conative human act. In a radically different set of cases, existence is totally the outcome of our activities. The meeting of a board of directors, for example, is an occurrence altogether dependent on human acts and practices. For no one is a director except in a complex social context, and no meeting of those who are directors is a meeting of the board unless its scheduling and convening follow established rules.

There are also intermediate cases in which human choice and action build on preexisting things or conditions to create a novel object. No person is fat apart from human judgment, yet corpulent people are not created by our perception or our whim. There is an underlying physical reality: the distribution of weight among the population. This continuum, ranging from those who weigh less than one hundred pounds to individuals who tip the scales at over five hundred, then receives a human contribution which breaks it into the loose categories of the thin, the average, and the fat. Such categorization, based on taste, tradition, and social purposes, is by no means trivial. It establishes new objects, namely, groups of people judged to be deserving of differential treatment medically, socially and in our personal relations.

In the human world, there are a very large number of cases of this third variety. The law and our social practices frequently call on us to draw relatively sharp lines to separate phases of an otherwise continuous process or to stress the differences among remarkably similar conditions. Such differentiations represent human contributions to physical facts: they express our choices and embody our values. The person who wants a fine lawn needs to kill noxious growths. But in its physical constitution, nothing is a weed. Weeds are physico-social objects, namely, broad-leafed plants that grow, undesirably, in the grass. The combination of independent existents and selectivity expressing human interests and purposes is evident here, as it is when we call someone smart or beautiful, or when we set the time at which a young person can begin to drive, or when we fix the end of the Middle Ages.

In which of the three types of cases does death belong? Although some people, Christian Scientists perhaps, view it as a human creation or illusion, it is unlikely that death lacks objective basis. Does this mean, however, that it is an exclusively physical event that "separates the process of dying from the process of disintegration"? Although this is the currently favored position, I do not think that it is right. Persons of scientific sophistication should have long had their suspicion aroused by the notion of death as an instantaneous point-event, for such presumed occurrences resemble humanly contrived termini much more closely than they do the unbroken temporal processes we find in nature. The function of determining the exact moment of death yields another bit of evidence against the purely physical view. Our interest in this is largely legal, not scientific: we want to know in order to establish criminal liability or, as in the case of multiple deaths in a family due to a single accident, to clarify the pattern of inheritance.

Death a Physico-Social Reality

The role this notion of the death-event plays in our common practices provides added confirmation that the object it identifies is not a purely physical reality but a physico-social one. Our primary purpose in applying the concept of death to people is to indicate a very important point of change in our relations to them. So long as people are alive, certain activities are obligatory while others are forbidden with respect to them. If we are members of their family or of the team that cares for them, we must, for example, attempt to communicate with them, to ascertain their wishes, and to aid them when appropriate. On the other hand, we are not permitted to open their safety deposit boxes and read their wills, to perform autopsies on them or to cart them to the cemetery for burial. The relations and the activities that embody them change in a radical way once death has taken place. It then becomes acceptable for us to treat our patients and loved ones in the ways our society deems appropriate to the dead.

No one would want to deny, of course, that there are important differences between those alive and the dead. These divergences constitute the objective foundation for distinguishing the two. But how much difference there must be and which traits or activities of the living must change in order for us to say that they have died are matters of judgment. Since the concept of death functions as a trigger or an indicator to alter our activities with respect to those to whom it is applied, it must involve a social standard of decision about when such change of behavior is proper. In developing criteria of death, then, we must do two things instead of the one usually supposed. On the one hand, we must attend to the facts of organic decline; this is an empirical inquiry about independently existing biological phenomena. On the other hand, we must also formulate a socially acceptable decision about precisely where in the continuum of decay to draw the line between the living and the dead. This is essentially a normative activity in which we bring tradition, religious and moral values, and social utilities to bear on important human relations.

Value Elements in the Choice of Death Criteria

The current line of thought sheds new light on the conflict between the whole-brain and the neocortical criteria for declaring a person dead. Advocates of each position tend to view the controversy as factual, namely, as a disagreement about when or under what circumstances death *in fact* occurs. It should be obvious by now that there is no factual solution to this debate and that both sides, when they insist on one, betray inadequate self-understanding.

There can be no objective solution because there is no empirical disagreement; neither side offers an alternative biology. The real opposition, though misleadingly couched in factual terms, is conceptual, and that conceptual conflict is grounded in incompatible value commitments. Advocates of the neocortical view tend to think of humans in terms of the category of persons and thus regard death as the cessation of such higher activities as feeling, consciousness, self-consciousness, and reflection. Proponents of the whole-brain thesis, by contrast, adopt the ancient and perhaps more inarticulate idea that humans are intimately connected with or inseparable from all of their integrated bodily acts.

This conceptual disagreement is but the cognitive expression of divergent valuations. Champions of the neocortical view prize consciousness and the activities it makes possible. The vehemence of their affirmation that a life lacking awareness (and related acts) is worthless sometimes takes the form of refusing to call biological existence without neocortical function 'life' at all. Their reasoning proceeds not from the objective recognition that cessation of higher brain functions is tantamount to death. Instead, though often only tacitly, they move in the opposite direction: initial commitment to the all-importance of certain activities makes them choose destruction of the organs supporting those activities as the indicator of death.

Advocates of the whole-brain criterion think in a similar fashion.

But their devotion, no doubt traditional and religious in derivation, is to integrated bodily acts. Factual considerations come in only when they try to establish the biological foundation of those acts. Cessation of the integrative work of the entire brain, then, is not the sign of when death in fact takes place; it is where we must place the point of death if we have an antecedent commitment to the importance of integrated bodily function.

We cannot, therefore, adjudicate the conflict of criteria in anything less than frankly normative terms. The question to ask is not when death *really* occurs but why we should draw the line between life and death at the higher cognitive rather than at the lower integrative activities. Recast in these terms, we can develop a better understanding of the differences between the criteria and hope eventually to resolve their conflict in a socially acceptable way.

Biological Facts, Social Decision

The essence of my claim is that formulating a criterion of death involves, in addition to factual considerations, a social decision. Whether the heart beats is an empirical matter susceptible of factual determination. Whether when the heart stops beating death has occurred involves the application of a social standard. This standard is not written into the nature of things and, accordingly, cannot be read off from the facts of biology. It is established by taking biological realities into account and then making a more or less conscious communal choice. The choice is not dictated by what we know of the operations of the body; religious, social, moral, and technological considerations also play a part. That, for example, we insist on the *irreversibility* of the cessation of heart, lung, or brain function is not a matter of recognizing what death is; it is an expression of our interventionist values. What it means is that we refuse to view anyone as dead so long as there is something we can do to sustain or restart the biological machinery.

In other cultures, the normative and religious milieu make cardiac resuscitation unthinkable; when the gods stop life, such people might believe, it is sacrilege for humans to interfere. Those who respond by claiming that our practice is superior yield the point at issue by moving to the normative plane. For then they agree that criteria of death are far from being purely factual: if irreversibility, for example, is not a part of them, then it ought to be.

Other Societies

If I am correct that locating death along the continuum of organic decline involves a social choice, it is likely that different societies place it at different points. And that is precisely what both history and anthropology show. People in some societies have, not unreasonably, decided that no one is dead until the next sunup after spontaneous movement ceases. In other cultures, expressing different values and divergent natural constraints, death has been pegged at the point where people get sufficiently weak to consume more social goods than they can produce. Primitive Eskimos might have had something like that in mind when they invited infirm old people to lessen the community's burden by walking into the blizzard or the night. Cruel and unacceptable as this might seem to a society in need of consumers, it was clearly reasonable and legitimate under then prevailing circumstances. I note that even there death had a physical basis, but it was supposed to occur relatively early in the process of decline and disintegration. The act of walking out into the snow was not suicide but proper acknowledgment of the fact that in the eyes of the community, one was already dead. Along with whatever weaknesses it displays, this view has an intriguing and beautiful feature. In industrial society, our last act is an involuntary movement of the heart, lung, or brain. Eskimo culture permitted many the privilege of a last act that was not only voluntary but also virtuous and noble.

My point is not to urge the superiority of Eskimo ways. I use their example to underscore the fact that the point of death can be situated at a number of places along the continuum of organic decline. Where we put it is a matter of choice determined by the beliefs, values, and circumstances of the community. The naively realistic view of death obscures this centrally important element of choice. Yet even the most fervent belief that death is something the criterion of whose occurrence can be discovered or read off from the facts cannot eliminate the element of social decision involved in formulating it. The naiveté of the realistic view, well exemplified in the report of the President's Commission, succeeds only in keeping the choice unconscious and hence uncriticized. The thought that we can discover the point of death conceals from us what we really do and thereby makes an intelligent examination of our activity impossible.

Death a Biologically Based Social Status

My argument shows that we have reason to think of death not as a simple organic condition but as a biologically based social status. Since the status is social in nature, there are public and community-wide standards for determining it. This is the truth behind the claim that the decision of when one is dead cannot be left to personal whim. The choice of which I speak is not, therefore, that of the individual physician or of the patient. It is a choice the community must make, or has made, as displayed in its rules and practices. The physician merely applies this customary or statutory standard. We need to remind ourselves that the presence of human decision does not remove generality, only the comfort of supposing that our ideas are replicas of reality and hence our beliefs accord cozily with the nature of things. The choice, moreover, is obviously less than unconditional or absolute: no society is free to set as the sole criterion of death a sneeze or a strong itch under the left armpit. The line of death must be drawn at some significant point on the continuum of personal decline. But such disintegration involves the change or cessation of a multiplicity of activities; societies have considerable leeway in pinpointing death at the stage where functions of particular interest to them become impossible to perform.

Activities and Costs

If the line between life and death is drawn on the basis of a social decision, what factors influence this choice? Two considerations appear to be always present. The first is, as I have just indicated, the identification of important activities that, when one can perform them no more, is a sufficient reason for thinking one dead. Declarations of death are, therefore, at once (though tacitly) statements about what the individuals involved are no longer able to do. The second consideration is the assessment of our responsibilities to declining people and of the cost of carrying them out. We have many duties to people who are alive; declaring them dead instantly eliminates a host of these obligations, imposes only a few new ones, and makes hitherto. unacceptable acts appropriate.

Lest I sound cynical in mentioning the cost of locating death at one place or another in the biological continuum, let us remember that societies hard-pressed have always set the point of death on a cost-benefit basis at the early stages of nonfunctionality. In many contexts, elderly Eskimos could still function reasonably well. But the cost of supporting them through debility and disease was thought too high for the meager resources of their community. When Europe suffered from the plague, individuals with the first signs of the disease were treated in ways appropriate to the dead: the health costs of providing treatment or even the comfort of companionship were judged intolerable. The long-term maintenance of numbers of humanly non-functioning biological wrecks is a luxury open only to rich and stable societies. I hesitate to infer from this that none but the very wealthy can do what is morally right.

It should be clear from these comments that the cost of what we would have to do for certain groups of people if they were judged to be alive is a factor, and sometimes the decisive factor, in formulating a criterion of death. But in many, if not most, cases the primary consideration in the social decision underlying the definition of death is what individuals at different stages of organic disintegration can do. The issue is in part one of technology: with the aid of suitable devices, we can now do more over a longer period of time than ever before. But for the rest, it comes to a question of our beliefs, values, and needs, or they shape our view of the hierarchy of human activities.

What are the acts and achievements absence of which has been supposed to render one dead? Even if we leave out the personal and idiosyncratic failures of function for which individuals have rendered themselves dead, we find a bewildering variety of activities. I have already mentioned relative economic unproductivity and the early signs (with minimal loss of function) of contagious disease. We can add loss of rational control over one's life, loss of strength sufficient to prevail in combat, permanent loss of consciousness, loss of pulmonary function, loss of cardiac activity, and loss of the integrated operations of the entire brain. At the spiritual end, we find irreparable damage to the proper work of the soul or to one's relations with God. At the other extreme, death is supposed to occur only when all biological activity, down to the cellular level, has ceased or when putrefaction sets in. There is hardly any significant human activity that some society or subculture has not thought crucial to life and whose loss has not been supposed to signal death.

Is Death Not a Biological Fact?

An objection is likely to be urged, perhaps quite impatiently, at this point. Those who insist on the pure factuality of medical science may indicate displeasure with the way I seem to mix the social and the biological, what to them appears as the optional and the compulsory. This tends to blur the distinction between ostracism, traumatic or destructive community practices, metaphorical senses of 'death,' self-sacrifice and suicide on the one hand, and the stubborn reality of the cessation of biological function on the other. Modern medicine takes little interest, I may rightly be reminded, in odd social rituals. Its gaze is fixed on the natural process that underlies human interaction and whose end destroys its possibility. Whatever a community does to or requires of its members, their actual death does not occur until their bodies give out. The definition of death should, therefore, reflect this primacy and ultimacy of the physical.

This is a serious objection, and although much of my discussion so far has been devoted to showing the dubiety of its assumptions, it deserves a straightforward response. I begin by happily granting the importance of biological process. My concern is only with our current supposition of its all-importance. Life is a very large collection of activities; the cessation of some, many, or most of these constitutes death. I want to stress that not all the operations of life cease at any point where death is supposed to occur: some residual activities and relations go with us to the grave. There is, therefore, significant selectivity in deciding which activities are central for life and which are peripheral. The President's Commission, for example, maintains that brain integration of biological function is essential; its absence is a sure sign, or is even the very nature, of death. By contrast, apparently on the theory that cellular activity is necessary but not sufficient for organized life, its continued presence is declared irrelevant to the death of the organism.* Those who favor cessation of neocortical function as the criterion of death, on the other hand, insist on the centrality of the cognitive and conative activities associated with consciousness. To them, continued organic process, even if systemwide, is insufficient to keep persons alive.

The Choice of Which Life Activities Are Central

* President's Commission, 28.

How are the 'essential' operations selected from among all those that compose human existence? All choice presupposes interests or purposes or values. The focus of physicians is the biological substratum of life, its roots and not its flower. Understandably, therefore, they give preference to causally central, capacitating processes. Are these, in fact, the crucial operations of life? Almost certainly, if we identify life with organic existence and thus adopt the biological perspective of medicine. But if we seek the fruit of life and not its sustaining causes, the view of medicine may well appear reductivist and inadequate. The activities selected as central to life will then be thought, emotion, and the other higher functions; their termination will constitute death just as really as cardiopulmonary failure does for the physician.

We can see, then, that the selectivity necessary for identifying central life activities inevitably carries us past the factually empirical. It introduces a set of interests and a system of correlated values. The biological perspective common to physicians is itself a social creation with its own underlying purposes. It is, by and large, the collective possession of an entire, important subculture in our society. And this society permits, encourages, even fosters the predominance of the biological perspective in the medical subculture because of the immense health benefits it provides.

None of this presents a problem if it is properly understood. But the precise factuality of science and vast success of medicine tend to make us forget about the interests and the selectivity that underlie them. Expertise is easily converted into truth: insensibly, we drift into thinking that biology and biochemistry and medicine provide an accurate, literal, and complete account of human reality. Medicine becomes, in this way, the final arbiter of life and death: we look to it for precise information, for solutions to our problems, even for reliable standards of when life, and not merely its biological support, ends.

Standards of Health and Death Socially Established

When we convert the results of this important but conditioned and limited enterprise into unconditional truth, we lose sight of the vital role social decisions play in establishing it and shaping its structure, and in setting the standards of health and death. This inattention is the source of the false idea that death is a purely natural terminus that involves no human activity other than the attempts of the health care team to retard or to reverse it. In fact, we cannot understand death and cannot even hope to establish rational criteria for it without putting it in its proper historical and social context. If we do that, we see at once the omnipresence of human activity, the way in which our choices and values surround, frame, structure, channel, establish, accelerate, and in some cases eliminate natural processes. The best way to remind ourselves of this centrality of human purposes is to call attention to the diversity of social practices. The absence of this cross-cultural or anthropological perspective renders much contemporary discussion of the criteria of death one-dimensional and the deliberations of the President's Commission sterile and unsatisfying.

My response, than, to persons who charge that in discussing death I mix social and biological considerations is warm congratulations. They have detected my strategy; I hope that at this point they can even see my arguments for it. If they do, they may come to agree with me that we are unlikely to make progress in this field without due attention to the social and normative context, that is, to the deliberate choices we must make and the reasons for them.

How to Choose a Death Criterion

How does paying heed to choice and value help us in assessing the relative merits of the whole-brain and neocortical views of death? First, it protects us from the misleading suppositions, fatal for inquiry, that the primary issue between these competing theories is either factual or conceptual. It is, of course, absolutely essential to get the relevant facts exactly right. And conceptual clarity and precision are equally important. But these are initial requirements only; without agreement that is hammered out of the traditions and beliefs of the community and that takes due account of social utilities, they are inadequate to establish the line between life and death.

In our society, the agreement is pursued and achieved within the confines of the political system in its broadest and most inclusive sense. This system can operate only if public discourse is free and enlightened. Such discussion of community policy, in turn, presupposes accurate information and an educated citizenry. The role of physicians is not to inform us of when death, in fact, takes place but to provide reliable knowledge of the stages of organic disintegration. And the job of philosophers is not so much to resolve thorny ontological problems about the personhood of human beings as to focus public discussion and political decision making by the critical examination of our beliefs and of the consequences of the values we embrace.

The report of the President's Commission was political in just this sense: it offered itself as a voice in the social dialogue, presenting a criterion of death that might be generally acceptable. But lacking a clear understanding of the central role of values in any such proposal, it attempted, erroneously, to pass off its results as supportable by scientific facts. Such a naively realistic approach may be thought to be rhetorically effective: who, after all, would want to contradict what physicians say about the objective realities that fall within their domain? Yet the conclusions of the Commission have succeeded neither in enlightening public discourse nor in stilling the controversy surrounding the conditions under which a person should be viewed as dead. Lasting agreement will not be achieved until we develop a reflective and public consensus of the relative strengths and weaknesses and of the costs and benefits of rival positions.

Whole-Brain or Neocortical View?

The Weight of Tradition

This is obviously not the occasion to work out the details of such an assessment. I will sketch only its outlines, calling attention to the sorts of considerations we must take into account. I have already indicated that these fall into three broad categories. First, any attempt to establish the line of death must reckon with our habits, traditions and established practices. These appear to be a mixed bag: some favor the more conservative whole-brain criterion, while others are readily compatible with the neocortical view. We have, for example, the deepest devotion to the human body, caring for it and treating it with respect well past the point where such regard can do the person inhabiting it any good. We also have habits of optimistic intervention that make it difficult for us to admit that anyone is past hope and nearly impossible to feel released of the obligation to continue to benefit them.

Such practices support the view that death cannot be thought to occur until centrally controlled organic activity ceases, or perhaps until even later. But other established forms of behavior point to permanent loss of the higher conscious functions as the proper dividing line between the living and the dead. Our spontaneous attitudes to people do, after all, undergo radical change when we find them unresponsive in a deep coma. And those closest to patients so afflicted, the members of their family and of their health care team, tend to deal with them in a way that is clear-eyed and unsentimental. This is amply displayed in the widespread practice of denying resuscitation not only to comatose individuals but also to those in advanced stages of senility and to terminal patients in drug-induced stupor.

The Role of Established Beliefs

Our shared beliefs show the same ambiguity as our practices. On the one hand, we have such a strong commitment to the value of individuals that the possibility of false positives—the survival, reversal, or misdiagnosis of the loss of higher conscious functions—makes us suspicious of the neocortical view. Although nineteenth century fears of burying people who seem dead but are somehow alive are no longer with us, we are reluctant to believe that individuals who appear physically intact and may even breathe on their own could, nevertheless, be irremediably dead. On the other hand, we also believe that people who have permanently lost consciousness have undergone a profound change and that respectful treatment of their bodies is largely the expression of residual respect for who they had been. When such treatment becomes protracted and burdensome, the people directly involved with it, who tend to understand the situation best, generally agree that though the body may linger, the person is no longer there.

Our beliefs in these matters were formed under the influence of our religious heritage. But the Judeo-Christian tradition is itself of two minds about the significance of the body for true life. It invites us to consider our physical nature as but the earthly shroud we should be happy to shed or as a prison we must be eager to escape. At the first reliable sign, therefore, that the human (not the vegetative) soul has fled, we should be comfortable in disposing of the body as we would of any other piece of unneeded matter. Yet, another powerful element in the tradition insists that the connection between person and body is far more intimate. If, in this world at least, the soul is inseparable from the body, respect for people is respect for their earthly forms. Moreover, it is not for us to decide when the physical tenure of persons comes to an end: we must support them without fail until God's will is made manifest by the total ruin of their bodies.

Social Utility

The line of death we draw should be conservative in the sense that it agrees, to the greatest extent possible, with our practices and beliefs. My discussion so far makes it clear that neither of these clearly favors the neocortical over the whole-brain criterion. The deliverance of the third central consideration—social utility—is, however, almost univocal. In every respect but two, drawing the line at the total cessation of the integrative activity of the brain entails vastly more cost than its rival. Of the two, one is purely economic, namely, the employment by the hospital industry of a significant number of people for the purpose of caring for permanently comatose individuals. Given the availability of more productive, alternative employment, this is not a compelling consideration. The other cost of a neocortical criterion is the possibility of error it presents. After all, it is conceivable that people who appear to have lost all higher conscious functions may, at some later time, astoundingly regain them. But additional vigilance readily reduces or eliminates this cost: the criterion must be so phrased and applied that the recovery of anyone about to be declared dead is only a logical, not a clinical, possibility.

For the rest, the neocortical view is vastly preferable. The suffering of patients who are capable of feeling pain but not of taking or asking for countermeasures, the protracted torture of their families, the sensed impotence of the health care team, and the unproductive use of social resources all point to the unwisdom of the whole-brain view. As any observer of the current scene knows, social choice between the two criteria is not easy. But if they are our major alternatives, rational assessment favors destruction of the neocortex as the better place to draw the line of death.

The Individual-Centered Multiple Criterion View

Are these views, however, the only major contenders? There is another one that has, for the most part, escaped the notice of philosophers. That it enjoys broad support is demonstrated by the spread of legislation permitting people to write living wills. Because we tend not to think of the criterion of death as chosen, we have failed to recognize the remarkable fact that such laws empower people to adopt their own criterion. The multiplicity of criteria from which persons can freely choose is necessary for the good death and particularly appropriate to the political system we have adopted. The matter is complex, so here I shall only sketch the nature of, and the arguments for, this individual-centered multiple criterion view.

If our exertions are mere motion without consciousness, there is no such thing as the good life. Similarly, if departing this world is a clinical point-event, there can be no good death. Although there are clear asymmetries between the good life and the good death, there are certain important similarities due, in large measure, to the presence in each of what makes for the good anywhere. At any rate, the good life and the good death form an integral whole. This is well expressed in Aristotle's view that a timely and fitting exit is necessary for the completion of a rich and satisfying existence. It is difficult to think of happiness as constituted by less than just such a structured and meaningful life. The sensible conclusion to which this leads is that death is a part of life (even though it may well be the last part), and that the good death is an indispensable element in the happy life.

The Good Death

Innocent as this view may sound, it has important political consequences. For combined with our inalienable right to pursue happiness, it implies that we have a similar right to seek the good death. Mindless legislation banning suicide violates this right. It is astounding that the President's Commission, though entrusted to deal with ethical problems, shows no awareness of the distinction between death and the good death, of the relation of the good death to the good life, and consequently of the right of individuals to self-determination in the matter of when, how, and under what circumstances they shall expire.

For those who do not favor the rhetoric of rights, the same point can be made in different language. In our country it is established public policy to promote such central values as liberty. Freedom cannot exist, of course, without limit. But the spirit (though not always the letter) of our laws, well supported by fundamental moral principles, is to restrict the liberty of each only where it infringes on the liberty or welfare of others, and to leave it unabridged in matters relating to the individual alone. Since death is paradigmatically a private matter, it follows that its determination should be left open to individual control to the greatest extent possible.

In a very general analysis, the good life has three basic conditions or ingredients. We must have desires and purposes, we must be fortunate enough to live in circumstances where they can be satisfied, and we must have the capacity and energy actually to achieve them. Without the convergence of will, luck, and power, the good life is impossible; even Stoic control and Eastern resignation presuppose certain aims and, if nothing else, the luck of having the internal strength to crush worldly desires. The lack of power yields envy and bitterness; the absence of will makes existence meaningless; without luck, life remains a frustrated quest.

The good death has the same conditions as the good life. First and foremost, we must be fortunate enough not to pass away before our time. We must avoid extravagant cravings, such as that for endless physical life, and frame sensible desires about the time and manner of our demise. Finally, we must have the power to achieve what we want either by taking direct action or by causing others to respect our will.

The coincidence of will and power makes for effective autonomy. The role of the state is to respect and to safeguard this autonomy in the choice of death no less than in the decisions of daily life. To afford people control over their own death amounts to giving them power to determine how they are to be treated. Autonomy in the choice of conditions under which we no longer wish to live, therefore, requires our legal and social empowerment to decide when members of our health care team are to cease their labors and begin to treat us in ways appropriate to the dead.

Choice of One's Own Death Criterion

If my earlier argument that death is a biologically based social status is correct, to say that someone is dead is partly to affirm that the person has reached a certain stage of organic decline and (most important) partly to indicate a change in our relations to that individual. As a signal, the declaration is meant to shape our expectations and to revise our obligations. Such statements must not be made lightly or without warrant. What justifies them is an assessment of which significant activities the individual in question can no longer perform. Who is to determine what these valued activities are? The decision is best left to the persons involved: only they can judge what is of paramount importance in their lives and when their existence is no longer worth its cost. In a pluralistic democracy, we can acknowledge this sovereignty of individuals over their lives and leave the timing and manner of death to personal choice. Instruction by competent individuals of their fellows about the circumstances under which they no longer wish to be treated as living persons does not require an instant funeral. There are stages in our dealings with the dead; the initial declaration, though it precipitates complex social and legal changes, may demand only the cessation of treatment or, more controversially, active steps to bring a recalcitrant heart in line with its owner's will.

There must, of course, be limits to such self-determination. The decision about the timing of one's death, though not irrevocable, must be serious and sincere. And there has to be an appropriate biological basis for the choice: those suffering from sinus colds or impacted wisdom teeth must be barred from the decision. But persons even in the early stages of terminal or degenerative ailments clearly qualify: cancer patients, for example, and those afflicted with Lou Gehrig's disease should be free to determine the criterion, fulfillment of which is an adequate sign that they are dead. We should, in other words, leave it in their hands to decide where in the natural process of disintegration life no longer serves their human purposes. The time at which heart, lung, or brain ceases to function is not, then, for those who decide otherwise the moment of their death; in their cases, these customary signs serve only as the physical confirmation of what took place before.

Where Autonomy Is Impossible

The individual-centered multiple criterion approach is obviously inapplicable to microcephalics, accident victims without living wills, and those in a persistent vegetative state. This third view focuses on the good death, and for people in such unfortunate circumstances, the good death is not possible. In their cases, the autonomy principle cannot be applied because they are not in a position to will anything or to act on their desires. For them, all we can hope for is an institutionally made humane decision.

The best place to draw the line of death in such cases is the cessation or, in some cases, the irreversible cessation of neocortical function. Our ability to sustain bodily processes beyond the point where they are of any conceivable personal benefit has generated a desperate need to distinguish between biological and human life. In view of the success of medicine and the sciences, we must make extraordinary efforts to remember that biological processes serve only as the support and substratum of human existence. When we unalterably lose the ability to will and do, to think and hope, to feel and love, we have ceased existence as human beings. The only humane course then is to declare us dead and to treat us accordingly. If the diagnosis is careful and accurate, we need have no fear that this harms anyone: once the human person is gone, in the faltering body no one is there.

CHAPTER 23

Human Natures

I f I drive south from Nashville, Tennessee, in less than ten hours I will run upon a large body of water. The existence of this sea is an objective fact: it was there before the first human being swam in it, it is there when no one beholds it, it will likely be there when we evacuate the earth and move on to pollute other planets. Even if, following some bizarre conception, a mad dictatorship denied its existence, its waves would continue to wash its shores, and its fish would still frolic over oyster beds. I offer no comprehensive theory of the nature of objective facts. For my purposes, it is enough to note that some things do not owe their existence to human thought or effort.

The body of water I run upon is called 'the Gulf of Mexico.' This is a conventional or choice-determined fact, a fact that depends on inter-subjective agreements. We could refer to it by the old, Indian name for one of its bays or call it 'the Gulf of Contentment,' or even, simply, 'Sam.' The water neither implies nor requires any particular name. Viewed from its perspective, therefore, what we decide to call it is not only contingent but arbitrary. From the standpoint of its history, of course, the name is anything but arbitrary: social, political, and geo-graphic considerations conspired to establish it as the generally accepted one. Yet it continues to be hostage to human decisions. The Florida Department of Tourism may well launch a campaign to rechristen it 'the Gulf of Florida,' and succeed in convincing everyone to use no other name.

It is not very difficult to identify objective and conventional facts. The distinction produces classes that are mutually exclusive and appear conjointly exhaustive. Many people, therefore, think that every fact is either objective or conventional and none is both. This view unfortunately overlooks a third, intermediate class of facts whose central significance has in any case been inadequately appreciated by philosophers. I have in mind facts whose constitution involves both objective elements and human decisions. Let us call these choice-inclusive facts.

Since the days of Kant, the idea of realities constituted by human beings has been commonplace. The facts to which I wish to call attention, however, are not transcendental but quite ordinary and empirical. They are determined not by the nature of human cognitive faculties but by contingent and reversible choices. Everyone is familiar with such facts, although because they masquerade as objective, their proper nature tends to elude us.

How, for example, should we view the claim that the body of water I run upon is a gulf? Objective facts set our parameters. We are dealing with a certain volume of salt water located in a specific geographical area. Shall we call it a sea? This is clearly what its size suggests. It is, in fact, larger than most seas and much larger than many. Its geographical peculiarity, however, is that land bounds it on three sides, making it appropriate for us to call it an inlet or a bay. But, though Hudson Bay and the Bay of Bengal are large, bays on the whole tend to be relatively small bodies of water. So, we may classify it as a gulf, which is a relatively large part of an ocean or sea extending into the land. Yet if it is a gulf, the Sea of Japan and the Baltic Sea, which are smaller and more bounded, should be gulfs also. The Gulf of Guinea, on the other hand, since it is much smaller and is bounded by land on two sides only, should not be a gulf.

The conclusion of this line of thought is obvious. It makes no sense to ask, "What is this body of water *really*? Is it *really* a bay, a gulf, or a sea?" Within limits, it is what we decide it is. The limits are imposed by its physical features: we cannot, without being silly, class it as a mountain range or a coffee pot. But we have good reasons to classify it a sea, a bay, and a gulf, and which of these carries the day is a matter of choice. The right question to ask, therefore, is, "Which is the best way to classify this body of water?" And this is a question to which there is no unambiguous, or even meaningful, answer to this question without a prior account of what we want the classification to do. In the case of the Baltic, with rival nations inhabiting its shores, it may well have been in everyone's interest to secure universal rights to navigation by declaring it a sea. Classification as a gulf, on the other hand, may have accomplished for the Gulf of Mexico the opposite desired effect, conveying to colonizing European powers the idea of a private American waterway.

There are several types and many instances of such choice-inclusive facts. All of them involve objective facts along with some decision, normally a social one, about classification. Some choices concerning how to categorize the objective facts are inappropriate or wrong: no large body of water is a flowering mimosa plant. But no single classification is exclusively right. The facts allow flexibility in our concepts: depending on what we wish to accomplish, widely divergent ways of sorting and grouping the bounty of nature may be appropriate and useful.

In saying that someone is fat, for example, we do not disclose an objective fact about the person. There are, to be sure, objective facts involved: the body weight of the individual and its relation to the weight of other people in the population. But we can also detect a decision, such as that to be fat means to exceed by 20 percent or more the average weight of people of one's height. We could, of course, decide to draw the line elsewhere, say, at exceeding the average by only 5 percent or by 50 percent. There may be good reasons to incline us in one direction or the other. But in no case do we accurately capture what it is *objectively* to be fat, for the simple and conclusive reason that there is no such thing.

Adulthood is another choice-inclusive fact. It involves both the age of individuals and the decision, recently revised to the chagrin of young people, concerning where to draw the line between (among other things) those who can drink and those who cannot. Nothing is large, hot, or heavy, and no one is poor, smart, weak, generous, tall, retarded, or even dead as a matter of objective fact. The reason is not that the application of these terms involves tacit comparisons between members of a class but that the comparison does not by itself justify the application. We also need a decision to specify the point in the relationship of the compared items where we first wish to permit the term to apply.

Such decisions are, of course, not arbitrary. Normally, they are public, subserve some shared ends, and involve a variety of formal and informal social mechanisms in their formulation. The decision about where to draw the line between the living and the dead, for example, is now being made through the political process. The traditional distinction, cast in terms of the cessation of cardiopulmonary function, had been rendered inadequate by the development of advanced techniques of resuscitation and life support. A presidential commission was appointed and made the novel suggestion that the irreversible cessation of whole-brain function be designated as the criterion of death. The new standard addresses some broad social concerns and is more clearly in line with technological realities than the now antiquated, traditional criterion. Accordingly, in the last dozen years or so, nearly thirty state legislatures have adopted the recommendation. With additional support, the new social decision about the point of death will be clearly in place, generating, as physicians declare people deceased, an indefinitely large number of choice-inclusive facts.

The continuing abortion controversy is also best seen as disagreement concerning the social decision about the beginning of life. There is no novel objective fact to be discovered in this sphere: no biological research or abstract philosophical reflection can tell us when human life begins. We need a generally acceptable decision about where, in the continuous process from fertilization to birth, it would be best to draw the line between merely biological and genuinely human existence. Too much is at stake for this determination to be groundless or arbitrary. The religious beliefs, personal values, and established lifestyles of people must all be taken into consideration, along with economic interests and the broad social implications of each proposed decision. The fact that consensus has eluded us for so many years is a result not of having failed to *discover* what we seek but of the intensity of the feelings involved and the complexity of the balance among values that we must achieve.

The currently popular categories of biology are also choice-inclusive in character. The full continuum of plant and animal life serves as the objective foundation of the facts their application creates. In addition, however, there is also a tacit choice to cut up the continuum in a certain way and not in innumerable others. We could, for example, classify porpoises by their habitat and method of locomotion, in which case they would be a sort of fish, or by their weight, in which case they would be related to cattle, or by their intelligence, in which case they would belong in the same group as humans and the great apes. Viewed in this light, our current classification, based on method of respiration and reproduction, loses its apparent privilege. Each of these arrangements is legitimate and useful; each focuses on some interesting features of the animals and highlights some of their signif-

icant relations to others. To say that one and only one of them captures the way things really are amounts to a slanderous impoverishment of the world. All of them illuminate a bit of reality, though not
necessarily the corner into which we wish to peer.

Biologists might respond, however, by contrasting our changing
purposes with the enduring value of truth. Some classifications are
simply better, they might argue, for learning the truth about animals.
If we focus on the respiration and reproduction of porpoises, for
example, we are more likely to discover their evolutionary origin than
if we study the ways they use their tails. The right classification is
like a key that opens the door to nature's secrets; when the key fits,
we know that our idea is not only useful but also true. If this is so,
our ordinary quests are not on a par with the search for the right classification, the pursuit of truth. Among other differences, their satisfactory termination presupposes that we get what we want. In the
scientific search for truth, by contrast, there is no room for private
whim or ulterior public purpose. When we operate under the constraint of objective facts, the only permissible desire is to ascertain the
way things are.

This line of thought is impressive. It plays on our suspicions about
our motives and appeals to our hunger for heroes. It depicts scientists as selfless devotees of truth and the rest of us as slaves to the
shabby designs of daily life. I, for one, do not have the problem many
philosophers experience today with acknowledging the independent
reality of facts and truths; I even take pleasure, when summer
approaches, that the Gulf of Mexico is there waiting for me. Nevertheless, it is worth remarking that not all truths are of the objective
variety: choice-determined and choice-inclusive facts are also appropriate objects of the search for truth. And the rigors of this search
have been much exaggerated. In fact, nothing is more plentiful and
easier to get than truth. We are surrounded by truths on all sides; if
we permit it, their sheer number will numb the mind. My car is made
of roughly eighteen thousand parts. This gives eighteen thousand
truths, if I care to enumerate them, along with millions more about
how the parts are related. A colleague concerned about his record of
speaking the truth told me that whenever he finds himself asserting
too many dubious propositions, he quickly recites the multiplication
tables to raise his daily truth average.

It is not truth we want, obviously, but relevant truths, general
truths, novel truths, or interesting truths. Inquiry must be guided,

therefore, by objectives and values beyond promiscuous curiosity, or else it will drown in truth. These values express the multiplicity of our concerns and enterprises; they identify the corners of the world where we want to look, the sorts of things we want to find, the kinds of uses to which we wish to put our results. The scientific enterprise is not a detached, indiscriminate search for truth. It is an organized human activity governed, like all others, by our needs and interests. The aim of at least portions of it may be purely epistemic: some scientists may want to identify those characteristics of objects that are central in the sense of connecting and concomitantly varying with the largest possible set of their other features. Such systemic objectives, however, express the long-term, deeply entrenched, need-based concerns of the vulnerable animals we are no less than do our more immediately practical interests. An omniscient God would pay no heed to central, unifying features; gods secure from injury would find their curiosity easily satisfied and consider the relentless search for knowledge an embarrassment. That porpoises breathe by means of lungs is no more of a truth than that they weigh about as much as cows. And the desire to determine their evolutionary origin is no less a contingent human purpose than the craving to study the engineering of their tails. However we relate and classify things, we will find some truths. Whatever choice-inclusive truths or facts we find, they will always have some purpose behind the decisions that give them structure or definition.

Now that I have angered those who believe in fixed and natural species with my comments about the choice-inclusive character of biological categories, I might as well proceed to infuriate the friends of human nature. The statements we like to make about what is and what is not a matter of human nature, about the identity of the human essence in everyone, and about the endurance of human traits also articulate only choice-inclusive facts. Since the facts are choice-inclusive, they have an objective component that imposes constraints on what can be called a human characteristic and who can be classified as a human being. But the element that is independent of our choice establishes only the outer, and rather fuzzy, boundaries of appropriate categorization. Within these parameters, the facts that surround us do not mandate any particular classification; they are rich and flexible enough to permit a variety of organizational arrangements. How we order them, therefore, cannot be determined simply by what they are. Their features and relations provide a jungle of opportunities for the mind. With or without full awareness of what we do, we must focus on certain relationships and to disregard others.

Whom shall we classify as human beings? Primitive tribes tend to be notoriously exclusive, many of them reserving for themselves alone the distinction of being human. Even the civilized ancient Greeks were tempted to view only themselves as properly human and called outsiders uncouth and imperfectly human "barbarians." Although the story of Adam and Eve suggests a single origin and a single nature for us all, the Old Testament leaves no doubt about who were and who were not worthy of special divine attention. The history of humankind is at once the history of denying human status to selected groups: to women, children, blacks, Orientals, Jews, Indians, Slavs, Infidels, Saracens, Christians, and Huns. The more civilized parts of the world have now reached consensus on the undesirability of such exclusiveness. But this humane agreement has emerged not as a result of the general recognition of a single human essence but due to the decision to stress certain telling similarities among us and to dismiss our differences as irrelevant.

The twin facts that acknowledgment of the humanity of all promises significant benefits and that the campaign for this concession has been waged with such passion should have alerted us that this is an area not of objective but of choice-inclusive facts. Important values are at stake, and these values shape our decisions about which similarities to stress and how to classify. The objective facts underlying the classification permit us to call everyone from Albanians to Zulus human no less than they allowed the exclusion of idiots and infidels. But they are not infinitely patient. Clouds and waves and slices of apple pie cannot reasonably be considered human beings, nor can home runs and the stars in the evening sky. So it is possible to be wrong about such matters, though not as easily and as often as philosophers suppose.

In certain other cases, it is not clear what the facts will allow. In such fuzzy borderline situations, the centrality of the decision presupposed by classification is plain to see. There used to be earnest philosophical discussions about whether humans could be but sophisticated robots and whether advanced machines could one day become human beings. Such questions masquerade as queries about objective facts. They cannot be resolved, however, on the basis of observation, of clever argument, or even of what a native speaker of our language could appropriately say. The fundamental flaw in the discussions is that the question generating the inquiry points in the wrong direction. It is unproductive to ask whether human beings might not, after all, *be* machines, and how complex a machine would have to be in order for it to *be* or *become* a human being. These are not matters of objective fact, of how things are. They are, instead, matters of conscious or unconscious human decision. The proper question to ask, accordingly, is concerning the circumstances that would have to obtain in order for us to decide that for purposes of classification, the obvious differences between human beings and machines can be overlooked.

What might such circumstances be? We must note, first, significant similarities between humans and machines. The leprechauns that were supposed to have driven the gears of old clocks were sufficiently like us to enable us to call them small human beings. The gears were not, nor are internal combustion engines and hair clippers. Next, something about machines might engage our concern or sympathy. We might, for instance, be struck by the fact that they are very intelligent or that they act as if they could suffer pain. This notion would activate our value commitments, and as a result, certain of our general beliefs, such as that intelligence is worthy of respect and that gratuitously inflicted pain is evil, would gain extension to machines. We would then examine the consequences of classifying machines, or at least some machines, as humans. Such classification has important social results: as human beings, computers and robots could no longer be sold and would have to be treated as employees or independent contractors rather than as inanimate tools. They would fall, moreover, under the protection of all the labor laws, guaranteeing them lunch hours, overtime pay, periodic vacations, and workmen's compensation benefits. At some point, advanced robots may even launch a campaign for recognition as beings with rights. Faced with such a situation, we may well decide that it is better to classify them as humans, with all the costs that involves, than to endure the consequences of continued differentiation.

Might it not be, however, that such a decision is merely the political acknowledgment of a reality? Perhaps machines of a certain complexity just *are* human and have been all along while we were trying to decide how to classify them. We do, after all, tend to believe that blacks were fully human before they were accorded that status with the abolition of slavery. Why should the humanity of machines at a certain stage of their development be any different?

This view has some initial plausibility. For, should we ever decide that machines are human, some people are likely to say, "I've noticed for a long time now that they are *so much* like us." And others may well announce, "I have *always* thought of them as human beings dressed in metal." But shall we consider this intuitive plausibility adequate to convince us that when we classify machines as human we merely note an objective fact? This decision depends at least in part on the similarities between the circumstances surrounding the two situations. Does the process that issues in the announcement that machines are human resemble acquiescence in objective realities more than it resembles decision-making?

On any careful and sensible examination, the answer to this must be no. Objective facts, such as the existence of the body of water we call 'The Gulf of Mexico,' are relatively easy to recognize. In such cases, we have little need for collecting evidence or for lengthy deliberation: the realities tend to impress themselves on us. Some earnest religious person might predict, for example, that the world will end on a specific date, say at nine o'clock in the morning. By one minute after nine, it will be blindingly clear to everyone that judgment day has not arrived: that the world continues on its merry way is an objective fact. Of course, there are some independent realities we cannot ascertain so easily. The presence of a planet beyond Neptune, the identity of Dwight Eisenhower's wartime lover, the whereabouts of Bonnie Prince Charlie were at one time or another all surrounded by uncertainty. But, even in such cases, something other than a decision is required to settle the matter. Once we catch Pluto in our telescopes or the general in the boudoir, the controversy is resolved. Stubborn inquiry graced by luck suffices to get straight about these objective facts. Choosing the outcome here is not only inappropriate but also disastrous, because it obstructs the needed investigation and makes what we want a cheap substitute for what there is.

This is not at all the situation with the question concerning the humanity of machines. Humanity is not a feature that stares us in the face, but a coveted designation we award on the basis of complex criteria and shrewd assessments. When the question is whether we should award it to machines, inquiry can reveal no additional facts adequate to develop an answer. To be sure, getting straight about the similarities of machines and humans is an indispensable element in moving toward a resolution, but the structure of the problem makes it impossible for this to suffice. For even if what machines do closely resembles our own activities, the issues of origin and ingredients remain. Machines, after all, are manufactured, while human beings are the results of more private and more pleasurable acts. And manufactured objects consist of non-living components, instead of the cells and organs that constitute our parts. The question of what level of resemblance in behavior, if any, is enough for us to overlook these obvious dissimilarities cannot be answered by reference to facts. It requires a decision and with it the assessment of purposes, desires, context, likely consequences, costs, and benefits. If philosophers declare, therefore, that machines cannot be human unless they are capable of falling in love or of liking strawberry shortcake, they are not stating objective facts, but affording us an insight into how high a value they place on such things as caring in a sexual context and fresh fruit with whipped cream.

These considerations reveal that there is no compelling similarity between accepting or rejecting the humanity of machines, on the one hand, and recognizing, noting or accepting objective facts, on the other. Might we not have compelling reasons, however, for deciding to treat questions concerning who is and who is not human as though they were queries about objective fact? We might, indeed, and we frequently do, though this can give no comfort to the objectivist. Making one's view appear to have a warrant in the very nature of things is an excellent strategy for convincing others and stilling one's own doubts. Declaring certain values natural rights, for example, puts us in a more powerful position than if we simply announced our intention to fight for them. Asserting that certain social structures, political arrangements or modes of behavior are direct outcomes of human nature makes them appear more weighty than if we merely said that we favor them. If we should ever decide that machines of an advanced design are really human beings, we could therefore greatly facilitate public acceptance of this changed state of affairs by insisting that they have been humans all along and that we are only paying our belated respects to an objective fact. Obviously, however, neither our objectifying tendency nor the decision to treat certain choice-inclusive facts as if they were objective, changes the nature of the facts. Although choice enters into the constitution of some classes of facts, to which class any given fact belongs is not a matter of choice.

The complex and variable criteria and the shrewd assessments involved in promoting certain groups of beings to the rank of humans were present throughout the long history of expanding the boundaries of our race. Little by little we, or influential groups among us, made decisions to overlook the differences due to class, race, sex, religion, national origin, intelligence, drive, and physical endowment, and to treat a very broad selection of individuals as equally entitled to consideration and respect. The objective facts permitted these decisions without compelling them. Slaves, for example, resembled their masters as closely before emancipation as they did afterwards, but resemblance is insufficient for classification as a human being. Accordingly, to say that they had been human before they were set free is a misleading, ontological way of stating the moral truth that they should have been classified as humans long before.

It is precisely the moral context and the value-consequences of such reclassifications that justified expanding membership in the human family. Clearly, we are all better off for having decided to treat blacks, women, members of different religions, persons with disabilities, and even our enemies, as full-fledged human beings. The benefits of this increase in the range of the concept of humanity, however, have been mitigated by two powerful trends. One is the failure to recognize that the facts about human nature are choice-inclusive rather than objective. This has left a simplistic ontology in possession of the field, in whose terms we continue to believe that all of us share a single essence and that granting people rights and respect is just a response to noting the presence of this independently occurring form. The second trend is supported by the first. Since we think of our concept of humanity as identifying a natural kind, we have failed to introduce into it the diversity needed to keep pace with the increase in its scope. We have admitted to membership in the human community a wide variety of individuals whose nature is at odds with established conceptions of what is properly human. Not having loosened these traditional standards, we now face a situation in which we fervently wish to continue calling such individuals subhuman and their practices unnatural, yet we cannot do so without revoking their newly gained status. This is the source of a fundamental ambiguity at the center of the modern world: we have come to accept the legitimacy of lives we cannot but condemn.

Important and valuable as it has been to embrace the idea of a single human nature uniting us all, we must therefore supplement it by the conception of human natures. The facts permit this manner of classification and our needs and our purposes amply justify it. The human landscape is adorned by variety; vast differences frame our similarities. Philosophers interested in generalization tend to overlook the full range of this diversity and resist being reminded of it by shunning empirical observation. In fact, however, humans differ significantly in feelings, values, and activities. The commitments their lives express vary not only from society to society and from age to age but frequently from individual to individual as well. Moreover, some (such as the severely retarded) lack the capacity for higher mental functions, while others are virtually unable to experience emotions. Some alter their responses unpredictably and without cease, while others (such as catatonic schizophrenics) are unable to change much at all. Some probably perceive the world in ways the rest of us cannot appreciate, or lead internal lives rich in private images and meanings. Some are incapable of significant communication, and some that we unhesitatingly classify as human (such as hydranencephalics) share with us none of the supposed differentiating activities of our species.

We must be careful not to suppose that every divergence among us is suitable as the basis of an irreducibly different human nature. The variations must be wide enough and central enough to enable us to avoid trivializing the notion. We certainly do not want to suppose that short and tall people, beer drinkers and teetotalers, individuals with 20/20 vision and with 20/40 vision are different by nature. The purposes that underlie our choice to distinguish human natures revolve around appreciating our dissimilarities and tolerating those who live by divergent values. Accordingly, the differences we seek must be generic disparities in the commitments and in the lives that express the commitments of groups of human beings.

Such differences are not difficult to find if we focus on the desires, activities, and satisfactions of people. A desire is a wish gone active: it occurs when as a result of prizing something, we develop a tendency to take steps to obtain it. These steps constitute the bulk of the activities of daily life: they are the seekings, the searchings, the habit-bound purposive routines, the dexterous moves and secret rituals that fill the everyday. It is a mistake to look for them only at the dramatic junctures of life. They constitute, first and foremost, the elements of our microbehavior, such as the adjustments of eye and hand when we reach for a slice of pie and the movements of jaw and tongue as we chew it. Focusing on microbehavior makes the connection between action and satisfaction particularly easy to see. Even simple activities consist of action-segments, each of which is carefully monitored to determine what change may be needed to move closer to the desired end. If the action-segment is satisfactory, the activity proceeds apace, as when I continue to turn to respond to a voice behind my back. The unsatisfactoriness of the action-segment, on the other hand, leads to rapid correction, as when I note that in whirling around, I have managed to turn too far.

Desire, action, and satisfaction constitute, in this way, an unbroken and interactive chain. In our grand passions no less than in microbehavior, desires generate activities and satisfactions ratify the action. When our exertions yield no fruit or produce it at too high a cost, we tend to question and eventually to revise both our desires and our activities. The early hankering to fly by spreading one's arms, for example, is abandoned because of futility, while the hunger for throwing baseballs through large windowpanes (an easily performed and highly satisfying task) is surrendered only with the worldly wisdom painful consequences produce. In an ongoing process, therefore, desires, actions, and outcomes exert a determining influence on one another. Whatever we choose to believe about the nature and justification of values, this process is their birthplace and their testing ground.

Human natures vary according to significant differences in the desires, activities, and satisfactions of people. That there are such differences is a matter of objective fact; that each defines a divergent human nature is a choice-inclusive fact. Stress on what is unlike about us must not, of course, be permitted to obscure our similarities. The differences, however, are so broad, so neglected, and so important to the growth of decency in the treatment of others that it is appropriate to dwell on them at length. Dissimilarities in desires, activities, and satisfactions make for different sorts of values that structure different sorts of lives. In honest moments, many of us quietly admit that it is unintelligible how others can act on the values and be satisfied with the lives they embrace. We know, however, that on reflection we must add that they surely feel the same way about us.

The desires, activities, and satisfactions, for example, that full-fledged membership in an acquisitive society requires render us human beings of an identifiable sort. The relentless drive to work, the incessant accumulation of new and old products, the savage haste make leisure as brief and rare as bird song on a cloudy day. Even in universities, where life is supposed to afford reflective distance, people move in a swirl, or haze, of exertions, devoted to serving the needs of the moment, chasing name and visibility, not antique perfection. Such a life, viewed from the outside, might seem impoverished or wrapped in frustration or lit only by feeble pleasures. Yet many of us choose it eagerly and find happiness in nothing but its movement.

We can contrast such desires and activities in the flux with the lives of people who seek peace and rest in monasteries or under the bridge. A human nature passive in the face of contingency or resigned to the will of God operates by different values and seeks dissimilar satisfactions. The large houses, fancy trips, and car phones that measure meaning for the person on the make are, to this soul, ashes in the mouth. Acquiescence replaces drive and will; what desires remain aim at a simple and wholesome mode of life. Attempts to manipulate people and the world recede, and the person, at one with nature, learns to move without motion, like a still bird carried by the wind. Some small percentage of the homeless, of welfare recipients, and of deeply religious people may well be such dropouts from acquisitive society. Spirituality and the simple life remain powerful ideals even in the worldly postindustrial age.

Adopting the view that there are multiple human natures removes one important line of support for dismissing unpopular values and alternative forms of life. It makes it impossible for people to claim that one and only one style of behavior is natural and right or that certain desires and activities and satisfactions are unnatural. To the extent that who we are determines what we value and how we ought to act, it constitutes the theoretical basis of a wholesome pluralism. In this way, we can at last secure the full legitimacy of our fellows: so long as they cause no harm, their differences from the majority in economic, religious, social, or even sexual values, or in the relative ranking of these values, will not justify their differential treatment. We will simply ascribe what appear to us as odd behavior and unfathomable bent to innocent differences in our human natures.

Modernity has taught us a double lesson. We have come to recognize that much in the world is contingent and that much of what is contingent can be improved. These discoveries were made first in relation to the physical world; only recently and gradually have we come to think of traditions and social and political arrangements as optional and open to intelligent control. It appears that we have not yet fully extended this recognition to our own thoughts and conceptual schemes. We continue to believe that there is one and only one correct or best way to think about things, and philosophers, unburdened by historical knowledge, tend to identify this with our current mode of thought. That is unfortunate. We must learn that our opinions, our distinctions, even the terms of our reflection lead conditional lives and may need to be replaced. In many areas of thought, we enjoy vast flexibility and vast power to adapt our ideas to our broader purposes. Only intelligent and imaginative variations in how we think can help us achieve our epistemic goals and do justice to the astounding richness of the actual.

CHAPTER 24

The Philosophical Significance
of Psychological Differences
Among Humans

Murphy, of whose laws our lives constitute continuing empirical confirmation, once said that the Golden Rule is simply
that he who has the gold makes the rule. Philosophers have
long been familiar with a version of this law and have employed it to
good advantage. Since nature determines function, whoever controls
the essence can prescribe behavior. The way to gain command over
the nature or essence of a thing, of course, is to recognize and to name
it. Adam's act of naming all creatures was a symbol of our knowledge of their secret and, thus, of human dominion over them. Similarly, whoever can define the hidden essence of humankind acquires
the power of deciding who and what is human and who and what is
not, and can thereby establish the parameters of acceptable behavior.
Whoever owns the essence determines which actions make sense.

The enterprise of searching for the single nature of any species
involves bold presuppositions. In their quest, philosophers have typically supposed that such simple essences define natural kinds, that
they exist independently of human choice and cognition, and that
they can be known with assurance. Such assumptions naturally led
thinkers to disregard the complexity of empirical facts, to underrate
the contribution of choice to understanding, and to overlook the pervasiveness of contingency and change. The positive conceptions they
developed suffer, as a result, from arbitrariness and excessive generality.

If we could, indeed, identify that central trait possession of which
guarantees humanity, or at least the traits that all and only human
beings have, we would be able to provide definitive and objective

answers to who is and who is not human, and to what norms all members of the species must observe. So far, however, no one has come up with such a single feature, and we have little reason to think that one exists. Moreover, what appears to mark the boundaries of the human is not so much a collection of traits all of us, but only we, possess as the degree to which we display a significant number of loosely interconnected characteristics. But even here, we must remember the continuity of our activities with the activities of animals and the way our picture of the properly human varies with the features we select for attention.

No simple answer exists as to where the animal ends and the human begins. Accordingly, concerning a number of beings that range from the prehistoric ancestors of humankind to certain individuals today, we cannot with assurance say that they are human or that they are not. The matter is best settled by a decision that takes into account not only the facts but also our purposes and values and that, for this very reason, remains open to change. The distinctions we draw between species are obviously not arbitrary; but admitting this still leaves us a long distance from the view that species are natural kinds whose existence we note and whose nature we discover. What we note is a bewildering variety of creatures and facts. We sort them into groups to suit our purposes and to meet the constraints under which we operate. The lines we draw have an element of invention in them: they reflect, at least in part, our decisions on how best to categorize—and that means to simplify—the bounty of nature.

The first thinkers who recognized the creative power of human categories reacted with philosophical hyperbole, announcing that the entirety of the structured world was the product of our cognitive efforts. Kant, for example, maintained that all the intelligible features of experience, which he did not adequately distinguish from the physical world, were due to the organizing activity of mind. According to this view, the properties of physical objects, including their spatial and temporal configurations, resulted from the sensory and conceptual grid with which humans, it was supposed, uniformly operate. Kant thought, therefore, that facts were constructions that make their own raw material unrecognizable: he placed the sensuous manifold out of which the world was made near the vanishing point, at the distant portal of the mind. About such unstructured, human-independent things, he too quickly concluded, nothing of significance could be said.

It seems no less surprising than it is unfortunate that such extreme positions continue to be held today. Deconstructionists, unable to see past a world of discourse, are in this sense also constructionists: they leave no room for any reality external to the human world. And even those supposedly devoted to good sense and clarity, such as Nelson Goodman, speak unabashedly of ways in which we create worlds. Goodman claims that all facts are fabricated by the use of "words, numerals, pictures, sounds or other symbols of any kind in any medium."* The search for an 'aboriginal'—that is, human-independent—reality is, accordingly, futile because each world is a system of symbols and the only alternative to such cognitive structures is blankness.† The raw material of any world is some other world already on hand, so nothing limits human creativity but the internal demands of symbol systems and our lack of imagination. Everything seems to be up for grabs to such powerful world creators as ourselves. No hard, environing reality constrains us; even "the felt stubbornness of fact" is just "the grip of habit."‡

Reading such things reinforces my fear that the two great requirements of doing distinguished philosophy are poor judgment and lack of a sense of reality. No sane person would wish to deny the power of symbol systems. But underlying them, surely, is a physical world, including our bodies, that we did not make. Those who speak of the primacy of action in life do not mean action as it appears in perception or as our understanding of it functions in some symbolic medium. As Peirce accurately pointed out, action is a brute encounter between forces, a clash that is, intrinsically, below the level of the sign-spinning mind. This is the sphere of existence that surrounds us with mindless, unjustifiable, absurd constraints. Symbols are draped around what there is or are invented to account for the absences we find. A slip on the ice that breaks a bone, hunger met by a bare refrigerator, a brick wall with my love on the other side, the March sun that kisses blossoms on my skin—these are the sorts of facts we did not fabricate. To be sure, someone built the wall and ate the food and will perhaps even set my bone, but not by putting "words, numerals, pictures, sounds or other symbols" together. I must, of course, use words to tell you about these oppressive or

---

* Nelson Goodman, *Ways of Worldmaking* (Indianapolis: Hackett, 1978), 94.
† Goodman, 100.
‡ Goodman, 97.

promising realities. But this converts them into words or symbols or meanings just as little as the fact that we cannot cook without heat transforms food into nothing but high temperature or flames.

Common sense, embodying the long experience of our species, rejects such extremes as the constructivist claim that all facts are fabricated. Philosophical good sense, on the other hand, enables us to see that the other radical view, namely, that all facts are objective realities existing independently of human effort, is not correct either. There are objective facts, such as that it is raining today, that are not human products: these we do not make and cannot unmake. But there also are conventional facts, such as that the strong atmosphere surrounding some mouths is called 'halitosis.' This is not the "right" word in any final or objective sense ('foul breath' will do as well); its appropriateness derives from the social practices of which our language consists.

A sensible philosophy must, then, acknowledge the existence of both objective and conventional facts. But whoever occupies this middle ground and remains sensitive to the teachings of experience will note that there also are facts of a third sort, intermediate between the first two. These interesting facts are not in any straightforward way either simply objective or simply conventional. Surprisingly, although they surround us, they have never received the philosophical attention they deserve. Typically, these facts have an objective and an optional component. Optional does not mean arbitrary, only that there is room in them, and need, for choice. And normally, there are ample reasons for the choices we make.

We divide all rubber-wheeled, combustion engine vehicles into the mutually exclusive categories of cars and trucks. Where do conversion vans fit? Like cars, they are used to transport people, not merchandise. But they are built on truck axles and utilize truck engines. If we stress their function, they are large cars; if we attend to their parts, they are small trucks. Which should we emphasize? That depends on our purposes. If we wish to sell a lot of them, we will praise them as the roomiest of cars. If, on the other hand, we want to remove their deadly effect on the attempt of manufacturers to comply with passenger vehicle fleet mileage standards, we will declare them to be trucks. Neither designation is wrong, nor is either just right. Concerning such issues, it is wrongheaded to look for an objectively correct answer because they are not objective matters of fact.

I call facts of this sort 'choice-inclusive' to indicate the element of discretion we enjoy in their constitution. Normally, the objective ingredient in such facts is a spectrum of individuals: cars and trucks in one case, individuals weighing a certain number of pounds in another. The element of choice consists in how we carve up the continuum. Within limits, a variety of arrangements is acceptable, so long as each meets relevant needs and purposes. But the objective factor imposes significant constraints: vans may be classed with cars or with trucks, but not with term papers or with Cuban cigars. An additional hold on wild categorization is that the choice is rarely private. Decisions about who is fat, intelligent, retarded, or dead are made by society as a whole or by groups of appointed specialists. Moreover, the decisions are open to adjustment: changes in technology and in moral beliefs have caused us just recently, for instance, to revise our ideas about where to draw the line between life and death.

The category of the human has undergone just such a gradual mutation. The initial tendency concerning application of the label runs to exclusiveness. To call people human is to impute laudable characteristics to them and to confer upon them the benefits of privileged status. It is natural to be sparing with such conferrals and to want to retain them for oneself and one's associates. That essentially has been the social history of the notion of humanity. Its application has been extended over the centuries only slowly and grudgingly. On more than one occasion, even when a tribe or race or nation had nominally been brought under its protective umbrella, its members continued to be treated as though they were not really human after all.

In other cases, there was genuine doubt about whether or not individuals of a certain sort were human. The first encounter of the British with West African black people occurred at the same time as their first contact with chimpanzees. Western travelers noted remarkable similarities between the monkeys and Britishers, but they saw an even more immediate connection between blacks and the apes.* Many thought of blacks as somehow intermediate between the animal and the human, sharing with us the gift of language but retaining the lusty disposition of beasts. Only after many years did white people agree that blacks were fully human, although they continued to treat them as though they were not. Admission of them to the human race was a social decision motivated by many factors. In spite of the

---

* Winthrop D. Jordan, *The White Man's Burden: Historical Origins of Racism in the United States* (New York: Oxford University Press, 1974), 16.

rhetoric of the controversies of the age, recognition that they were, as a matter of objective fact, human was not one of them.

The reason for this is that there exists no uniform human essence that those who advocated the humanity of West Africans could have discovered. What they noted was the pervasive similarity between white Britishers and black Africans. Sympathy and good feeling may have directed attention to the similarities; religious belief, tradition, and self-interest could all have contributed to kindling the generosity. At any rate, the claim that blacks were human was not the expression of a blinding intuition but a savvy judgment about how to classify groups of individuals.

I offer two considerations in favor of this view. The first is the excessive improbability that Britishers of the seventeenth and eighteenth centuries were able to have intuitions of such essences, while we can neither have them nor intelligently explicate what they would be like. The second is that although West Africans were very similar to Britishers in some respects, they were also different in others. Were the similarities more important than the dissimilarities? Answering this question requires a decision about how to weight each, and that, in turn, mobilizes the values and purposes of the community. The coldly cognitive quickly leads, in this way, to the normative for its supplementation. Whether we view blacks or others as human beings is, therefore, more nearly a moral issue than an epistemic one. At least an element of choice or will is involved in such classifications, and choices are better or worse, not true or false. At this point, one might attempt to introduce the notion of relevant similarities to avoid my conclusion. But that does not help. For we must already know the human essence to be able to tell which similarities are relevant to it. Without such knowledge, relevance becomes a matter of judgment guided by values and purposes.

Does it make no sense, then, to talk of a single, uniform human species? If we have in mind a large collection of creatures all of whom share the same essence, it does not. However, we can sensibly speak of a group of individuals who resemble one another to varying degrees in a wide variety of ways, all of whom are accorded rights, and to all of whom we attribute dignity. The primary significance of the notion of a human nature shared by all is, therefore, moral. Our motivations for inventing the idea and for admitting various groups to 'the human race' may not be moral in the sense of being pure or unselfish. The issues involved, however, are clearly moral in that they center on actions that have a profound impact on the good of others.

Since facts about who is human are choice-inclusive, the continuum of individuals clearly permits us to dignify a single, large group with the name. The larger the group, however, the more vacuous the designation becomes because of the wide differences among its members. Some, whose physical appearance does not diverge much from the average, lack all higher mental functions. Others, outstanding in perception and thought, operate with severe affective deficits. With respect to every discriminable feature, at least some individuals, in evolutionary subgroups and even today, are indistinguishable from animals. The intellectual content of calling someone human and the location of the line that separates the human from the animal are, therefore, always dubious. The richness of the actual renders every wholesale attempt at classification inadequate.

We can make more headway if instead of exploring human nature, we concentrate on discerning human natures. How shall we distinguish these natures from one another? To say that there are as many natures as there are individuals amounts to declaring the bankruptcy of thought: theory cannot operate without at least some generalization. Yet when it comes to differentiating one sort of human being from another, we do not want to fall back on old and discredited categories. It would make no sense to say, as I once heard a colleague sigh with exasperation, that women constitute a different species, or that blacks or the French or Aryans do. Such distinctions subserve certain purposes, though not ones we would wish to adopt. Since our primary aims are to understand and to appreciate our differences, we must look for fundamental valuational disagreements. If nature determines function, function that fulfills reveals nature. To learn who we are, therefore, we must explore what satisfies us. What we like, what we do, and what we like to do separate us into groups with natures that are, if not incompatible, at least significantly different.

The valuational differences of which I speak permeate nearly all aspects of life. They consist of the varieties of desire and satisfaction that constitute the psychological differences among us. Even here, of course, we do not want to classify humans as having divergent natures on the basis of every minute difference in what they seek and enjoy. We must look for significant differences and thereby make sure that those who prefer fried fish to the broiled variety, for example, do not end up classified as different sorts of people. The problem we face is that no general formula can be developed to determine which differences are significant. How much difference is enough to reach significance is a matter of purpose and need and decision deeply influenced by the particularities of context and the values at stake. In the case of devoted hunters of ducks and of deer, for instance, the difference in objects of pursuit is inadequate to warrant their classification as individuals with different natures. When we deal with deer slayers and unregenerate killers of humans, by contrast, the diversity in the objects targeted is ample justification for viewing the latter as different by nature and deserving of differential treatment.

The situation is similar with sexuality. Whether gentlemen prefer blondes or brunettes is a matter of little significance for their classification. But if gentlemen prefer gentlemen, we may have good reason to see them as people whose nature is different. And if we find some individuals who have little or no interest in sex, we may not want to hesitate at all in saying that their nature is quite unlike ours. Thinking this way reveals two mistakes Freud committed, probably under the influence of bad philosophy. The first was to assume, in his search for the human essence, that all of us have the same basic drives. This made him refuse to accept empirical evidence to the contrary. The refusal started him on the journey of postulating repressive structures to account for the apparent absence of what he knew had to be there. The desire for perfect generality about human nature makes for no better psychology than philosophy.

Freud's second mistake lay in declaring as a universal standard the proper display of the human nature he thought he had found for us all. Once a norm of health or adjustment takes hold, it becomes easy to dismiss conflicting ideals and behavior as deviant. Organizing a broad range of cases in this way highlights one sort as optimal or right and relegates the others as variously flawed to different levels in a hierarchical structure. This makes it impossible to appreciate multiple perfections or even to see ideals and practices different from ours as legitimate. In discerning human natures, by contrast, we automatically legitimize a multiplicity of directions in the search for meaning in life and, with that, a broad spectrum of fulfillments. These varied perfections are not arranged in any weighted order of good and bad, or even of better and worse. They are seen simply as different, each well suited to please those who need or want it.

Although no one can provide an algorithm for which dissimilarities among humans are adequate to credit them with having different natures, I can make at least one general comment. The valuational differences that form the basis of classification cannot be insular. Truly important desires and satisfactions tend to have a profound influence on the entire economy of one's life. A stray craving, no matter how odd, that turns into an isolated vice (such as the passionate collection of fur-lined boots), is not enough to make one into a different sort of person. But when the passion for collecting spreads and fills one's life with needs, demands and goods, we can reasonably think that a different human nature is emerging.

Talk of desires and satisfactions might suggest that we are dealing with hidden or private phenomena. Nothing could be farther from the truth. Public activities bridge the distance between cravings and fulfillments; rightly interpreted, they tell us everything we need to know about the varieties and the complexities of human nature. There is, of course, no shortage of dissembling and deceit among human beings, nor would I dare assert that we are always correct when we infer what people want and what pleases them from what they say and do. But desires, activities, and satisfactions are so intricately and intimately connected that the material is at hand for careful observers to draw reliable conclusions.

Philosophers have too often thought that they can learn more about human nature by scrutating the murky depths of substance and faculties than by interpreting the obvious evidence. The result has been not insight but oversight of the marvelous subtleties of experience that betoken the deeper differences among us. Even those philosophers who look to experience for information tend to study the interconnection of desires, activities, and satisfactions in macrobehavior without proper analogies derived from the investigation of constituent routines. Yet only microbehavior shows the truly intimate connections between the elements of action. Focusing the eyes, for example, involves complicated feats of interrelating aim, performance, and assessment of the result. The purpose to be achieved initiates the activity but passes control of it to the relation between the actual and the desired conditions of the eyes. Continued assessment of the adequacy of what we do keeps the eyes moving and adjusting until full focus is achieved; cessation of relevant efforts marks the attainment of satisfaction. Purpose and the degree of its fulfillment are, in this way, hovering presences throughout the duration of the activity: they are as organically connected with what is done as it is with them.

If we think of all desire-action-satisfaction complexes as connected in these intimate ways, it becomes relatively easy to note the differences on the basis of which we may decide to classify individuals as having divergent natures. For the actions in which we engage and their terminations can then be read as telling evidence of what satisfies us. And the fulfillments we seek serve as good indicators of who we are.

Let me examine two cases of unusual behavior to show how the classification of human natures might proceed. The first concerns a twenty-six-year-old male who goes to public rest rooms to retrieve the feces of people he finds attractive. He achieves sexual excitement by playing with his find, and then he masturbates. He is single, holds a steady job and, though somewhat shy, appears otherwise unremarkable.* According to the latest diagnostic system of the American Psychiatric Association, this person suffers from fetishism and from atypical personality disorder.

Few conceptual structures show the looseness and the choice-inclusive nature of classification better than the categories of psychiatry. Admittedly, the reported behavior borders on the bizarre. There is no reason to suppose, however, that the person displaying it is sick, unless we made a prior decision that whoever seeks help with a psychological problem must suffer from some disease. Such a decision, made perhaps to enhance the likelihood of help through 'diagnosis,' nearly obliterates the distinction between problems and diseases. It also entails the paradoxical consequence that hypochondria may lead us to mistaken beliefs about having physical ailments, but we can never be wrong if we think we are mentally ill.

This young person strikes me as neither sick nor appropriately classified as having a different nature from the rest of us. His bizarre behavior is isolated and appears to have little effect on the rest of his life. It reveals a peculiarity about his likes in a narrow area of endeavor that is relatively free of social effects. If there were many people like him and they organized into groups attempting to extend the scope and structuring force of their values, we might reconsider and decide to view them as having or developing a different nature.

---

* Robert L. Spitzer, Andrew E. Skodol, Miriam Gibbon, and Janet B. W. Williams, *DSM-III Case Book* (Washington, D.C.: The American Psychiatric Association: 1981), 193–95.

Given the relative inertness of this single desire-action-satisfaction complex, however, we have reason to say only that a portion of this person's behavior is different, not that he is.

The second case is that of a recently deceased captain of industry. Throughout his life, this man displayed a vast drive to acquire money. He made hundreds of millions of dollars, much of which he never spent. He permitted his fine collection of paintings to be shown only at museums whose curators were beholden to him. He hired yes-men to head his companies; whoever among them made independent decisions or disagreed with him was instantly removed. He loaned, not gave, needy members of his family small sums of money and involved them in expensive lawsuits if they did not repay on time. He did not hesitate, on the other hand, to make large donations to politicians, especially if these bought personal influence or glory. He allowed no one around him to make a decision concerning his life, but he tried to make as many as he could concerning everyone else's.

We recognize in the behavior of this person many tendencies whose germs we find in ourselves. In his case, however, these impulses could grow unchecked. As a result, the exercise of power became the central value in his life, and he developed into a thoroughly nasty, obnoxious old man. Moral condemnation, however, is the easy route to go. It is much better to view him, without rancor, as a person whose nature was different from ours and whose fulfillments, consequently, appear to us empty and unsatisfactory.

One great advantage of such a classification is that it enables us to understand, or at least to accept, that what seems to us hollow and wrong may be, to another, the only worthwhile thing in all of life. Acknowledging the reality and conceding the legitimacy of such alien enjoyments may not incline us to be a party to them or even to embrace those who are. But we will understand people better, and even if we give them wide berth, we will be more disposed to tolerate them.

CHAPTER 25

Persons and Different
Kinds of Persons

mong the neglected treasures of American philosophy, Borden
Parker Bowne shines with the regal color of the amethyst. The
color mix is rich, pulling hues from divergent parts of the spectrum, but always warm, favoring humane, even spiritual, interests. It
was not by accident that amethyst became the symbol of spiritual authority and found its way into the rings of bishops. Its message is
that the ordinary world of physical existence and a deeper, personal,
moral reality intersect. We live at the crossroads and must choose.
Even if we reject full ecclesiastical hierarchy, as Bowne was apt to do,
the power of the amethyst confronts us with a hierarchy of values and
invites commitment to what is, in any case, our birthright and our
destiny.

Our birthright and our destiny, I say, because we are persons and
personhood immeasurably transcends everything in the mechanical
world. We are *persons*—the idea satisfies, even if it is not clear. How
can we give some content to it? Bowne obliges: "The essential meaning of personality is selfhood, self-consciousness, self-control and the
power to know."* This statement is, of course, terribly general, and
Bowne himself denies that we are abstract intellects or abstract wills.
In a more concrete vein, he offers this description: "We are living persons, knowing and feeling and having various interests, and in the
light of knowledge and under the impulse of our interests trying to
find our way, having an order of experience also and seeking to

---

* Borden Parker Bowne, *Personalism* (Boston and New York: Houghton Mifflin,
1908), 266.

understand it and to guide ourselves so as to extend or enrich that experience, and thus to build ourselves into larger and fuller and more abundant personal life."*

This is an excellent description—it connects with a great deal in my experience. We all know many people just like this though, of course, not everyone answers to every part of the description. Some persons I know, for example, make no effort to understand their experience. Others wish neither to enrich nor to extend their lives. And how many in this culture, never mind the South Seas, take no interest in making their personal existence "larger and fuller and more abundant"?

Should we call individuals persons even if they do not show all these marks of personhood? And what if they lack some of the more abstract features, such as self-control? And what about those who are neither self-conscious nor enjoy the power to know because they are in a permanent vegetative state? These problems pale, however, by contrast with a devastating fact: Bowne's concrete account provides a perfect description of my dog, Lou. She knows me, members of my family, and the woods around the house. She has feelings of joy, sadness, and perhaps even shame. She has "various interests," focused largely on playing, eating, and being loved. Her experience is ordered—perhaps rigidly so—taking her from morning naps to afternoon meal and the evening chase. She tries to find a way to extend and to enrich her experience by acquiring better control of the petting hand. To do this, she had to discover and now understands what works best: grateful licking from finger to wrist combined with uncontrolled wagging of tail. I have no doubt that she wants to achieve a more abundant personal life. Why else should she constantly ask for more food and love, lie in the deep leaves in the fall, and roll on her back to turn her belly to the sun?

Lou is unquestionably a person, then. Actually, even without such philosophical warrant, I have always believed this. Occasionally, in a mood of wonderment about wild metamorphoses and reincarnation, my wife and I ask just who Lou really is. The answer to that, however, is obvious: she is Lou, the sweetest and fattest black Lab-like dog we know.

Bowne would not be satisfied with this promiscuous readiness to call dogs persons. But what reason could he offer to deny them the

* Bowne, 263.

designation? "Personality and corporeality are incommensurable ideas,"* he says. Perhaps so, but if that means no one with a body can be a person, both Lou and I will fail to qualify. In fact, Bowne himself shrinks from such an implication: he is happy to talk about the bodies and souls of persons and thinks that they can interact. So a more promising line is to explore what justifies us in assigning personality to humans and to contrast that with how we relate to dogs.

Bowne asserts that we are "quite sure of one another's existence and of our mutual understanding."† How do we achieve this? "Our thoughts of our neighbors arise within our own minds as a mental interpretation of our sense experience,"‡ he says. Sensory clues must be taken to reveal a deeper, nonsensible reality. This is what we do with speech when we construe sounds as disclosing the presence of other minds.§ Communication with these minds justifies the belief that the beings to whom they belong are intelligent, living persons.

This account of how we come to ascribe personality to perceived others strikes me as generally correct. We enjoy sensory contact with objects, we observe their behavior, and when it meets certain standards, we declare them to be or to be closely associated with persons. The sensory clues, the necessary interpretations, and the relevant standards are complex and subtle. Speech or communication of some sort doubtless plays a central role in the ascription. But none of this means that only and all humans are appropriately designated persons. For whatever conduct marks the presence of self and mind, that conduct is there in Lou. And if intelligent exchange (of which what we think is speech constitutes an unduly restricted form) is the ultimate criterion, my communication with her is richer, more precise, and far more satisfying than anything I can achieve with a baby. I readily grant that when I discuss philosophy or the stock market with her, I get only a lick and a stare. Concerning such matters, however, I do even worse with humans: they stare just as much but they never lick. I also admit that though I speak English to her, she does not respond in the same tongue. Nevertheless, she and I share other languages: those of expressive sounds, meaningful looks, and a wide variety of bodily attitudes and motions.

I conclude that Bowne faces the following difficult situation. Whatever criterion or set of criteria is chosen for ascribing personhood, some humans will not qualify under it, but some animals will.

---

* Bowne, 266.   † Bowne, 80.   ‡ Bowne, 74.   § Bowne, 76.

Some very young and very old people are neither self-conscious nor self-controlled, for example, while—after a moment of indiscretion—Lou appears to reflect on what she has done, determines that she got too excited, and will exercise more self-control from here on. One response Bowne might make is to convert his American personalism into Native American personalism by extending to dogs some of the respect and courtesies, such as a place in heaven, normally reserved for humans. This, however, will not really resolve the problem because dogs are by no means the only animals that qualify as persons, nor are all that qualify animals. If we read the sensory clues, machines of a high degree of sophistication must also be classified as persons. Even without *Star Wars* fantasies about the future, we can say that some of our advanced, self-moving, intelligent mechanisms give signs of knowing, feeling, and seeking in a controlled way to "extend or enrich" their lives. If this is so, however, how can personality and corporeality be incommensurable or even incompatible ideas? With this step, Bowne has to give up too much for his position to remain intact or even identifiable.

Problems of this sort are not unique to personalism and to Bowne. Similar issues arise, for example, in the abortion controversy, where the personhood of the fetus carries a heavy ideological burden. This is not accidental but grows naturally out of the concept of person itself. For this idea is neither like that of being present nor like that of the timeliness of filing an appeal. Whether a student is present or not is a purely objective question. It is easily answered by calling the roll or by looking around. Nothing is a matter of choice in such cases: if, once the door is shut, Susie cannot be seen among the students eagerly taking notes, she is simply not present.

The question of the timeliness of an appeal, by contrast, cannot be resolved by reference to objective factors. To be sure, issues of objective fact arise: we need to know, for example, when the documents were actually delivered. But this becomes relevant only when placed in a context of conventional decisions. We or designated individuals in the legal system must determine what shall count as an appeal and decide how many days to allow for it. These are matters of choice and agreement; nothing about them is objectively right. Thirty days for appeal is no more correct than sixty or ninety-five; delivering them to the Clerk of Court is not more nearly right than sending them for redistribution to a post office box in Seattle. The point is that here decisions create the reality: without the rules we make, nothing could *be* an appeal, and no appeal could be timely or otherwise.

Someone's being a person is not an objective matter along the lines of his or her presence in class. It is also not a conventional matter of the sort timeliness of appeal constitutes. Interestingly, it appears to fall between these two categories, involving both choice and significant objective considerations. That certain types of beings are persons is not discovered; hence it is not a simple objective fact. It is also not created out of whole cloth, however; hence it is not a fully choice-determined, conventional fact. In such intermediate situations, we make choices about how to carve up a continuum of objective cases we find.

Following Bowne, we may begin by observing the conduct of a range of living creatures. In doing so, we are certain to find striking parallels, continuities, and similarities. Some of these will recommend themselves for special attention because in our own case we find them associated with particularly valuable or painful experiences. We may wish to highlight a few of these by establishing a group to which only those who display such similarities may belong. Our purpose in classifying in this way is frequently, though not always, practical. We may wish to protect or to promote certain traits or else to stamp out or at least to reduce the incidence of others.

An example of what I have in mind is the way we classify certain birds. We note a number of them tend to roost in city parks and by their noise and droppings make a nuisance of themselves. We generalize that, by and large, any bird that behaves in this way is undesirable, and we take action on this judgment. This classification of birds expresses a purpose, let us say the control of pests. In doing so, it may subvert or disregard other purposes, such as that of scientifically correct classification or that of categorization in terms of aesthetically pleasing colors and shapes.

I have called the facts that result from the imposition of optional categories on objective continua 'choice-inclusive facts.' A significant number of the facts we distinguish in the world are of this sort. There are at least two elements of choice involved in such facts. The first is to stress some feature over others by creating classifications on its basis. The second is to determine the degree of similarity necessary to gain a place in the group. The first thus establishes that there shall be a certain sort of class; the second defines the range of its membership.

The recent history of the concept of person strongly suggests that its application creates choice-inclusive facts. For it has come to function as a term of commendation or of congratulatory contrast between humans and animals. Humans (according to some, even human zygotes) are supposed to be persons; animals can never reach this lofty status. How do we know that we are persons? Is this something that a careful examination of our experience of ourselves discloses? Is personhood something that if only we manage to look in the right place, we can find? Certainly not. To call ourselves persons is to express our resolve to set ourselves apart from the rest of creation as somehow special and precious.

How do we accomplish this? By focusing on some high-level accomplishments of human beings, such as knowledge, self-consciousness, and self-control, and declaring them to be defining traits of personhood. We choose these particular features rather than irritability, year-round sexual appetite, and predisposition to weather-influenced mood swings precisely because we want to maximize our distance from animals. But is it reasonable to suppose that all humans enjoy or are even capable of these rarified achievements? Of course not. Once we declare that all humans are persons, however, we no longer have to demonstrate the presence of these traits. Instead, our possession of them is assumed and thus assured, and we can proceed to find reasons why their display is inadequate or altogether absent in some cases.

If special purposes did not motivate our ascriptions of personhood, we would be satisfied with empirical findings. It is perfectly clear, for example, that people in advanced stages of degeneration and in permanent comas lack knowledge, self-consciousness, and self-control. If this fact were taken at face value, we would concede that such folks are no longer persons and thereby remove a powerful obstacle to treating them and their families compassionately by helping them out of their misery. Many of us refuse to do this, however, because we think—mistakenly—that their personhood is an ontological or objective fact about them rather than a temporary status that is socially conferred.

If we understand the personhood of people as a choice-inclusive fact about them, we can lay bare the way such predicates are ascribed. We are confronted with a continuum of individuals, both human and nonhuman, that display a variety of types and levels of knowledge, self-consciousness, and self-control. Those, such as C. S. Peirce, who show these features in abundance qualify preeminently as persons. Others may qualify to a greater or lesser degree, requiring a decision on our part concerning whether they resemble Peirce and others closely enough. That some qualify more or less does not mean that being a person is a matter of degree. Whoever is judged to be a person is a person completely, with all the benefits and privileges that status confers. But his or her qualifications for personhood may be partial or weak and it is a matter of social decision as to where we draw the line between those who are persons and those who are not, that is, how weak a qualification for personhood we shall consider enough.

How do we know where to draw the line? In answering this, we must remember that there is no right place. Depending on our purposes, we may want to be restrictive or expansive. The history of the concept of person shows that we started out in a fashion that limited the application of the idea sharply. Over the last several hundred years, we have become more permissive, admitting into the human race and to personhood large numbers of people who do not look, do not think, and do not behave the way we do. In the West, we have long thought of God and of God's angelic companions as persons, but we have not been able to get ourselves officially to confer personhood on the likes of Lou and on machines.

Are these limits justified? Not if people in comas are honored as persons. But circumstances may arise in which we may want to restrict the notion to intelligent and sophisticated human adults. Alternatively, the contingencies of life may occasion us to expand it to several species of mammals and perhaps even to certain types of manufactured objects showing machine intelligence. Such expansions and contractions would be justified by the circumstances and the purposes we wish to accomplish. None of them is just right, though they can be good or bad and they can achieve or fail to attain our purposes. Can we ever be wrong in such matters? Of course, and in many ways, though not in the way in which it is wrong to say that Susie is present when she is not. We can embrace the wrong purposes, choose inept means to attain them, and be inconsistent in our application of the concept. We can also extend the idea too far, assigning personhood to everything that moves, or not far enough, retaining it for the two of us and seven balding friends. The point, however, is that we are never wrong in that we fail to recognize personhood where it exists or see it where, in fact, there is no trace of it. We are not wrong, in other words, in a recognitional way, though we can be wrong in how we think and what we want and how we go about things.

One vast advantage of viewing personhood as a choice-inclusive fact is that it demythologizes an area of concern that now suffers from fuzziness of thought. The fuzziness derives, at least in part, from the sense that we tread on hallowed ground, and therefore a careful examination of claims is inappropriate. In celebratory discourse pickiness constitutes bad form, so we stand back, swallow hard, and learn to live with inadequate thought. As a result, we extend the notion of personhood too far and not far enough, and few dare to challenge such traditional confusion. We extend it too far because we seem to think that personhood is an essential possession, and thus, even those humans reduced to mere biological existence continue to enjoy it. We fail to extend it far enough by overlooking the obvious similarities between humans and higher mammals, thus categorically rejecting the possibility that the likes of Lou can qualify. Misery and cruelty flow from both errors: humans who would be better off dead are forced to live, and animals who need protection are denied all standing.

The fundamental idea that needs to be assailed is that personhood is an ontological condition invariably attendant on humanity. Such a species-specific and species-limited idea is not likely to have an empirical origin or to be responsive to empirical counterevidence. The proper antidote to it is recognition that even belonging to a species is a choice-inclusive fact. At any rate, if being a person is a choice-inclusive fact, we are reminded that the criteria for ascribing personhood are not only contingent but also within our power to adjust. Moreover, we are then constantly led back to daily experience to determine whether any given individual or group actually displays the characteristics we require for personhood.

There is no need to be concerned about the moral consequences of the possibility that one's status as a person may with time be lost. Sensible criteria of personhood and fair application of them should safeguard the values we hold dear. The argument that if we yield an inch about the humanity or personhood of people on the far edge of life, then no one's rights or existence will be safe again has always struck me as tendentious and exaggerated. Contingency and security are not incompatible; the fact that the criteria of personhood are open to choice does not mean that they are arbitrary. And the fact that at some point we may cease to qualify by them does not place our lives in constant jeopardy. In any case, absolute proscriptions have not had a distinguished history of success in protecting people; it is too easy to declare those unlike us or our enemies nonpersons and, as such, beyond the reach of sheltering rules.

On the contrary, recognition that ascribing personhood is a decision should be an energizing and empowering act. It empowers by enabling us to take conscious and critical charge of activities we had performed without full understanding before. It energizes by the realization that without our input, such important decisions may not go the way we want. Conscious, critical, and energetic contributions to the social choice of criteria of personhood and to their fair application provide far greater assurance of personal security than rigid adherence to an absolute code.

The stress on security achieved through control of consequences raises the issue of the relation of personalists to pragmatists. These two remarkable systems of thought constitute the pride, the most original elements, of American philosophy. Moreover, pragmatists and personalists share commitment to the central value of the individual, to the democratic creed, and to many of the highest spiritual activities developed in the history of humankind. It is unfortunate that these two philosophical currents have never combined their flow to make better progress toward their common sea.

The reason for this, I suspect, is that pragmatists tend not to be realistic enough and personalists are too deeply devoted to a transcendental order. My own version of objective and choice-inclusive facts should remedy the pragmatic abhorrence of realities that are unconnected to human activity. Personalists, in turn, need to give up their transcendent ontology, along with the disparagement of ordinary experience this involves. They do not have to abandon the beautiful idea that much of human life occurs in the "invisible realm."* The moral and communicative relations that obtain between us are, indeed, invisible, and they constitute the most important facts about human beings. But is there a reason to suppose that this invisible world is different and more real than the one we normally inhabit? Do we gain anything by supposing that the personal world of consciousness is incompatible with or at least distanced from the physical realm in which we suffer and thrive?

I suspect that these views constitute the Kantian and idealistic residue in personalism, which is a historical and dispensable accre-

* Bowne, 274.

tion. If they were dropped, nothing required for personalism in the full sense would be lost. The primacy of the invisible world would become the primacy of moral and communicative relations among us in this one. Our minds, our freedom, our purposes, would be resettled from transcendent exile and become central, meaningful aspects of our natural lives. All it takes to accomplish this is not to view the natural world in the worst possible light. If this world is completely mechanical, we simply do not belong. But we are here, so it cannot be just an inhuman machine.

EPILOGUE

To Have and To Be

In an incident Aesop did not record, three animals were lamenting their fate. "If only I had more to eat," said the pig, and he imagined himself buried under an avalanche of fragrant victuals. "If only I had shorter hours and less work," complained the ass as he rubbed his aching back. "If only people had more things and I greater skill to steal them," whispered the fox, for he did not want to be found out.

The god Zeus, known for his cruel sense of humor, heard their complaints and decided to grant the animals what they desired. The pig's larder was overflowing with food: he had so much that he had to ask the fox to store some of it for him. But soon the pig could no longer enjoy these good things. Eating too much had caused indigestion, and he could not even think of cooking or of food. The ass's workday was reduced; his master bought a small truck to do his heavy work. But soon, instead of concentrating on all the important things he had said he would do, the ass fell asleep and spent his day in a stupor. The fox did not fall asleep, but once the initial glory and excitement of plucking defenseless chickens had abated, he grew indifferent to the charm of pillage. He was bored.

The fable has, of course, no moral for anyone who thinks that boredom, stupor, and the glut that comes of over consumption are integral parts of a good and human life. No good has ever come of the fanatic claim that only one's own ideas are right and only one's own values authentic: if there are people who wish to adopt the fabled pig's desires or share the fox's fate, I will be glad to have them try. The ultimate test of living by the right values is satisfaction or equilibrium, and satisfaction is an individual matter. It is possible that undisciplined consumption is the good of some, while others find happiness in the indulgence of their orgiastic passions. Nothing could be farther from my intention than to censure such behavior. Nature continues to laugh in the face of those stern moralists who strain to set bounds to human plasticity.

I will, then, not condemn a way of life, and I will not categorically reject the set of values that it embodies. Nor will I recommend the universal acceptance of another, possibly quite dissimilar, set of principles or aims. I will restrict myself to a critical appraisal of some of the values by which some people in our society live, and for which too many may be willing to die. A critical approach need not lead to criticism: it is merely the dispassionate attitude of the investigator who attempts, in this instance, to determine the value of certain values. As sympathy can be aroused only in humans who share a certain concern and possess imagination, values can be discerned only by persons whose natures coincide and who are endowed with sagacity and insight. For this reason, my conclusions will have no validity at all save for those whose nature—being similar to mine—prescribes for them a similar way of life, who are able to achieve the self-knowledge that is required to recognize this and, eventually perhaps, to muster the courage to carry it out.

If the values of the pig, the fox, or the ass satisfy you, I will not argue: surely, nature will out. Your satisfaction implies that in truth you are a human pig, or a human fox, or an ass. But what of the rest of us who live amidst the ruins of values that were our fathers'? Tossed in an ocean of conflicting obligations and alien pressures, many of us survive by makeshift, impermanent adjustments: we live without settled principles, without a private attitude to life, without a planned pattern to our being. We are not trained to divine the demands of our individual nature, and as a consequence, many of us lack the inner unity that is the unmistakable feature of a *person*. There is nothing mysterious about this inner unity. Morality is a kind of hygiene: it is a cleanliness and unpromiscuity of mind. As children learn the simple facts of animal hygiene—to eat only what nourishes and to reject whatever does not agree with their nature—adults have to learn, sometimes through tragic experiences, the importance of acting by a single principle and living by a single plan, assimilating and dismissing as their nature commands. A healthy conscience is but the inner demand for consistency that makes one's life the history of a person instead of a disconnected series of events.

There is a current fallacy whose prevalence I do not feel called upon to discuss. This specious but unuttered principle is best expressed in the phrase "To live is to make a living." All the values of our Consumer Age are implicit in this phrase. "To make a living," of course, means to earn enough to be able to purchase the goods necessary for life. But what are the goods necessary for life? According to what I shall call the Consumer's Fallacy about the Ends of Human Life, enough food to avoid hunger and enough shelter and clothing to keep warm are not enough to live in the full sense of that word. Implicit in the Consumer's Fallacy is the claim that we do not even begin to *live* until we have the right or approved kind of food bought in a good store, fashionable clothing, and a cave as good as our neighbors'. This, of course, is only the beginning. For there are characteristically human needs, such as the need for fast cars, the need for heart-shaped bathtubs, and the need for the envy of one's fellows. We *live* when we have as many of these and other goods as our fortune will allow or our stratagems create.

The possession and the use of manufactured physical objects have become primary and fundamental facts in our culture and in our lives. They have penetrated our thought to such an extent that the attitudes appropriate to ownership and use have come to be the model for our attitudes to the world at large and to other human beings in it. Our attitude to almost everything we have or wish for is the attitude of a consumer. We use not only cars and washing machines, but also reputation and the goodwill of our neighbors. We possess not only typewriters and television sets, but also security and the loyalty of our children. It is, of course, natural for the human mind to reify the intangible: to substitute images for attitudes and concrete objects for abstract relations. But when such conceptual aids cease to be merely that and begin to penetrate our mental life and to govern our actions, when human beings begin to be considered physical objects and human feelings things to be consumed, the result is that the good life becomes a life filled with goods, and our attempt to live it culminates in a rage of possessiveness.

At the basis of the Consumer's Fallacy are the suppositions that people are what they have: that happiness is a function of the goods we possess and the things we consume or that it is the result of urges satisfied. Thus Hobbes, an early exponent of the Consumer's Fallacy, writes, "Continual success in obtaining those things which a man from time to time desires, that is to say, continual prospering, is what men call FELICITY."* If this is true, the introduction of mass advertising and of credit buying are the two greatest steps ever taken to promote the happiness of human beings. Advertisers create new desires, and consumer credit makes it possible for these desires to be readily satisfied. The unbroken cycle of guaranteed desires and satisfactions amounts to the "continual prospering" that people call 'felicity.' Continual success, which is happiness, is the share of Americans who desire, purchase, and consume in proportion to the installment payments they can meet. And lest my point be misunderstood, what is purchased need not be a manufactured object; it may be love. And the installment payment need not be a sum of money; it may be time to listen to another's troubles or a promise of security.

If Hobbes and his contemporary soul mates are right and happiness is but the satisfaction of desires on the basis of wisdom in trading, I wonder why so many Americans, shrewd businesspeople at work and in private life, remain unhappy. If Hobbes's analysis were correct, the successful consumption of physical objects and of human emotions should suffice to make us happy. How is it, then, that so many of us are successful as owners and consumers, even as consumers of human feelings, but unsuccessful as human beings? The answer to this question is not to be found by an examination of the means we use to achieve our ends: it resides, instead, in the nature and inadequacy of our current ends. Similarly, human dissatisfaction is cured not by concentrating on increasing our possessions or by combating the natural urge to have, but by relegating possession and consumption to their rightful and limited place in a comprehensive scheme of human values.

The Consumer's Fallacy and the accompanying tendency to treat human feelings as commodities and human beings as serviceable objects are closely connected with our current veneration of progress. Progress is a kind of motion: it is motion in the direction of some desirable goal. What differentiates progress from mere movement or change is its directionality. Direction, in turn, implies a fixed point of reference: some state of affairs for which we strive, an objective that is deemed worthwhile. I do not wish to assail the apologists of progress on the issue of mistaken standards: that some of the objectives in terms of which we measure our "progress" are insignificant or worthless is too obvious to require emphasis. It is as easy to suppose

---

* *Leviathan* (Cambridge: Cambridge University Press, 1904), 37.

as it is barbarous to assert that the possession of two radios per family or the development of wash-and-wear, warm-yet-light, no-ironing-needed underwear is the yardstick by which human advance is to be judged. My immediate concern here is not with such mistakes, but with two even more fundamental errors that the indiscriminate veneration of progress promotes.

The first blunder is best expressed in the scandalous slogan "Progress is our most important product." Progress, in fact, is a movement, not a product, and its sole importance derives from the importance and the value of its goal. No progress is valuable in and of itself: only the end of progress is of any worth, and only by reference to this end may any change be called 'progressive.' The value of progress is, in this way, entirely derivative: it is wholly depends on the value of the fixed objective at which progress aims. This single reflection should eliminate the mistake of supposing that progress can or ought to go on indefinitely or, in other words, that progress can be its own end. As all forms of transit, progress aims at a destination, not at its own self-propagation: its object is a state where progress will no longer be because its goal will have been achieved.

I am, of course, not denying that progress is a 'good thing' in some sense of that ambiguous phrase. But good things are of two sorts: those that we want for their own sake or as ends, and those that we want for the sake of other things or as means. Comfort and pleasure may be things we want in and of themselves: if they are such *ends*, they are valuable. Coal and electrical generators are *means* to these ends. They help to bring about our comfort and pleasure, and though not intrinsically valuable, they are at least useful. Progress is at best useful; it is not intrinsically valuable. It is good as a means but not as an end: it must have an end or objective other than itself. Hence progress can never be the goal of progress and no progress can be indefinitely sustained. Progress makes no sense at all without the possibility of fulfillment or attainment, and the more fervently we desire the attainment of our goal, the more we look forward to the time when progress, having got us our aim, will have ceased to be.

The sharp separation of progress from its goal is the source of the second mistake to which I alluded. We believe that it is important to progress and pride ourselves on being a `progressive' nation. We tend to overlook the fact that 'progress' is not a term of unqualified commendation. Progress is movement in the direction of what we do not have and what, at the same time, it would be good to have. Its existence implies a current lack along with the hope of future con-summation. For this reason, any society committed to progress is at once also committed to the future, and whoever is committed to the future ceases to live in the present. Yet it is impossible to live in any-thing but the present. People who attempt to live in the future end up by not living at all: their present is saturated with a heavy sense of impermanence, worthlessness, and longing for the morrow. Their concentration on what is yet to come blinds them to the satisfactions possible now. Their desire to come closer to their goal makes their present a chamber of horrors: by hastening the passage of the days, they wish their lives away. And not only is their longing agonized; after such fierce desire, each attainment is an anticlimax. Unreleased emotion paints in hues reality can never match. The object of desire once possessed is only a pale replica of what it was to be.

The meaning of life is not to be found in the future, and the charac-teristically human malady of trying to find it there leads only to dis-appointment and despair. Caught between the incompleteness of striving and the essential insufficiency of the possessions that flow from desire and hard work, future-directed people live with a perva-sive sense of insecurity, anxiety, defeat. The paradigm is the grotesque figure of the man who works so hard to provide for his retirement that he dies of a heart attack when he is forty-two. I will call the belief, fostered by our veneration of progress, that the means and the end must be distinct and separated by time, the Fallacy of Separation. The combination of the attitudes of ownership and use implicit in the Consumer's Fallacy with this Fallacy of Separation issues in disastrous effects on the attempt to lead the good life.

The Fallacy of Separation is so deep-seated in our thinking that it is difficult for us to conceive and almost impossible to admit that means and end may coincide. But this admission is the foundation of all sound ethics, and accordingly, it is found on the first page of Aristo-tle's great work on the subject. There Aristotle says, "A certain differ-ence is found among ends; some are activities, others are products apart from the actions that produce them."*

As a result of our commitment to the future and of our interest in 'products apart from the actions that produce them,' the concept of activity has been virtually lost to Western civilization. An activity is a deed, any deed, that is performed for its own sake. It is an action

---

* *Nicomachean Ethics* 1094a3–5.

done not as a means to obtaining some ulterior end or producing some product. Simply put, to engage in activity is to keep doing things without getting anywhere. But why should we wish to get anywhere if we are satisfied with whatever we are doing? The desire to get somewhere, our everlasting restlessness, betrays a sense of dissatisfaction with what we have and what we do and what we are. If we find something worth doing, it is reasonable to enjoy doing it and to ask for no more. If we are satisfied with what we do and are, looking to the future and hoping for improvement and progress become unnecessary .

Because the concept of activity is alien to us today, we tend to think that whenever change ceases, stagnation sets in. If that were true, no one would be more stagnant than the Christian God, who is free of desire and eternally changeless. However, to be without the striving that characterizes the infantile romantic mind is not necessarily to be static or inert. Striving might come to an end not only because of exhaustion or disgust but also because the condition of all striving, the separation of means and end, of creative act and created product, is eliminated. Activity is not the sequestered sleep of the impotent: it is, instead, achievement unfailing and instantaneous because in it alone the human act is its own reason for existence. I readily admit that all activity is useless, and hasten to add that this uselessness of activity is the best indication of its great value. The useful merely *produces* good things without being one. Activity, on the other hand, is good in and of itself. Too often, our actions are useful to bring about ends that are worthless. When these actions cease to point beyond themselves, like poisoned arrows, when they begin to function as ultimate ends, they acquire a worth that places them in the category of what is useless but, because of its intrinsic value, also priceless.

If the good life is a happy life, the pig, the fox and the ass are guilty of two fundamental errors. The first is an error of attitudes, the second an error of aims. The Consumer's Fallacy prompted the animals to extend the attitudes of ownership, use, and consumption to areas, such as leisure, happiness, and the emotions of human persons, in which they are inappropriate. The Fallacy of Separation prompted the infelicitous beasts to look for aims and goals that are other than activities, for products of the human act instead of the enjoyment of the act for what it is. In short, the pig, the fox and the ass all wished to *have* and not to *do*. But human beings are built to be bustling engines: they are agents and only action can satisfy them. Possession is not action; it is a passive state and, as such, at best a substitute for activity.

There is no clearer instance of a possession that functions as an activity substitute than what is now commonly called a 'status symbol.' To *be* a developed person is to engage in a sort of characteristic and appropriate activity. Nothing is more difficult than this, since it involves self-knowledge, spontaneous action, and self-control. Thus, the majority of us settle for less, while we wish to appear as if we had not compromised. If we cannot *be* someone, we can do the next best and *appear to be*: and we do this by acquiring the possessions that seem to go with being a person of distinction or a developed individual. On the level of the popular mind, the confusion is even clearer. Each status symbol reveals an attempt to substitute having for being, ownership for activity, possessions for character: each is a visible manifestation of our endeavor to be someone by having what he or she has.

A question spontaneously arises in my mind, and I am sure it has already arisen in yours: What cure can we prescribe for the three beasts? My answer is as simple as it is disarming. I cannot prescribe a cure for animals. If satisfaction attends their lives, I congratulate them; if they do not interfere with mine, I will at least tolerate them. But how could I prescribe a mode of life for forms of life as alien from mine as oysters are from migratory mice? I can speak only for myself and for anyone else whose similar nature demands a similar fulfillment.

For us, my counsel is to be. Life itself is an activity, and we should not approach it with the attitude of the devourer of experiences or with a possessive violence. We must develop attitudes appropriate to activity, to self-contained, self-validating human action; nothing short of this can make a life happy, spontaneous, and free. Finally, we must engage in appropriate activity. Which activities are appropriate for us is determined by our nature and may be discovered by self-knowledge. The two rules of the personal hygiene of the mind are to know oneself and to concentrate on the exercise of human powers for its own sake and not for its products or its usefulness. By knowing ourselves, we will do the right things; by concentrating on the exercise of human powers for their own sake, we will do them for the right reason. In this way, each moment of life acquires meaning and inalienable value. In this way, death cannot cut us off or leave our lives dismembered. For under these conditions, each moment of existence shines like a total crystal: each is an appropriate, meaningful, and completed human act.

INDEX

273

JOHN LACHS IS THE AUTHOR, EDITOR, AND TRANSLATOR of many books, including *George Santayana* (Macmillan, 1988), *Mind and Philosophers* (Vanderbilt, 1987), and *Intermediate Man* (Hackett, 1981). He has played an active role in the American Philosophical Association and the Metaphysical Society of America and was one of the founders of the Society for the Advancement of American Philosophy. He holds degrees in philosophy from McGill University and Yale and has taught at the College of William and Mary. Lachs joined the Vanderbilt faculty in 1966 and was named Centennial Professor of Philosophy in 1993.

THE RELEVANCE OF PHILOSOPHY TO LIFE

was composed electronically in 10 on 12 Palatino,
with display type in Optima;
printed on 60-pound, acid-free, Thor White Recycled paper,
with 80-pound colored endsheets and dust jackets printed
in 3 colors,
Smyth-sewn and bound over 88-point binder's boards
in Roxite A-grade cloth,
by Thomson-Shore, Inc.
Both book and jacket design are the work of Gary Gore.
Published by Vanderbilt University Press,
Nashville, Tennessee 37235.